My Father's Voice

My Father's Voice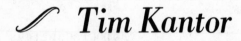

MacKinlay Kantor
Long Remembered

 Tim Kantor

McGRAW-HILL BOOK COMPANY

New York   St. Louis   San Francisco
Hamburg   Mexico   Toronto

1 2 3 4 5 6 7 8 9 DOC DOC 8 9 2 1 0 9 8

ISBN 0-07-033276-2

Library of Congress Cataloging-in-Publication Data

Kantor, Tim.
  My father's voice.

  Bibliography: p.
  1. Kantor, MacKinlay, 1904–   —Biography.
2. Authors, American—20th century—Biography.
I. Title.
PS3521.A47Z77 1988   813'.52 [B]   87-36670
ISBN 0-07-033276-2

Book design by Kathryn Parise

TO DIK BROWNE

*Without his urging I might
never have begun this book;
without his enthusiasm and support
I might never have finished it.*

Contents ⌒

Author's Note ⌒⟩

Perhaps one percent of the dialogue in the main body of the text is taken directly from my father's published books and unpublished manuscripts. The rest is drawn from stories which were told to me, from what I myself remember, and—largely—from what I know of the events recounted and the personalities involved.

On rare occasion I have used initial capital letters with certain words which today are not usually so capitalized. In most cases this conforms to the usage of the past; in others it reflects my personal taste.

The following are fictitious names:

Nan (I hope that the lady still thrives; she might not wish public recounting of private celebration long ago.)

Dr. Heinrich Von Krog (So my father named the man when he wrote about him in a memoir of childhood, *But Look, the Morn*; out of sentiment I use the same name now.)

Glenda, Hester, and *Kelley* (They are entitled to anonymity.)

Jake and *Harry*

Mike Loewenthal

Jim

         *   *   *

To all those fond friends—of my parents, of the family, and of my own—who are not mentioned, both the living and that legion of the dead, my apologies. I wanted to write a family memoir, but it was my task to write a book.

We learned the legends; we became a part of them, and they of us.

—MacKinlay Kantor
Cuba Libre (1940)

Preface ⌒

All my life I have spoken in my father's voice. His peculiar pitch, his resonance, are mine by nature and, when I was young, his presence was so strong, and my clay so weak and I so bonded to him, that I slavishly absorbed the rhythms of his speech as well, his every lilt and pause. I use that voice now when I say that over one hundred years ago, in 1884, near a prairie town in Iowa, Effie McKinlay lived in a house beside a mill. She helped her mother at her work, as best a four-year-old could do, and sheltered in the hymns her mother sang. She sensed, and profited from, her father's labor in the mill. She waited, fearfully, for Indians to ford the stream and pass by on the dusty road beside the mill, or to come begging at the door. And she tended her dolls, especially the one with muslin dress and a china head, with the same strident, loving care she would later lavish on her children when they came to her, in time.

On a summer's day during that same year, in Karlskrona, Sweden, John Kantor—an engaging, spoiled and nasty little boy of five—ran away from home. He made his way to the piers and, by the time his father found him, he had gathered an audience of older boys, of idlers and young stevedores, and they were listening, entranced, to false tales he told of coming from across the sea. The more they listened, no matter that they laughed and sneered, the more stories he invented. And, as his father watched, ashamed, John Kantor lied, and he lied, and he lied.

1

The Workroom

I last touched my father the day before we died.

My sister and I went to the nursing home, where he had been deposited a few days before, after visiting our mother in the psychiatric ward across the street. He was lying in a hospital bed with the sides drawn up—an oversized crib—and his wasted body was drawn in upon itself, curled in a fetal position. I do not know if he was conscious of our presence, but his fingers exerted some slight pressure upon ours when we held his hands. Hands which had once been gentle, once been clever, once been almost cruel.

"Hi, Dad," we said. "Hi, Daddy. We love you."

His eyes did not open, but he moaned, as a baby might cry. *"Aaanh."* This was the man I had nursed for months and nurtured on his way toward death. He had sired me, had loved and nurtured me as best he could. I had loved him, and he had daunted me. He had encouraged me, supported me, diminished me. He had enriched me, as no other ever could have done. He had been the warden of my prison: a prison which I, myself, had built, bar by weak and foolish bar.

Across his face there came an almost-smile. I wondered in what strange regions his mind—his brilliant, kindly, angry, frightened mind—might be wandering. I hoped that he was roaming through tall fields of the long ago.

Down behind our house stretched a mighty cornfield. By midsummer the corn was grown to be a wilderness. I took my gun, cocked it, saw that the cork was set firmly in the barrel. Quietly as any hunter might stalk, I crept barefoot through grainy black soil with that thick

1

jungle of corn extending overhead. Leaves scraped and rustled. Perhaps there were Indians prowling beyond, or bears... solemnly I shot three Indians and one mountain lion. Then I was hungry, and pulled broken cinnamon rolls from my pocket, and ate lunch.

We kissed him, and left him there.
"Aaanh."

My father's name was MacKinlay Kantor, and he had been a man of note—at one time almost as important in popular estimation as in his own. He had been born of a mixture of charm, lust, deceit, and innocent, misplaced love. An uneven mixture, for his mother was incapable of deceit and his father was incapable of love. He was a prisoner of sentiment, and of fantasy, throughout his life, and never fully understood either the wounds which maimed him or the victories he gained. I was very proud of him, and fond. Indeed I loved him, reluctantly, sometimes resentfully, but just as fiercely and compulsively as he had hated his own father. But when he died I was relieved. He had taken so long to die, body fighting will in odd disharmony—oh strange, gaunt shade which had haunted the house, fouled the bed, for so many weary months—that we were all, wife, daughter, son, exhausted.

But there were calls to be made, and so I made them. For many years he had lived, had gloried in, a public life. That recognition, and the books and stories which had earned it, had been in his own mind and in ours the justification, even the excuse, for what he was. I felt that it would be a shame for him, and a hurt for us, if his death should go unnoticed. I sat at his big desk, in his workroom, and, feeling like a usurper, I used his phone. First to call the local paper, the *Sarasota Herald-Tribune*, and then the wire services, the major newspapers, and Max Maxon at the *Daily Freeman-Journal* out in Webster City, Iowa. Dad would have risen from out his shriveled body in full wrath if I had forgotten the *Freeman-Journal*, and the town that gave him shape.

Already I had told my children—had stopped by the home which was no longer mine and said hard words, and hugged them, sharing their grief—our grief. In sensible division of labor, my sister was calling his sister and the other relatives who must hear the news from us. As for friends—they were legion, they were far too many. I reached a few, and shrugged about the others. They'd hear soon enough: from television, radio, newspapers across the country. Across the world.

He was dead, and I was free.

I shook my head. He was not dead at all. With every echo, every imitation, every act of denial, he lived and breathed in me. Just as, despite all Dad's intent, his wretched father had lived and breathed in him. I had been a captive, and so had he.

Now he was free, not I.

I was numb. The telling all was done, and I raised my eyes and stared about his room. A big room, enormous, which had served as a stage for his labor and his laughter, his hearty, insistent dominance and, later, his defeat and his decay.

The walls, what one could see of them, were of pecky cypress—from trees which had aged long years under swamp waters, before they'd been retrieved and milled. There was a big picture window on the west, looking out to Big Pass and the Gulf, and the huge desk was placed before it, facing into the room. I sat behind the desk in a large swivel chair with casters on its paws. There was a long bank of windows on my right, and another in front of me, over thirty feet away, behind which jungle menaced and invited. There was a suggestion of partition, halfway down the room, which had once demarcated living room from dining room in the house I'd known when I was young. On my near left there was a big coquina-rock fireplace, and in it a witch doll hung by her neck, dangling from the damper, to mark that it was closed. High over the mantelpiece a big poster blared, in red letters, FUCK COMMUNISM, and—on the mantel itself—there were placed handmade birthday cards which various grandchildren had presented in the past.

Arranged on the walls, amassed upon the desk and tables, was a sea of artifacts: his world, his life, as he had chosen to remember it. Photographs, paintings, illustrations, things. And books: the forty-four books he had published and their reincarnations in over a dozen other languages, the anthologies in which his stories had been included, and also his tools—his instruments of research. *Godey's Ladies' Book, Pioneer Families of Missouri,* the folk song collections of Allan Lomax, regimental histories from the Civil War, memoirs of escaped prisoners or survivors of Andersonville, a *Home Medical Companion* from the 1880s, Catlin's *North American Indians,* a field guide to butterflies and moths, another to mushrooms, the ripe lies of Stuart Lake's *Wyatt Earp, Frontier Marshal:* America's history, the very texture of its undisciplined but still unpolluted past, marched in haunting, mildewed disarray along those shelves.

Song and violence abounded in that room as I got up and wandered, with my father looking on—glaring out, laughing out, crying out from every photograph, every bomb pin, every Minié ball, every page.

Shrill of fifes and thrum of drums. Young Mack Kantor—gangling, earnest, and nineteen—is marching along Ohio Street with the Fife-And-Drums of the Grand Army of the Republic. Cemetery-bound, in Webster City on Memorial Day; is that "Turkey in the Straw" they're playing, or "Jefferson and Liberty"? The fifes in front, Mack and two veterans keening away, and then the drums, veterans all, with the other old soldiers, so impossibly young for 1923—and who was at the Wilderness, who got hit at Petersburg, who hid from anger, guarding sutlers, all through the war?—straggling along behind.

That was the last time my father ever marched. I glanced across to a corner of the room where there stood three canes, leaning awry—as though in search of that same support which once they had offered him. In the July following that Memorial Day, a car filled with six young people had driven off a hillside near Lehigh, Iowa, and fallen into the trees a hundred feet below. Dad was not driving, he did not bear the guilt, he did not break his back, as others did, but his left thigh was smashed. After the months of healing there came osteomyelitis to plague him, through sixteen operations during nineteen years.

The seventeenth operation worked, and the sloughing of bits of bone, the seepage of pus through open wounds, were stopped. But when I was a little boy I thought that the signs of manhood included a long, dangling penis, a hairy bag below, and an oozing, bandaged wound upon the thigh.

The wounded god! Certainly he seemed a god to me. He cherished that role, and played it eagerly.

From across the room, where an illustration of a drummer boy hung upon the wall, there came a long, hallucinatory roll of drums. There were fifes upon the mantelpiece, and I remembered that he would play them for me when I was small. I picked one up, and blew and fingered, but could make no music at all.

The late afternoon sun, slanting through the window, illuminated objects on the desk. There was a simple tin can, painted with a white and blue design, which one of my kids had presented for use as a pencil holder. (He was so much easier with my children than he had been with my sister's, earlier, or with us. Age, or fatigue, had gentled him.) And the crudely shaped, painted clay somethings which the children—knowing that he liked paperweights—had also given. And other paperweights, at least eight or ten: a Minié ball, plucked off the field at Gettysburg; several elaborate, colored, blown-glass fantasies; a little dime-store Snoopy in a miniplastic universe which created snow when shaken; two hearts entwined, carved out of quartz; and another small glass weight, from a convention of the Grand Army of the Republic, with a legend inside, reading *Iowa—51st Volunteers*. There was also a paper-knife—or as such Dad used it—which was in fact a utility knife, fashioned from a file by a Union prisoner in Andersonville prison; his grandfather's (Adam McKinlay's) pocket watch in a little bell jar; ashtrays, pipes—there were over a hundred in that room—a humidor, tobacco pouches; unanswered correspondence which he had not had wit or strength, and my sister and I no time, to answer; a Dictaphone; and a few of the big, soft lead pencils which he loved to use for manuscript revision. His huge typewriter was on a stand nearby. And, amidst so much more, the heavy, solid Zippo lighter which a friend had presented upon the completion of his novel *Andersonville* (*"To Mack—Who Won The Battle Of Andersonville—May 25th, 1955"*; and there was a citation for the Pulitzer Prize, framed and hanging on the wall, to prove that claim).

It was the desk, the room, of a successful man, a famous man, in a house which seemed to testify to wealth. Hidden away in a corner of the leather blotter holder I discovered a small piece of white notepaper, folded over. I picked it up and opened it, and recognized his writing. As I read, my stomach griped, and wind from a desolate heath seemed to blast my ears. "When we are born, we cry that we are come / To this great stage of fools. —*Lear*, IV:6." Oh, crumbled king! Oh, God! And below that quote, in an uncertain hand: "Jan.—April. No income." Poor Dad, poor man.

And how much responsibility did I bear for that plaint, and for that desperation? And... *"Aaanh, aaanh, aaanh!"* All of us cry when we come into the world, but I cried more than others. And longer. *"Aaanh, aaanh!"* I cried the first time I sought for nourishment at my mother's breast, and for months thereafter. I was born with a spastic pyloric valve, which governs the passage of food out of the stomach. Every time I nursed, within minutes that valve would complain, and so would I, my belly jumping so fiercely that the twitch could be seen across the room and my lungs alternately distended and gasping for yet more air with which to scream. *"Aaanh!"* It took the doctors weeks to make a proper diagnosis, it took them months to find, and adjust, the proper medication, and all that time, after every feeding, I yowled, I yawped, I hollered. My mother had already been exhausted by a difficult pregnancy and a long delivery; and she was more exhausted now. She had a primitive apartment to see to, a husband and a four-year-old daughter to cosset, and a fractious, agonized brat. Half the day I screamed, and half the night. At night my father, himself nursing a toothache, nursing worry about overdue rent and unpaid bills, nursing the idea for a short story which might help to relieve that worry, would walk me back and forth across the floor, chanting a gravelly lullaby. "Hush, Timmy. Hush, hush." He had a notion that the warmth of his strong body might ease the hurt in mine, and so he'd slip me inside his pajama top and press my belly close to his. *"Aaanh!"* "Hush, Timmy, hush."

And still I rambled, in a cavern called The Past. In the northwest corner of the room there hung a town plat of Webster City, Hamilton County, Iowa, and a map of the County itself, both dating from the 1880s. Above, in a little window recess, there was a statuette of a Pioneer Mother, standing straight and dauntless, with a Little Girl and Boy clinging to her skirts, and her arms sheltering them. Ah, Effie! I thought of a wide prairie sky, with cumulus clouds in stately, vast procession, and of mill wheels grinding, mill sluice rushing, and prairie wind moving through corn of the fields, elms of the town. Always, when I myself was small, that bronze piece, more than any photograph we owned, evoked the grandmother I had never known. Standing there in that sad, brave room, I felt it must have done the same for my father as well.

On the same shelf, palm trees and a blue Florida sky visible through glass behind, there stood another statuette, this one a time-crackled porcelain of a kilted highlander, wearing the MacKinlay tartan, with a blurb for MacKinlay's Scotch Whisky on the base. I smiled out of darkness. How typical of Dad, who loved the Scots and Scotch as well, to have acquired that totem somewhere along the way. I heard the drone of bagpipes in my head, their lilt, their skirl, their haunting bray, but I couldn't quite get the tune. Was it "Courtin' in the Kitchen"? ("...Courtin' in the hall, courtin' in the little room underneath the stair.") My father was a great one for courting. Or was it "A Hundred Pipers," or "The Blue Bonnets," or...

"When your mother and I were in Great Britain in the summer of '37—the time when you were in Camp Owaissa and swallowed the penny and we all met May—they were still bringing bodies—skeletons—home from France. And in Edinburgh one morning, we saw a funeral procession: slow march, or half step," he moved stiffly back and forth across the room in emulation, "with a riderless horse being led, coffin on a carriage before, and the officers with arms reversed, and the pipes were playing 'My Lodgings in the Cold, Cold Ground.' Sometimes they call it 'My Home in the Cold Ground,' or just 'My Home.' It's a coronach, a dirge. You know the one. The tune Tom Moore stole for 'Believe

Me, If All Those Endearing Young Charms.' *Dah-di-daah-di-di-daah-di-di-daaah-di-di-daaah*. It was so goddamned moving. I had tears in my eyes." And then a fiendish grin, all gaiety and strength, and he no more than thirty-nine, and looking forward to combat and the chance to prove—as always he must prove—that he was not just Effie Kantor's little boy. "If I get killed over there they can play that for me. I'd like that. *Dah-di-daah-di-di-daah*..."

I moved to another picture-covered wall, and the pipes receded in volume, their drone replaced by another—that of engines at high altitude—and the crunch of flak and harsh stutter of .50-caliber machine guns filled my ears. Flying Fortresses. B-17s. He went to gunnery school in England and qualified, in direct defiance of Geneva Convention rules covering war correspondents, because, in those rough months in '43, the Eighth Air Force was reluctant to take along dead weight on bombing missions—they often had enough dead weight coming home, those who did return—and he wanted to go. To risk, to share, to defend the countries that he loved, to be in fact a veteran and thus redeem an ancient lie. Here was Dad with the crew of *She's a Honey*, I didn't know what happened to them, and then with Rogers's crew, and they went down though some came back later, and Dad standing with some young men from the RAF, and with the aircraft commander he flew with in Korea. And here was young Sid Lovitt (oh, gay, oh, eager, vital Sid, lead navigator and lead lover, with more missions than any other man in the entire Eighth Air Force) pointing at the hole in his flak helmet, wearing a bandage on his head and an amazed, delighted smile.

Shock rolled through shock. It occurred to me that I could put a name to almost every face on that wall, on every wall in the room. And when I couldn't supply names for a particular photograph or illustration, I could recall a story to go with it. I had heard so much, remembered so much, *knew* so much, about my father's life and those who had entered into it. It was as though for many years I had shared in his identity, rather than risk establishing my own.

Next to that photograph of Sid Lovitt there was another—a vertical shot of three B-17s at altitude, in tight formation, amid malignant bursts of flak, and one of them was trailing smoke from its number-one engine, a long white plume. And next to that, pinned to the wall, was a small piece of bruised and twisted metal. "That's from a '17 that crashed on landing," my father had said once, and now I suddenly realized which plane it must have been. The one in which he was scheduled to ride, except that there had been a snafu, a foul-up, and his orders hadn't come through in time. So he had stood on the platform around the tower and watched the ships take off, and, hours later, had stood there again and watched the lucky ones come home. But that ship, *his* ship, had had too much of flak or fighters, perhaps its landing gear had been damaged beyond all use, and so, instead of touching down and rolling neatly to a halt, it had hit the runway hard and squealed and sparked and made a nasty mess. He'd stood and watched it burn.

I went to the bar in the living room and made myself another drink. Beside the bar there hung two photographs I had made in Latin America in rather nasty circumstances. I looked at them a while and then walked back to the workroom, toasting lives I couldn't fully understand. My fingers riffled through the pages of a dictionary spread open on its stand. How he had loved and honored words! And then my eyes strayed to my own service cap, and two of his, hanging on the wall. He had also loved and honored uniforms—always had, from his Scout days and even before. I opened a closet door, opened a box, and touched the rough fabric of a khaki shirt. (It seemed for a moment that I touched again the flesh of the man who had nurtured and almost overborne me.) There were fourteen merit badges sewn on the left sleeve of that shirt, and one of the badges was for lifesaving.

My father was twelve years old when he joined the Boy Scouts and earned that badge. I think it was the same year that he first met Charley Morean. Charley was tall for his age, and strong, and shambling in his walk, and—although his skin and hair were fair, and his eyes the brightest blue—the boys all called him "Chink," because those eyes were vaguely slanted. He was a lonely boy, a victim like my father of a then-exotic malady called divorce, and he lived on a farm with his grandparents. He was not the quickest boy at sports in all that Scout troop, nor the ablest at games, but surely he was the most popular, for he was warm and eager, and there was no malice in him. Dad and Herbert Arthur, his closest friend for many years, became fond of Chink Morean and they all spent a lot of time together. One hot, sky-blue, corn-gold summer's day when Dad was thirteen, he and Herbert hiked out to the farm where Charley lived and wheedled his grandparents into releasing Charley from his chores, and then the three boys went swimming. They laughed, they splashed in the warm and sluggish water of early August, they swam across the river and rested in the shade. Then they started back. Charley Morean was last in line and, halfway across, the splash of his dog paddle turned into a wild thrashing and he made an awful sound. Young Mack Kantor was closest to him. "Hey, Chink, what's wrong?" and he swam back to try to help him. ("Approach the victim from the rear.") Perhaps Charley Morean had a cramp. Certainly he had gulped a lot of water, and hysteria can make strong boys stronger yet. He grabbed Dad and pulled him close; kicking and flailing, he pulled him under. No air, lungs bursting, under all that water. ("Kick free from the victim and surface, and try again, approaching from the rear.") Charley's head broke water one more time, his arms stretched high, and then he sank again, and drowned.

Two weeks later Dad was in Chicago, spending a few days with his father, John Kantor, for the second time in his life. John Kantor was an important man: he dressed importantly, walked importantly, talked importantly, and he was a friend of the Mayor and of the Chief of Police. (He had known many other police officers in the past; he would meet many others in the future.) He took his son to lunch, to be shown off to some of his important friends. Seated at the table, with all those important faces turned reverently toward him, John Kantor said, "My dear son has recently had a dreadful experience. He went swimming with his closest friend, and that friend became ill and, because Mack did not know the right thing to do, he allowed his friend to drown." Eyes teared, face flushed, my father felt that he was drowning too. "It is too late to save that poor boy—what was his name, Mack?"

There were all those other faces at the table, there were all the other faces in the room, but my father could see but one. The face of *his* father, heavy, grave, and solemn: the countenance, wholly superior, mildly benevolent, largely unconcerned, of a smug and distant god. "His name was Charley Morean. But, Daddy, I *knew* what to do! He was just too big, he was too strong."

"I have instructed my son as to what he should do if, in the future, he has the opportunity to save another friend. Mack, stand up and show the gentlemen."

"But, Daddy—"

"Mack, do not embarrass me in front of my friends. Stand up and demonstrate what I have shown you. Tell them what you would do to save another Charley."

Miserable, shame-faced, my father stood up, thrust his left arm out in front of him, as though to ward off a flailing body, and clenched his other fist. "I'd—I'd hit him, I'd knock him out." (Oh, treading water all the time.) "And then I'd dive and grab him, and take him to the shore."

"That is good. You have learned your lesson well." John Kantor, who could not swim a stroke, who had never tried to save another soul in earnest, nor ever would, nodded his head in sober self-approval. And, while his son stood there, damming up tears, John Kantor smiled upon his friends with just a touch of rueful weariness, and they all applauded him.

And so my grandfather was a bully and a fraud. Poor Dad. I put away his shirt and, turning for solace to the walls, I saw a picture of the two of us. Dad, eager and confident in his correspondent's uniform, and me—eleven years old, chubby, and uncertain. Poor me. Poor all of us. Bound by the chains that were forged for us, bound by the chains we forged for ourselves. Bound by the chains we allowed to be forged.

But other and happier bindings were represented in that room as well. Pictures of his friends were everywhere: his first publisher, agents, editors, his lawyer, cops, airmen, friends who had remained close since childhood, and dogs whose love he had valued as much as that of any human. And here were three snapshots, in fading, dying color, of Miguel and his parents, Miguel at school, Miguel with his wife. Miguel was just an eager little Spanish street kid, whose parents could not afford to give him an education, but Dad thought he was so nice and so bright that he deserved that education, and so he gave it to him. And here was my sister, wearing cap and gown and holding flowers, on her graduation from college. And here was my mother on the cruise ship *Stella Polaris*, dressed as a harem girl—looking youthful, wistful-gay and sexy—holding a full champagne glass on top of her head.

Youthful, wistful-gay, sexy, bright and eager. The sad and nasty thought obtruded of how she'd seemed that noon, when we had gone to the psychiatric ward to tell her of Dad's death. A psychopharmacological disaster: a product of too much anxiety, too long a grieving, and outrageous psychiatric ineptitude. I wondered if ever she would paint again, small hand holding the brush so firmly, first thought so sure, and I glanced again above the mantel, below the "Fuck Communism" slogan, at the watercolor she had painted years before—"The Tiger in the Streets"—as a cover for Dad's police novel, *Signal Thirty-Two:* a boy clutching a girl, the sights of East Harlem street life, all night and muzzy, and the Tiger coming out of it all, lying in wait.

As Tigers lay in wait for us all.

In yet another frame, of all that vast, romantic array, appeared photographs of Dad playing the guitar and singing, with Mother singing also and, from the wistfulness that enveloped her, I knew they must have been singing their favorite duet ("Aura Lee! Aura Lee! Maid of golden hair! / Sunshine came along with thee, And swallows in the air."). And then, Dad singing some song with his older sister, Virginia, whom he had so resented in early youth, and so loved and cherished through all his later years.

"Aura Lee! Aura Lee!..." I turned and looked at his guitar, which now leaned, long idle, in its case against the wall. And I saw, as in fact I had so often seen, his calloused fingers thrum its strings, and I heard his voice resound.

2

Daddy

That good voice will rasp forever in my mind. He was a laughing, raging, driven man who seemed to my sister and me, when we were small, and not so small, to be another natural phenomenon, like the sun which warmed us, the snow which chilled—the very wind itself, in all its gentleness and sometime fury. And his voice, baritone and tenor improbably snarled together—blaring, hushed, eager, angry, gay, and always vibrant—still lingers in my ears, even as it thundered then.

"Goddamn it, you kids, wake up!" The rough words tore me out of sleep, blasted dreams away, and I opened my eyes to sunlight bouncing off the yellow paper on the walls, and the sight of my father standing in the hall beyond the open bedroom door, beaming. Again his loud voice boomed, "Goddamn it, wake up! It's six o'clock and the morning's bright and there are things to do. We're going on a picnic!" I jumped out of bed—all five uncertain years of me—and heard my sister stirring in the room across the hall. And the bustle, and the shouting, as we put on clothes and made ourselves ready, and the warmth which moved us all. Mother—all busy eagerness—stowed provisions in a wicker basket and Daddy packed the car, and we drove off into the promised warmth of an Iowa summer's day.

The place was Webster City, the year was 1938, and we were visiting my father's home town for my very first time—seeing the house where he was born, the house where he was raised, traveling the streets which he had known, exploring the woods which had enraptured him when he was as small as I.

He parked the car beside a creek which wandered through a glade among tall trees. We unpacked the car while Daddy built a fire, and then put in sweet ears of corn, still in their husks and long soaked in salted water, to roast among the coals. He helped Layne and me to build a rock-and-pebble dam across the creek and, later, I listened without listening as he lectured upon the distinctive markings of the various butterflies I chased and almost caught. I remember sunlight and green life flourishing, and my father delighting in our delight—and in his dominance.

Briggs' Woods was a wonderland; we had a fine time that day.

It must have been earlier in the same year, because I know that I was five. And it was a Special Occasion, for Daddy was not sitting at his desk in the living room, nor was I banished to play outside or in my room because Your Father Is Working. Rather, we were out on the side porch of our house in Florida. Mother was sitting on the rattan couch with its aqua cushions (ah, how she loved that soft color, which seemed to echo both the green of the jungle all around, and the blue of the water along the beach) and Daddy was sitting in a chair. I was standing, facing him—and thus my face to his face, almost on a level—and we were having a Conversation. Which was most unusual, for he regarded small children as an alien breed, and found it hard to talk with them. Most often, during our early years, he talked *to* us instead.

But, this time, a Conversation, and I was thrilled at his attention. His voice, his eyes, the man himself—so vital and so easy—enveloped me, and warmed me with his fire.

We were talking about whatever the years have forgotten until, suddenly, thought of The Future came into my mind—that impossibly distant time when I would be as big as he. "When I'm grown up I want to have a grocery store, like Mr. Cheney, or maybe a drugstore like Mr. Boylston has." The dim interior of Cheney's was filled with the richest smells imaginable; and Badger's Drugs offered the sweetest ice cream sodas.

"You'll do no such thing!" Daddy's face had suddenly darkened, and his words flashed out with all the harsh intensity of lightning from the sky. "Groceries! Drugstores! You're a bright little boy and, when you're a man, you've got to do great things. You must never settle for what little people do!"

In the sudden chaos within my mind I focused on one phrase. "Little people?" Like me? But Mr. Boylston was big, and he was a family friend. My face was hot, and I felt like I'd been slapped.

Daddy was away, and so the house on East Eighty-fourth Street seemed empty. His voice did not rampage through the house, as in ordinary conversation, nor did murmured words issue from behind a closed door, as they did when Daddy was dictating—a comforting sound, like the surf on the beach in Florida—nor was there the thunderous silence which occurred when he was Thinking. Simply an emptiness, a void, though the sound of Scots bagpipes did issue from the phonograph, as I prepared to march to war.

He was often absent in those days. He kept a mysterious place called a "work apartment" somewhere, because he Couldn't Work Around The Kids, and he spent most days there, working with his secretary, and sometimes he went to Washington, to do research at the Library of Congress. Frequently he was absent at dinner—nor was he always there to say good night when I went to bed.

The steely winter light of afternoon filtered through the curtains as I marched around the living room, and my mother sat there on the sofa, wearing a long blue dressing gown. She was darning socks, with a basket full of mending beside her. "Farewell, Mother," I said, as I shouldered my yard-stick-spear—for she was Mother in this fantasy, as in reality as well—"I go to fight the foe!"

The bagpipes skirled around us. She sighed dramatically, and then, "Be brave, my son," she said in tragic tones, "and beat the English but, Oh, come back to me." I kissed her face, and strode away to the beat of drums, but with puzzlement lodged within my mind.

We both *knew* that it was only a game that we were playing, and yet the tears on her cheeks were real.

Another year, another rented house, this one three blocks north and one block east, at 522 East Eighty-seventh. It was late at night, and Timmy was asleep, perhaps lost in that strange, green-black nightmare which pursued him through those years: being forced down long stone steps, with noxious mossy walls closing in around, toward a barred door behind which bad things threatened.

But sister Layne was still awake. The sound of talk and laughter down below had tantalized her for hours, and she had crept out to the top of the stairs, to sit and listen. For long minutes now her father had been Reading. There had been no voice but his.

. . . Mr. Morley's hands shook violently, but somehow he got the wrappings loose, and then he had the box open.

The dial was pure and glistening, but the neat numerals buzzed and trembled when he looked at them. He turned the watch in his hands. It was a long while before he could read the inscription: TO TYLER MORLEY. FROM HIS FRIENDS. CLASS OF 1922. S.H.S. "BLESSED BE THE TY."

He knew that he must say something aloud, even though there were only the empty room and the happy little watch to hear him. He mumbled hoarsely, "Why, why—why they must have put in fifty cents apiece!"

He sat down in Letty's old rocker.

The watch ran on. It spoke busily, as if assuring Mr. Morley that the spirit of his children would stay close beside him, no matter whether he went to Lexington, Nebraska, or a great deal farther away.

There was silence for a moment, and then a gust of approval, with many voices intermingled.
"Mack, that's wonderful!"
"Marvelous!"
"Darling"—our mother's soft, rich speech—"it's magnificent!"
Then other voices overrode, with our father's overriding all. And drowsy Layne went back to bed. The world was as it should be. Daddy was reading, Daddy was talking while others listened, Daddy was home again.

A jungle night in Florida, and we had gathered on the screen porch. Daddy was reading aloud. Outside the screen, drawn by the light of the lamp which stood at his side, I could see big moths circling, but I paid them no mind. My concentration was caught by the words uttered, words from Ernest Thompson Seton's *Rolf in the Woods*, which Daddy loved—and so did we. He loved to read aloud, and happily we listened.

"Quonab, I am going out to get her a partridge."

"Ugh, good."

So Rolf went off. For a moment he was inclined to grant Skookum's prayer for leave to follow, but another and better plan came in mind. Skookum would most likely find a mother partridge, which none should kill in June, and there was a simple way to find a cock; that was, listen. It was now the evening calm, and before Rolf had gone half a mile he heard the distant "Thump, thump, thump, thump—rrrrrrr" of a partridge, drumming...

We could hear that partridge drum.

We had heard the crack of John Ridd's musket in *Lorna Doone*, the laughter and the tears of *Little Women* and *Little Men*, Oliver Twist's request for "More," all that and so much more beside. Good books filled the shelves of whatever home we occupied, and good words filled the air.

But sometimes Daddy could be selfish. After Rolf had voyaged to Albany and met the governor's son, I was kissed good night and sent to bed. Lying in the sweltering darkness of my room, I thought of another night, during the previous winter in New York, when he had—at first—refused to read.

For over a week he had been reading from *Under the Lilacs*. (And *Under the Lilacs* was, like so many others, a special book. On its flyleaf I could read, in fading pencil, "From Gramma to Effie, on her 13th birthday, October 19, 1892," and "Gramma" was Rachel Bone, and "Effie" was *my* grandmother, Effie McKinlay, and 1892 was very long ago. Even before Daddy was born. In another century!) Then he had had to go to Washington, to do research at the Library of Congress, and we kids—eager to hear how Bab and Betty and young Ben and his father fared—had begged Mother to read a little during his absence. She had agreed, and Daddy had come home to find betrayal: the book was almost finished.

At dinner he complained, after telling about his adventures on the trip. "God damn it, I want to know what happened, too! I want to read it again." And it was only after pleading from us, and apology from Mother—and a chance to skim the pages he had missed—that he had consented to read the final chapter.

The closed gate where the lonely little wanderer once lay was always to stand open now, and the path where children played before was free to all comers, for a hospitable welcome henceforth awaited rich and poor, young and old, sad and gay, Under the Lilacs.

The richness of his voice had brought the words alive and we were immersed in sentiment, which was not, in itself, a wicked thing.

"Jesus Christ! I hate Christmas."

A Florida December, and I was lying on the living room floor, poring over the pages of an F.A.O. Schwarz catalog and wondering if I had chosen wisely when, weeks before, I'd made my dream request. Mother was sitting on the couch, wrapping presents with help from Layne-o. (For so Layne had been dubbed long ago—in the days when panthers prowled the woods, and I had not been born—in rough parody of some forgotten song: "Layne-o, Bayne-o, the bane of my life." And sometimes she was Layne, and sometimes Layne-o, and sometimes even Bayne-o—when Daddy was feeling especially fond.)

"Oh, Mack!" said Mother, and Layne-o giggled. Daddy found the letter he'd been seeking, amid that jumble of ribbon and wrapping paper on his desk which had triggered his outrage, and stalked out of the room, fuming.

He did hate Christmas. He could not, he said, understand for the life of him why people wanted to make such a fuss about an essentially dreary day. His own mother, he would add in tones of fond derision, had insisted upon making a great to-do about the whole damned thing. There had been much talk, both at home and in church, about the Spirit Of The Season, but as he remembered it that Spirit had been harsh and cold and gray. There had also been talk about presents, and much "I know something *nice* about Mack," but when Christmas morning came, the presents had mostly been meager and practical. And his grandmother and mother and sister had persisted in singing carols about "Joy to the World" at a time when he saw little joy in theirs. He said he remembered Christmas Eves when his mother had had to work late, behind the cash register in that store on Main Street, being nice to all the fortunate people who *didn't* have to work, and then rushed back through the snow to be nice to everyone at home. Besides— and here his voice dropped and his fire seemed to wane—his mother had died on the day after Christmas, and he hated to be reminded of her death.

And so I knew he hated Christmas, but—also—I knew he loved to play the role of Scrooge. His first "Bah! Humbug!" had been snarled in earliest December, when Mother had announced that it was time to buy a Tree. "Good God, Irene!" he'd roared. "It's weeks away." But Mother primly insisted that *she* loved Christmas, and always had, and couldn't understand why Daddy was being such a grouch, and trying to ruin everything.

Then had come the search for the Tree, the carting of it home, with grumbling from Dad that we'd have to cut a hole in the ceiling to let it stand. As always in such matters, he'd been right, and he'd had to cut off a portion of the base of the thing instead.

"Bah! Humbug!"

Then had come the decoration of the Tree, with Christmas carols playing on the Magnavox, and humming in the air, and Layne and I as eager helpers—and Daddy taking refuge in the car, driving off to dictate to his secretary. And discussion of the Christmas dinner, and shopping expeditions.

"God damn it, Irene! I don't know how I'm going to pay for all this."

A few days before the special, hated day, about the time when he began to read *A Christmas Carol* to us in the evenings, there came a change. Delivery men brought mysterious packages to the door, and Daddy smiled as he signed for them. And he took himself off from the house—but not to dictate—and came back carrying shiny parcels, leering and snarling as he bore them in. And then the caroling on Christmas Eve, and no one sang more jovially than he; and on the following morning we Had The Tree.

There was Wonder on the white sheet spread below (along with the crèche, and the Christmas village, and the icy silver-mirror pond, with leaden figures skating on it) and Excitement, hidden by Daddy himself the previous night, in branches up above. He presided, beaming, in his chair as the presents were doled out: many presents, lavish presents, for Layne and for myself (I got the Army camp, complete with armored cars, for which I'd yearned), and Something Special for Irene, for Reno, for Mother—that year it was a chest of silverware, from Black, Starr and Gorham.

That night he read to us the last chapter of *A Christmas Carol*, and his voice was moving, gentle, as he read. But it did not have the zest it had held when, nights before, he had read the first.

"Merry Christmas! What right have you to be merry? What reason have you to be merry? You're poor enough."

"Come, then," returned the nephew gaily. "What right have you to be dismal? What reason have you to be morose? You're rich enough."

Scrooge, having no better answer ready on the spur of the moment, said "Bah!" again; and followed it up with "Humbug!"

"I remember..."

"I remember when..."

Daddy remembered everything and, constantly, he proved it. The names of birds, of butterflies and moths. The names of generals in the Civil War, and words from favorite passages in books he'd read. The words of every song he'd ever heard, every limerick, every dirty joke.

The very taste and substance of his youth.

"I remember, when we were kids, we'd hike down to Uncle Jas Bell's mill. Dick Whiteman, Bob Richardson, and one or two other boys. And we'd camp out overnight, in the woods near the mill, and then, in the morning, we'd go knocking at the door. Uncle Jas would welcome us, and his wife would say, 'My, I bet you boys are hungry. I bet you're ready for a real good breakfast.' And she'd cook up eggs and ham, and slice big slabs of bread—oh, the smell of that fresh-baked bread, and the other food—and we boys would gobble away. Then we'd do some chores, in pay.

"Now, Uncle Jas had a dog. He was a grand old collie dog, almost as nice as Beverly"—he rubbed Beverly's stomach with his foot as he spoke—"and he had only one bad habit. Unlike Beverly, who has many." More rubbing ensued and Beverly, four legs thrust into the air, shivered in ecstasy.

"That dog loved to chase cars. Any time a car came by the mill, that dog would go after it, hell for leather—barking, and snapping at the wheels, as though each car was a whole tribe of Indians, bent upon attack.

"In those days, cars didn't have hubcaps, but they did have wire spokes—to support the wheels. And finally that damn dog succeeded in what he'd been trying to do all along. He bit the wheel! He actually caught one of the spokes with his mouth. And"—big whirling gestures with his hands, and Beverly was now forgot—"Uncle Jas said the dog flew through the air for forty feet, at least, before it landed. Then he got up, kind of slowly, shook himself, and looked after the car as it drove off. Then he staggered off and hid in a crawl space underneath the house.

"Uncle Jas said he didn't come out for three days. And ever after that, whenever a car came by, that dog would just lie there beside the door and look the other way."

He remembered the kind of weather there had been, on the early morning when I was born; he remembered the way Mother had looked and walked when first he saw her; he remembered the overbearing pomposity his father had displayed on the day they met, when Daddy was seven; he remembered both the color of a gingham dress a farm girl had worn to school, long years before, and the details of a conversation he had had the previous night.

"I remember when..."

"I remember..."

*   *   *

He was the most famous writer in the world. I knew that for a fact. The teachers in school spoke of him with awe, and other adults I met had reverence on their tongues when they repeated my name and asked, "Timmy Kantor. Are you *MacKinlay* Kantor's son?"

Daddy did nothing at all to challenge my belief; he encouraged it, instead. "Come here, you kids, and listen to this." He held up a letter. "They sent this on from Coward-McCann. It's about *Valedictory*. 'You have written a beautiful thing, finely wrought. Your integrity as an artist is sound and fine. Thank you for a story that cannot be forgotten.'" And his big smile warmed the room.

"Listen to these! I just got some reviews on *Gentle Annie*." Ah, I remembered Annie. I remembered her anguished voice made incarnate, when he had read to us, in his own dramatic tones:

Annie made a little scream—a rabbit-sound. "They'll catch him! They'll—"

"Not on what he's riding!" I cried. "What's the blackest and fastest horse in all the world... outside the world... in heaven or hell?" I asked them. "What's the blackest horse?"

"This is from the *Boston Globe*. 'A combination of riotous mischief and blundering tragedy that plays lightly upon the unending questions of right and wrong.'" A sudden glower, with grins as its parentheses. "By God, I do know something about right and wrong. I remember that son of a bitch— my father. And this is *The New York Times*. 'Kantor has done a first rate job...' And, *The New Yorker*, June 27, 1942. 'Since Mr. Kantor is a better novelist than most writers of Westerns, this is a better Western.' And that's just for a book I did to make some money.

"Which we did!" He pointed toward the wall, where there hung the framed photograph of a check from Metro-Goldwyn-Mayer, for $25,000.

So Daddy was rich, and Daddy was famous. That gave me a lot to live up to, and earnestly I strove.

He hadn't spanked me since I was five, and both he and I were proud of that fact. He hadn't needed to. A *look*, with his handsome features cor-

roded by disdain, served better than one swat on the rear—or five, or ten—
to make me stop whatever childish act had spurred his anger. The *look*
said, "You are ridiculous, you are disgusting." The *look* said, "I do not
love you." The *look* said, "You make me physically sick."

There were carrots offered, to accompany that ocular stick: his admiration, his attention, and his praise. And—all grimaces avoided or dismissed—his affirming, warming love.

Growing slowly in the shade he cast, I seemed to thrive. Teachers,
once I had decided that the sound of his voice was not enough and I must
learn to read, commented on my brilliance. Among boys my age, in the
schoolyard and elsewhere, I was a leader of the pack: in the second grade
I established a classroom fad—a mania—when I pulled up Patsy Rosen-
bloom's skirt, in order to display her panties; and, in the first half of the
fifth grade (after rugged initiation by the boys in school who were *really*
tough), I routed the class bully and won the love of a pretty, dark-haired
girl, whom I kissed three times, behind the woodpile at our house when
I had a party.

Daddy was enormously pleased by all this. He laughed, quite proudly,
when he told his friends, and I floated on his praise.

In the second half of fifth grade we moved to Beverly Hills, and I went
to the Hawthorne School (the sixth school of my young career—we moved
a lot, in those years, as his fortunes and his whims demanded). I did well
in school and, one Saturday, a girl named Virginia invited me home and,
as we sat facing each other in a two-seated swinging rocker, she leaned
forward with her blouse half unbuttoned. For minutes I stared, face flushed
and eyes transfixed, at the most beautiful, the most wonderful sight I had
ever seen—a nipple on the scrawny chest her open blouse revealed—and
all the time she smiled.

As Daddy smiled, when I told him of this adventure. And smiled again
when I bested another bully.

Then he went to war, and I wilted. The next fall, at yet another new
school, I was victimized on the playground, allowed myself to be bullied
on the bus; and the little girls seemed to turn away and titter whenever I
came near. I had been king of the schoolyard, had stood strong and tall,
but then he went away and I discovered that I had no legs at all. I had
been standing on his battered, borrowed limbs, and would have to grow
new ones of my own.

*   *   *

Night, and the liquor flowing, and the guitar held firmly in his grasp.

> *Oh, years have blown like Spanish moss.*
> *And other hounds will cry*
> *Beside the dark Myakka's stream*
> *Where once Old Flint went by*
> *. . .*
>
> *And other lady dogs will lie*
> *Beneath the live-oak tree....*
> *But in the dawn I hear them still:*
> *Old Flint and Beverly,*
> *Old Flint and Beverly.*

Everyone applauded.

"That was wonderful, Mack."

"Sing another."

Daddy loved to add new verses to old songs or, as in this case, to write his own, seizing the tune from any likely source and the theme from his own experience. Beverly Hills Mosby-Coleman Kantor had been our second collie. She had been named after the town we lived in when we found her and also after a friend—Beverly Mosby-Coleman, who was both a young naval officer and, more important to Daddy, the grandson of the leader of Mosby's Raiders during the Civil War. And, one time, Old Flint had truly courted Beverly, although "the heat of Nature's flame / Would never come till May."

He also loved to sing the songs of others. He seemed to know the words of every folk ballad or popular song that had been sung from the time of "gude Sir Patrick Spens" to the days of "Captain Jinks of the Horse Marines", and—lustfully, tenderly, eagerly—he sang them all.

> *He was a braw gallant,*
> *And he rid at the ring;*
> *And the bonny Earl of Murray,*
> *Oh, he might have been a king!*

"Barbry Allen", "The Union Forever," "I Am a Roving Gambler," "We're Marching to Zion," "Casey Jones mounted to the cabin / Casey Jones with his orders in his hand."

I sat entranced, as did others in the room, singing along quietly when

I knew the words. All lust, all loss, all longing, all history itself seemed palpable in that thrilling air.

Through the years, his voice enchanted, raged, ranted, and cajoled.

"My father was the cruelest man I've ever known." Mother's features tightened, but Layne and I settled down on the couch in eager anticipation. We loved to hear stories about Grandpa. "God knows he tormented me plenty of times when I was in my teens, and even before, but I think the worst thing he ever did was that time in Montreal, Layne-o, just after your mother gave birth to you."

He was intense, but also he was smiling, as though remembering some wonderful dirty joke.

"She had a long, hard time of it, and I had a long time waiting, and then they brought you out. You had blond hair, and that jailbird pout of yours, and I thought you were wonderful.

"And then I went to see your mother. I kissed her, and told her that I'd seen you, and that I was so happy. She was still woozy from the anesthetic, and needed to sleep, and so they kicked me out of there. Said to come back in a few hours. I went straight to Dad's office, to tell him our wonderful news, and then I went on to the Consulate, to register your birth. I don't know why it seemed so important to do that right away, but it did.

"I guess it made you official. And then I sent some telegrams to Iowa and to Chicago, telling about the arrival of Carol Layne Kantor at eleven forty A.M., weighing six pounds and fourteen ounces." He beamed upon Layne, he beamed upon me, proud of us both and proud of his memory.

"When I got back to your mother's room at the hospital, and went in, she was lying on her bed and she was weeping—sobbing hysterically."

Mother's face tightened further. Even at fourteen I knew that she did not find it easy to abandon the anguish of the past. When she spoke of her own mother's death, when she was seven, or of the death of her younger brother Kenny when he was fifteen, the tears still came to her eyes. "The old bastard had gotten there before me. He'd been there, lied and gone."

Mother took up the story. "I'd fallen asleep after your father had gone," she said. "When I woke up I didn't remember that he'd been there at all. And that man, that awful, pompous man, was standing by the bed. He looked at me so solemnly, and he puffed his cigar, and he shook his head.

'So you have a baby girl,' he said. 'I know that, I was informed. Your husband is brokenhearted.' And then he went away, and left me crying."

Daddy had been restless while Mother spoke. In truth it was her story, it had happened to her, but it was his dreadful father the story was about and, anyway, he did not like to sit silent. "That's the way your grandfather is. No theft is too big for him, and no meanness too small."

He looked at me. "I'll never forget how, when I was your age and we were in Chicago, he loved to humiliate me in public, in front of his friends."

And then he laughed, and the warmth of his laughter made the very thought of John Kantor seem amusing and ridiculous. He told another funny Grandpa story, and Layne and I were delighted. We felt privileged—as we knew he intended us to—to have such an ogre for a grandfather. We sensed a hurt in Daddy, but he kept it hidden. We knew only that Grandpa was a brilliant, twisted man, and one of the great con men of the time. He had been wanted, at various times, by the police of Canada, France, Great Britain, and the United States. He had been locked up in the Cook County Jail in Chicago, The Tombs in New York, and he was just completing a long stretch in Sing Sing. He had stolen eighteen dollars from a small-town Indiana minister during the worst of the depression years—a loss which Daddy had made good—and he had presided over the theft of millions, to the harm or ruination of thousands of people. Not another kid in school could boast of a grandfather to compare.

But certainly we were glad that Daddy was not like him in any way.

Time had shortened Daddy's name to Dad, but still he loomed above me, both physically and in thought. We had, we both believed, a warm and easy relationship, and surely he was proud of the uniform I wore. I was home on leave from the Air Force, and the folks were having a beach party in my honor. The stars were clear in the sky above, and a bonfire, which I had helped to make, offered warmth and light. Earlier there had been food, which was wonderful, and now there were drinks and a gentle breeze, and close to twenty family friends sat around the fire. Once more there was singing, with Dad's voice leading all the rest.

He delighted in singing in falsetto, at least an octave above his natural range, and yet his voice was firm and certain—even when he was drunk, as now he was. Mine was not. Too often I sought for notes and landed in between; that had been a source of family amusement for years. But always

I had sung along when others sang, and always my uncertain contribution had been welcome.

"It was down in old Joe's Barroom / In the corner by the square, / The drinks were served as usual..." I loved "The St. James Infirmary," and joined in with perhaps too much enthusiasm. Too much sound. Suddenly Dad stopped singing, stopped playing as well.

"What's wrong, Mack?"

"Mack, go on!"

He did not look at me, but glared—sullen—into the fire. "I will," he said, "if Timmy will stop his braying and let us sing." ("Mack, do not embarrass me in front of my friends....Tell them what you would do to save another Charley.") There was an enormous silence, until I walked away.

The singing soon resumed and, even far down the beach, I could hear his vibrant blare. "When I die, please bury me..." I didn't want to die. I wanted to live until I could sing as well as he. I also wanted, strangely, his forgiveness for what he had done to me.

Later I went back to the group around the fire. But as the others sang, I just whispered the words.

When I graduated from Cadets, ten months later, he gave me a car, and—as always he had, as best he could—he gave me his love.

In the summer of 1955 I lived near Dow Air Force Base, in Bangor, Maine, in a house I shared with three other young officers. I had shiny silver bars, tarnished silver wings, and a wondrous, golden love. Her name was Nan.

Nan had soft, dark hair, tough blue eyes, a nice little body, and a very quick mind. She also had two children, from a disastrous early marriage, and she lived with her parents in a house on the coast, across from Bar Harbor. The mother was a warm and earthy soul, the father a shy and reticent man, possessed of considerable intellect and great courage. I enjoyed them all, children, Nan, and parents, and spent as much time in that house as I could. And Nan and I stole off for celebration of our love as often as *we* could—but that was a different age, and Nan's divorce decree was not yet final, and privacy was sometimes hard to find.

During that July or August Dad sent four bound galley proofs, containing the complete text of the novel he'd just finished—after lamenting, on the phone, that he couldn't read it to me the way he'd like to. I thought the book was wonderful and so did Nan, when I passed the galleys on to her.

Her father, who had long enjoyed Dad's books, was overawed when she passed the galleys on to him. Her mother also thought the book was wonderful, almost as wonderful as the thought that I, the son of a rich and famous writer, might marry Nan.

The thought, the fear, of such a marriage had also occurred to my mother, who had already met Nan. The idea that Tim might celebrate his twenty-third birthday by Throwing Away His Life in marriage to an Older (by one year) Woman With Two Children appalled her. (I suspect that Nan already knew what it would take me months to discover: that I was far too immature and unformed to undertake such commitment.) So Mother fumed, and Mother rued, while Nan and I played happy games.

In late August Dad wrote and offered invitation. He and Mother were going to spend some time on Cape Cod, and he'd love to meet this wonderful girl he'd heard so much about, and couldn't Nan consign the kids to her parents for a weekend, and couldn't I get leave?

And we said yes.

We left on a Friday evening, and drove through the late summer light. We stopped at an old hotel near Augusta, registered as Mr. and Mrs. Kantor, and passed the night in revelry. I think we reveled in the morning too, for we were young and eager, and certainly we reached Woods Hole later than we'd intended.

Mother was icily polite, but Dad couldn't have been warmer. He was hearty, gruffly man-to-man, with me, and he courted Nan with fervor. I don't believe—with the possible exception of his sister—that he ever met an attractive female past the age of puberty whom he did not treat as a potential sexual target. He kept us up late with talk and drinking, he used all his gaiety and charm, and even Mother thawed before we said good night.

Nan was enchanted.

We had separate rooms, of course—Nan and I were across the landing from each other, on the second floor of the inn where we were staying, and my parents were settled down below. But young love breathes of lust as well as innocence and, in the morning, I woke up firm and needful. I went knocking at Nan's door and, smiling, she welcomed me. And then, after kiss and touch, she welcomed me in other fashion. We were going at it, playing the ancient heel-and-toe, with all the love and energy we owned, when we heard a rapping from across the landing, and my father called my name. When there was no response, he stomped across the floor, and beat on her door instead.

He shouted, in a voice that could be heard throughout the inn, "God damn it, you kids, knock it off! You can screw later. It's eight o'clock, and you promised to have breakfast with us, and Irene and I are hungry!" I shriveled, both in fact and metaphor, but I managed some reply, and we could hear him chuckle rather smugly as he walked away.

Nan, her shattered face damp both from recent striving and now from strain, gazed up at me. First she shook her head, and then she managed a wondering smile. "Your father," she said in a very tiny whisper, "is a *most* extraordinary man."

3

Prairie Song

"Your father's in prison!"

The shrill, hateful voice cut through the rich April air like a knife through butter, pierced it like an ice pick through the heart.

"Your old man's a Jew!"

Little Mack Kantor was running home from school, along the sidewalk on Willson Avenue, pursued by three taunting, jeering boys. Two of them were older, larger—grimy oafs from some riverside shack—and the other was a smaller child who capered and yawped under their protection. But Mack was almost home now, almost safe for another day.

"Your old man's a nigger!"

Outraged beyond all bearing, in shamed desperation, he turned to attack his tormentors. Hysteria drove him into a whirl of fists, made all the worse because one of the bigger boys stood behind the smallest, and held the child's arms and used his fists to do the striking. "Yeah, yeah, can't even fight a baby! And your old man's a Jew! Your father is in jail!" Blows landed (I feel those blows now, as if they were landing on my own flesh, bruising my own skin), tears oozed, until Mack's grandmother heard or saw the ruckus, and came to shoo off nastiness.

But even in the warm comfort of her arms, even in the safety of his home, the tears and sobs continued. His father *was* in jail, or had been—more than once he'd heard his mother and his grandmother discuss that infamy in plaining whispers; more than once he'd heard his grandfather speak with contempt and anger when John Kantor's name was mentioned. And his father—that unknown being, that *word*, which each night his mother insisted he mention in his prayers—was a Jew. And Jews were foreign, monstrous creatures. Oh, Mr. Louis Frank was Jewish, and he was respected in the town, but he was different—he was a Pioneer. Jews were alien; they were Christ-killers.

His father was not a Negro. That particular libel—worse even than the others, in that time and in that place—was spread by ignorant folk who had heard that John Kantor had a dark complexion. Which was true. He was tall and handsome and slightly swarthy; his mother was a Margolis, and her ancestors had come from Portugal. But little Mack Kantor knew nothing of Sephardim or Ashkenazim.

He did know there were gibes. He lived with them; not every day, but often enough to hurt. And, unlike other boys, he had no father to avenge those gibes, or to protect him from them.

He did have a *grand*father, but Adam McKinlay was a remote and dour soul, whose warmth and eagerness had been stunted first by a brutal childhood, then stinted even more by later disappointment. Through energy and thrift he had managed to build up a respectable small-town competence. He had seen that slowly dwindle, as the grain elevator replaced the flour mill in the prairie economy, and dwindle further when he lent money to his father-in-law (never to see either money or father-in-law again), and further still as he wrote check after painful check in a small cramped hand, to repay his son-in-law's bad debts, or to repay the defrauded—in order to keep that son-in-law out of jail, or to bail him out if already he was there. Now Adam McKinlay—miller's apprentice, miller, mill owner—managed a grain elevator in a nearby town, for someone else and for meager pay, and he came back to Webster City late on Saturday night, and left again on the early Monday train.

So, in that kindergarten year, as in so many others, Mack Kantor lived in a house full of women—swathed, bathed, laved in assertive femininity. He slept on a day bed in Effie Kantor's room, and his sister Virginia— three and a half years older than Mack and somewhat of a mother figure herself—shared a larger bed with their mother. Their grandmother, Eva (which was short for Evalyn, and thus the e was also short), shared the only other bedroom with Adam, when he was home.

On wintry Sunday mornings, after Grandpa had gotten up to set the hard-coal burner going and to take his bath, sometimes Grandma would lie abed, and then Mackie might creep into her room and crawl under the covers and they would play silly games and recite nonsense rhymes, and he loved the scent and warmth of her. And sometimes, when his mother was away from home, "doing" for some birthing farm wife or doting granny—to earn a few precious dollars to substitute for the support payments which

John Kantor almost never sent—Mack would retreat into the closet in his own, his sister's, his mother's bedroom, and nestle among the long dresses and undergarments hanging there, and smell them and hug them tight and think of her, and long to have her near.

But there was more in his world than school and bullies, more in his home than the smother of soft love or the comfort of a dress. There were boys to play with—Robert Richardson and Herbert Arthur and other boys who lived nearby, and who did not revile him—and ardently he played. There was a garden to be tended and chickens, which he loathed, to be fed, and a cornfield just south of the house—oh, high the stalks, come August, and he so small—in which to hunt for Indians and hide from bear, and all around the house, as old as the house, were the guardian maple trees which he adored. Green, the leaves, but also golden when they blocked the sun and cast their shade. He thought they might be gods.

Within the house, along with want and worry, there was music. Often, on Sunday nights when Grandpa McKinlay went early to bed, he would call down, "Effie, play the Glory Song." Effie would go to the old Hallett and Davis piano in the front room and sit down, and her firm, strong hands would strike the keys and fill the house with joy. "... When by His grace / I shall look on His face, / That will be Glory, / Glory for me."

And there was laughter there, and there were tales.

"Mack, did I ever tell you how my father—your great-grandfather, Mack—fought the Indians?"

"Mother, did you ever tell Mack about that time down at the mill, when I was small, and that man came skulking, with an ax?"

"Mack, did I ever tell you...?"

"Mack, did I ever tell...?"

Eagerly Eva told, eagerly Effie told, and eagerly he listened to the legends which, when he was grown and I was small, my father told to me.

It hangs now from a nail on my kitchen wall: a small chopping board, unevenly fashioned—about three-fourths of an inch thick, nine inches wide, and fifteen inches long, with a six-inch handle at the top. It has been handled, well handled, for over a century. There are knife and cleaver scars upon its surface, cracks within the grain, and one corner was long ago charred by flame from an ancient stove. It was homemade, hand-carved from a single piece of wood, and its rough shoulders and the pierced circle at the top of the handle suggest an Indian totem. Whenever I use it I think of prairie schooners struggling westward, of prairie clouds and a prairie sun, and a prairie wind to beckon.

I also think of my father slicing onions or mincing green peppers on that board, to go with the quartered tomatoes in his favorite relish—Chicago Hot. Clumsy chop, chop, chop of the knife, seeming so small in his big hands, and he turns to me, smiling. "Do you know where this board came from?" A rhetorical question, with no answer expected or awaited. "It came from Zanesville, Ohio. A long, long time ago—back in 1848—your great-great-great-grandfather, Alanson Bryan, cut it out from the bole of a bird's-eye maple tree. He carved it and shaped it, and he gave it to his daughter, Rachel—your great-great-grandmother—on her Wedding Day."

Rachel Bryan was seventeen—a pretty, dark-haired woman-child—when she married Joseph Bone. He was one year older—a tall and eager young man with the gift of charm. Maybe he was kin to Daniel Boone (spelling was lax, idiosyncratic, in those days, and Dad liked to believe that there was some connection) and maybe he was not, but certainly he had great dreams and he had the urge to wander. As did many in the nation that year, and in the year which hurried after. Word had come from Sutter's Mill, in California, of gold nuggets to be found for the taking, and Zanesville was on the National Road, and the National Road was the main route westward. All day long Alanson Bryan and Joseph Bone could hear the squeal of wagon wheels, and smell and taste the dust which the wheels and the teams kicked up, and they felt the wish to follow.

They were both millers by trade, though millers of grain, not wood—unlike the man who had built the mill and found that gold at the foot of the High Sierras. In 1849 they and their wives packed up their children, their possessions, and their dreams and joined an immigrant train, headed west toward Iowa.

They did not dream of gold, nor ever did they find it. They found a new land, they made new lives, instead. But those new lives were purchased from adversity, as most lives were and are, and the cost was dear. The prairie wind again, come a long way off the Plains, from Kansas or Nebraska, and traveling even farther, making lonely music as it whispered past their ears and set the windflowers all aquiver. Windflowers, the kind which grew in Iowa only where the prairie sod had not been stripped away—torn off the loam with mule and chain—in order to clear the land for planting, or for burial. Rachel Bone bore a total of thirteen children and, while the names and fate of few of them have filtered through the years, I know that diphtheria, the measles, croup, and other childhood banes flourished in that undoctored time and place, and scattered loss and sorrow as they throve.

But adversity can toughen the soul, just as wind and sun can toughen the skin, and Rachel Bone endured. In 1861 she gave birth to her ninth child, my great-grandmother, Eva. Three years later her husband took a Cheyenne arrow in his shoulder. The Civil War had come to tear the nation in two, and Joseph Bone had volunteered to fight the Rebels—the damned "Secesh." But still the wagon trains were crawling westward, and still the retreating tribes resisted these incursions on their land, and First Lieutenant Joseph Bone was assigned to Company G, Seventh Iowa Cavalry, in Nebraska Territory. He was wounded in a skirmish and, as so often in those times, the wound became infected and he caught fever, and the surgeon thought that he might die. So Joseph wrote to Rachel, and asked her to fetch him home.

When Rachel received the letter, she herself was fevered, suffering from a painful abscessed tooth, and in no condition to travel. And there was no doctor nigh. She took a steel knitting needle, heated it past red to palest yellow in the kitchen fire, drove it into the swollen, angry gum to lance the abscess, and killed the nerve which plagued her. Rachel left her oldest child, a girl of fourteen, in charge of all the others, and rode the stagecoach west.

Lieutenant Bone was still agued—still hot and cold and hurting—when she reached him. They were assigned a covered wagon, with an escort of six time-served troopers, to make the journey back. Joseph lay and slept and ached within the wagon, and Rachel tried to comfort him. Halfway across Nebraska Territory, on their trek to the Missouri River and to Iowa, the little group crested a ridge and stopped. In the valley below them they saw a small wagon train halted, wagons clustered, under attack by a large band—to their frightened eyes it must have seemed a swarm—of Indians. They were too few to render help, too few indeed to protect themselves if the Indians saw them, and so they retreated behind the crest, left the wagon and tethered the horses, and took refuge in an abandoned sod dugout nearby. Peeping over its crumbling walls, like children watching a puppet show, they saw tiny figures misbehave. They hid, and watched the massacre. They hid, and watched the wagons burn.

Later they dug a long trench, and buried the bodies.

I have seen the site of that massacre. When I was thirteen or fourteen I stood upon a barren ridge, above a brown and desolate valley in Nebraska, and my father pointed it out to me. He was as scrupulous in absorbing and reporting the facts of history—the glorious, reverenced Past, complete with names, dates, places, and those small details which might give that Past an exactitude and vigor approaching life—as he was fanciful in reporting more personal, familial history. In such reportage he was apt to change happenings to the way he thought they should have been, and to change the personalities of those he knew and loved to nature's which he felt they ought to have—with which he felt comfortable. But on this occasion he spoke his own truth, and that of history, I know. We were some six miles south of Lexington, and roughly three miles east—not far from the Platte. The stream in the valley is called Plum Creek, and it lent its name to the massacre.

There were other tales to be told. Legend rained from the trees around the house, dripped from the eaves, whispered through that field of corn with the prairie wind behind it, and lingered in the bread his grandmother baked—bread redolent and fresh from the oven, the very oven on which the chopping board was scorched. Tall, lean old men visited the house— veterans of the Spirit Lake Relief Expedition back in 1857, over fifty years before—and answered Effie Kantor's questions about blizzard and frostbite and desolation, to Mack's delight and wonder.

"Frostbite!" He would grow tall and lean also, but still so young and vital. "When I was nine years old, and first had that paper route, I got frostbite too. The wind can blow mean in an Iowa winter and, for some reason, my right cheek always seemed to feel it more. I'd arrive home from delivering papers, my face frozen stiff, and Grandma—your great-grand- mother—would apply an old Pioneer remedy. She'd take a handful of snow and rub it all over my face." He rubbed his cheek as he spoke, in dramatic emulation. "Rub hard! I think, poor dear, she made things worse when she wanted to make them better. My cheek still aches whenever it gets cold."

There were the gray-beard, blue-clad stories of the honored elders of those days, veterans of the Civil War. Cannon spoke, men shouted in fear or exultation, Minié balls whistled through his mind whenever the Old Soldiers rambled in reverie—stumbling over their proud truths, or telling smoothly those fictions which, through iteration, had ceased to be lies.

And then the family stories: Lieutenant Joseph Bone and Alanson Bryan bringing their families north to Hamilton County, and buying mills just a few miles south of town, along the western bank of the Boone River. Ah, *Boone*. That word again. The name was haunting, informative, in my fa- ther's life, and even in my own. I can hear him now, reading aloud when I was six or seven, from a slim blue book with wonderful illustrations: *A*

Book of Americans, by Rosemary and Stephen Vincent Benét. Reading aloud, in nasal imitation of Steve Benét's tenor voice: "When Daniel Boone goes by, at night, / The phantom deer arise / And all lost, wild America / Is burning in their eyes." I could see those eyes, glimmering fey out of darkness as he read, and there *had* been deer along the banks of the Boone. There had also been bear and panther, and Indians to hunt them. And then had come the Pioneers; and Alanson Bryan and Joseph Boone had been among them.

He learned less about the background of his grandfather, Adam McKinlay, for Adam was not garrulous, and he did not like to linger on his past. But, yes, he had worn the kilt when small, and that was exotic. His father, William, had been mayor of Epworth, Iowa, for many years, and that was impressive. His mother had been a Miller—Jane Miller—and wasn't that ironic, for Adam had become a miller. And when his mother died, Adam's father had married a cruel woman, a thorn misnamed a Rose—Rose Wilkerson. She had beaten Adam a lot, particularly when his father was away from home supervising construction gangs on the railroad, and that was sad. He had run away from home for the last time when he was sixteen, and come to Hamilton County and found work in the mill which Joseph Bone later bought. Then Adam worked for Joseph. When she was sixteen and he was ten years older, he had married Eva, the miller's daughter. And that was wonderful. That was marvelous, almost overwhelming. For, two years later, they had their only child, a baby girl, and they called her Effie, after Adam's younger sister.

Effie. Mack's mother! She was tall and brave and busy, but so exciting to talk with and so gentle when she cosseted him, and her long hair was dark and coarse and lustrous and, on winter mornings, it crackled when she combed it.

He loved her dearly, and he always would.

And she loved him. Just as, despite all broken promises, deceit, and infamy, she would always love his father.

He was six when he first heard his father's voice. It was evening—"a cool evening," which makes it spring or fall in 1910—when the miracle happened. It was a typical weekday evening: Adam was out of town; Effie and Eva were busy in the kitchen, clearing away supper; dutiful, studious Virginia was doing her homework; and Mack was sitting on the sofa and playing with some long-since-forgotten toy. And then the phone rang, and filled the room with a counterfeit wonder which, almost thirty-seven years later, he described—with all the strange confusion of that night still working in him as he wrote.

It was my father. I do not know what his purpose was in calling just then; he had never telephoned before, to my knowledge, and did not do so again for a long time. I suppose that something had happened to awaken in him a mood of affection... maybe he wanted to hear my mother's voice again. After I was grown, I heard him declare that my mother was the only woman he had ever loved—but also he made a great many other declarations which were completely untrue.

This particular night Mother talked to him on the telephone; then he asked for Virginia; she talked. I watched entranced from the sofa. The room seemed resounding with a strange presence. The furniture, the old red-and-gilt wallpaper—nothing looked the same. It was not the same world in which I had watched a moment before. Everything was different... other people had fathers right with them all the time... I did not have any father with me.

Somewhere, off beyond that wooded eastern horizon which turned lonely and plum blue when night crept up from the prairie, somewhere far over the leagues of cornfields and towns and smoke, there was a strange place called Chicago, and my father was in it.

Now I was being pushed up to the telephone, I was standing on a chair to reach it: a little black phone fastened against the wall next to the front door. The receiver was planted at my ear.

Mother was whispering beside me, "Say, 'Hello.'"

"Hello."

A great sonorous echo came back to me; it sounded like no voice I had ever heard before.

Mother whispered, "Say, 'Hello, Daddy.'"

"Hello... Daddy."

"Hello there, sweetheart."

I stammered when I said it again. "H—h—hello, Daddy."

"Do you love your Daddy, sweetheart?" the deep resonant voice blatted in my ear. Mother had her own ear close beside mine, so that she might hear what my father was saying.

"I—I—" Then adjured to politeness by my mother, I said, "I love you, Daddy."

He laughed. Through all the years I can hear the fatuous rumble, the oily conceit of his voice. "Daddy loves you, sweetheart. Daddy wants to send you something. What do you want your Daddy to send you?"

I did not know what to say. This was not real, it was all an imagining and a mistake, a peculiar contrivance of nightmare. The great black voice blurting inside the sweaty receiver...father...I did not know. What should one ask of a father whom he had never seen?

"I don't know," I said. "I—I don't know."

"How would you like to have a bicycle? Do you want your Daddy to send you a bicycle?"

I whispered, "Yes." And then as the magnitude of this proposal flashed upon me, I yelled it at the top of my lungs: "Yes!"

"Very well, I know that you are a good boy, so I will send you a bicycle tomorrow."

Tomorrow! The oleaginous voice had also promised Virginia a present. Eagerly she waited for the mailman to come, eagerly Mack waited for the green express cart or the delivery wagon to come rumbling down their street. They rushed home from school each day, they kept watch from the windows of the house, the sound of horses in the street would distract them from their play.

They waited for weeks, and weeks, and weeks, but no bicycle ever came, nor ever did a present.

They were young. Days passed slowly for them, each with its own varying quota of distraction, of loss and gain, and so, in time, pain could be forgotten, or at least be deeper buried. And, in the months that followed, Mack found an honest wonder to enchant him.

He learned to Read.

In the first grade, confronted with a phonetic stew of *ad*s, *ed*s, *id*s, *od*s and *ud*s—all printed neatly, meaninglessly, on charts in the front of the classroom—he had failed in that task totally, and had been considered one of the class dunces. But in the second grade, with a new superintendent of schools, and thus new readers and new methods of instruction, and the ridiculous charts discarded, he made almost miraculous progress. He jumped from laboriously puzzling out passages from *McGuffey's First Reader* to flaw-lessly deciphering adult books—Dickens, Macaulay, and others—within months. He was put on display—perched on the big desk in the Superin-tendent's office, reading from a big book, feeling scared and proud—as a model of the excellence a more sound approach to the teaching of reading could produce, whenever officials from other school districts came visiting. In the spring he was skipped two grades—to the "lower fourth." Which was more tragedy than triumph, because for years he would suffer as the youngest and the smallest boy in his class.

But he had learned to Read.

Books were treasured in his home, and they had been for many years. (Eva had been named secretary of the Pleasant Hill Literary Society when it was formed way back in 1888, in the area around Bone's Mill, and she left records of meetings and debates—neatly written on lined notepaper—to prove it: "Question: Resolved, 'That George Washington deserves more honor for defending his country than Abraham Lincoln.'") Effie loved to read aloud, and the children loved to listen, but now Mack could read for himself, and that was even better. He was fascinated by words, their sound, their meaning, the flavor he encountered as he curled his tongue around them, and in them he found a certain power. He and Virginia learned to cherish words, as did their mother, and they learned to honor them.

Far more than ever did that distant voice—their father in Chicago.

Another evening, another year—the fall of 1911. The children were seated at the table, finishing their meal, and Grandma and Mother were looking at them and smiling, though perhaps Eva's smile was not as bright as Effie's. Effie asked, and her eyes were shining, "Would you like to go with me to Chicago, and see your father?" Jaws dropped, and spoons rattled on their plates. Mack and Virginia stared at one another. Many months had passed since that unfulfilled and now half-forgotten promise. Virginia could think only of the father she had last known when she was three years old. He had held her in his hands, and lifted her high, and smiled the most wonderful smile, and he had been so grand and kind. And Mack could only think of the absence in his life of that presence, being, word which almost every other child he knew possessed: a father. "Oh, yes," they cried. "Oh, yes! When? When?"

"Tonight!"

"But how?" Chicago was so far away. It was the center of the world, all glittering and bright.

"On the train. And in a sleeping car! Your father sent the money."

A sleeping car! Very few of their friends had ever ridden in a sleeping car. And Chicago, and their father. They were possessed by excitement, almost tormented by it, and rushed off to tell their friends the incredible news.

It was late when the train departed and, by the time they had reached the depot and boarded the sleeping car, their excitement was a little abated. They knew that their father had sent money for the trip, and that he was rich, but it seemed that his riches were limited. He had sent only enough money for one lower berth, and so they must share it all together. But still, Chicago the next day, and Father, and the rattle of the train: there was magic in the night, and they found it hard to sleep.

Grandpa McKinlay, who bitterly disapproved of this venture, was a practical man, responsible and thrifty, and it was because of those characteristics that Joseph Bone—who admired especially those qualities which he did not himself possess—had encouraged Adam's courtship of his daughter, Eva. Their daughter, Effie—now lying rigid in the middle of that lower berth, trying not to toss, with her children nestled close—also displayed a tough practicality, but hers was born of native strength responding to necessity. It was not inherited; at heart, at the core of her fiery, insistent soul, she was a romantic. She had loved John Kantor when she married him, she had loved him when he got children in her, she loved him now, and—in all trite and foolish truth—she would love him until she died. She was also an optimist. There had been phone calls, there had been flowery, entreating letters, and it seemed that a reconciliation might be possible.

It is hard to fit together these shards of memory from past generations. So many years, so much reticence, so many half-remembered tales have encrusted them that it is hard to sort them out, and make a pattern. To reassemble vanished lives is not easy; sometimes it is painful. But I think I know her mind. A woman needed, *she* needed—in proper married state— her loved one; her children needed a father; and perhaps John Kantor had at last become what he had always sworn he was: an honest man.

The train moved through the night, bearing them nearer and nearer to Chicago. Virginia concentrated on memories of wonderful, kindly—he had just forgotten about that present, he had just forgotten—regal Daddy. Maybe now she would live with him always.

Caught in a mixture of fear, reluctance, and expectation, staring into darkness, Mack listened to the sound the wheels made as they rode the rails. *Clack-clack-clack*, they went. *Clack-clack-clack*. "Chi-ca-go," they said. "Chi-ca-go. Chi-ca-go." And then, "My fa-ther, my fa-ther." He would see his father in the morning.

"My father, my father, my father, my father.

"My father!"

4

Come We That Love
The Lord

John Kantor, the eldest son of a Talmudic scholar whose ancestors for eleven generations had been cantors in fact as well as name, stood under soft, yellow lamplight on the corner of a damp, muddy street in Chicago and watched soldiers of the Salvation Army strive with brass and song to redeem lost souls from shame. It was a late afternoon in the winter of 1894, and he was fifteen years old. The band had finished "Onward, Christian Soldiers," and now they were playing "We're Marching to Zion." He found it hard to follow the words—he had learned a great deal of English in the last two years, but still it was difficult for him to capture all the meaning of the words when they were sung—and he did not approve of the lilt and bounce of the music. It did not seem *religious:* it was so sprightly and gay, unlike the more stately songs and chants he was accustomed to hearing in the synagogue, that it seemed to lack all dignity. But he was impressed with its effect on those gathered around him, and on those passers-by who stopped to listen, standing still and rapt, though the chill, dank wind from the Lake blew harsh about them. It was obvious that the music had power.

John Kantor was impressed by power.

He was more than impressed, he was enchanted, when the band stopped playing and their officer began to speak—reaching out with his words and with his voice to touch sinners in the crowd. And they all loved it, both the sinners and the saved; the poor fools ate it up, devouring every word and every tone. John kept his face sober and grave, it would not do for a Jewish boy to be seen sneering at a Christian sermon, but inside he laughed to see the smiles which came to some faces, and the tears which appeared in the eyes of others. *That* was power.

He turned his head to watch the speaker. He imagined himself up there on that box, speaking to these sheep with all his own resonance and force. The vision warmed him despite the wintry air; it shone bright within his mind, bright as the silver buttons now gleaming in lamplight on the Salvation Army uniform the officer wore. But he, John Kantor, would not wear a uniform. No. He detested uniforms, especially the Western Union messenger's garb he was wearing now. It hid his uniqueness, his own special quality. If ever *he* stood before a huge crowd of dolts—ten, twenty, fifty times the size of the crowd assembled now—urging them to come forward to accept Christ as their Saviour, and they all came forward with their eyes glowing in wonder at the beauty of his sermon, he would wear a simple business suit, very quiet in cut and color but obviously expensive. The cut would display the stately dignity of his own manly carriage, and the color would set off the flash of his own brown eyes, the grave composure of his own handsome face.

The fools would love it. They would love the clothes, they would love the sermon, they would love him.

His brothers loved him, and they were fools, but his father was the greatest fool of all. He was a learned man, of course, and everyone in the congregation respected him and called him Rebbe Joseph, but he had no money. He *had* had money, lots of it, but that had all gone, and the beautiful house in Karlskrona (John had thought of it as *his* house), and the business of haberdasher, by appointment, to the King of Sweden. Now they lived in a cramped apartment in Chicago, and his father sold tailors' trimmings, and John had to work as a messenger boy. All because his father's partner had been cleverer than he was, and smarter, and stolen all his money.

When John grew up, he would be smart too.

A few months before he had considered someday becoming a rabbi, or a cantor, like his grandfathers. It would have been fun to preside over the congregation in shul, to lead them in their prayer. But in a world filled with goyim, that would not have been smart, that would not have been clever.

Four years later John Kantor was touring the Midwest in a Revival Show, speaking as The Converted Jew and telling the audience about the falsity of Judaism and the joys of Christianity. The audience loved him.

In a small town in Iowa, at a church social after the Meeting, he met a wealthy, pious farmer, and the farmer's pretty daughter. Before many days had passed the farmer was so taken with the sincerity of The Converted Jew's Christian convictions and the strength of his vocation, and the daughter so affected by the warmth of his romantic insinuations, that the farmer offered to send him to Drake Bible College in Des Moines.

It was there, at Drake University, that he met Effie McKinlay. She was a slim young woman, rather tall for that time (Adam McKinlay was a short man, but Joseph Bone had been a giant), and she moved with a purposeful grace. Her face was long and bright and well-modeled, with a touch of the Irish about the eyes, and she was quite beautiful. And she had the gift of faith: the romantic's tendency to be credulous, in matters both of the spirit and of the flesh.

During the previous year, in the spring of 1898, while John Kantor was publicly washing himself in the blood of the Lamb, and gaining the sympathy and admiration of many while he did so, Effie had also been emoting. The Webster City High School senior class play that year was *The Merchant of Venice*, and Effie had been chosen to play Portia. When she did the "quality of mercy" speech she brought down the house. For days afterward, her father heard nothing but praise for her apparent courtroom talents. "By Gad," his cronies said whenever they encountered him, "By Gad, Adam, that girl ought to be a lawyer!"

Adam had certainly cared for Effie ever since she was born, but also he had resented her—for being a girl rather than a boy. Why, in that Victorian time, he should have taken such idle urgings seriously, I do not know, but he did. Effie did not. She knew herself better than that. She had, when she was not misled by romantic or charitable impulse, a passion for the truth; but it was the whole truth, the journalist's truth, which she sought, not the lawyer's clever parsing of that same truth into precise, equivocal pieces. She also loved the beauty of the world around her, and already she had made some pretty drawings which had brought her praise. She wished to study art, not law.

Some compromise was reached, and she entered Drake in January of 1899. There had been no need to compromise about the choice of school. That had been inevitable. It had a good reputation, it was only sixty miles away, and it had been founded by the Disciples of Christ; both Bryans and Bones, and later Adam McKinlay, were ardent members of that sect. She entered Drake University, and she met John Kantor, and her life was enchanted, was blighted, from that time on.

He was handsome, dark, and over six-foot tall. His short, black hair was closely curled, his mouth was small yet somehow full, appropriate to the fulsome speech he uttered, and his large nose was slightly hooked. His big brown eyes bulged with sincerity from under heavy lids, and his rich, deep voice coated all his words with honey. He had a fierce intellect, an enormously retentive memory, was widely and curiously well-read, and had all the warm and melting charm of Cagliostro himself. He was, or promised, everything which the beaux of Webster City had lacked, and she fell in love with him—or was overwhelmed by admiration, physical attraction, and what she took to be love—on the day they met.

Perhaps he also thought he loved her. It is difficult, even foolish, to ascribe emotions other than fear or joy to certain stunted people—they are not concerned with love or hate, they are concerned with *use*—but I think that, of all the wives and all the affairs of later years, he was more *aware* of her than any other. Certainly he forgot the farmer's daughter. She had served her purpose.

He and Effie were married on November 29, 1899, and, shortly after or before, John Kantor took a small pastorate in Sheldon, Iowa. He had not graduated from Drake, he had not been ordained, but that did not matter to him; he told the congregation otherwise. It did not matter to the members of the congregation either—they loved his sermons, the rich, ripe words he used, the sound of his deep and unctuous voice—until six months later rumors spread and they found out the truth. Effie, who had not, in her avid innocence, understood the nature of his charade, was mortified.

She was also pregnant.

Virginia McKinlay Kantor entered into her particular allotment of joy and tears on November 4, 1900. (Still, as I write this, she is vital and vibrant, and through the years she has grown far wiser than ever was her brother.) Now Effie had a love, a child, a problem.

The love, in response to her own need, and to charm, physical passion, and words of explanation which seemed wonderfully true and logical if she did not examine them too closely, grew ever more compelling. The child needed her father's love and presence, but also needed security. The problem, the product of John Kantor's congenital dishonesty, festered for over three more years, through other false pastorates and other defrockings, through unfulfilled business deals and petty defalcations, through unpaid bills and a series of evictions, through pleas to her father for assistance and his grudging compliance, through arrests and jailings and the need for bail, through words of exculpation and promises of reform. Three times, at least, she left him, and each time she returned—drawn by the honey of his tongue, drawn by the touch of his hand.

*   *   *

She made the final break in December 1903. She and Virginia had taken refuge in the Chicago home of Eva Corbett, a classmate from her brief days in college. John Kantor was in jail, or he was not; he was also in Chicago, or he was not. Effie was always reluctant to speak of this period and, if ever she gave more specific detail, in later years neither my father nor his sister remembered. It does not matter.

He was not there. And, for the second time, Effie was pregnant. She had no money, no money at all, and yet she needed provision for Virginia, for herself, and for the unnamed being who now was restless in her womb. And John Kantor was not there to provide, he was not there to help.

She wired home for money yet one more time, received it, and she and Virginia took the day coach back to Webster City. She went back to a bleak house (it would be a year before the family moved to that other cramped but homelier house which memory would later enshrine as home for both Mack and Virginia), and to a stern greeting. "You can come back, Effie," Adam McKinlay said, after first making much over Virginia, "and you're welcome to stay. But, if you go back to that man one more time, I never want you to come back again. Ever." So this was a watershed in her life, and one that shed bitter water. For not only was her father firm in his weary, understandable resolve, but also her mother lay abed. She was sick, and the doctors said that she was dying.

Eva had also been to Chicago. Victoria Evalyn Bone McKinlay had had a difficult time carrying her daughter Effie, and an even harder labor. According to family legend, she had suffered "lesions" during delivery. She and Adam shared a double bed during all the years of their marriage, but I think they may have practiced abstinence. I think the doctor may have given Eva a *warning*. I have a mental picture of Eva sleeping with her face and body turned away from him, and of Adam lying there, rigid, suffering Calvinistically the pains of a tumescence never again relieved, never again fulfilled. Certainly it is true that they had no other children.

During the summer and fall of 1903 Eva suffered pains, and other "problems." Her doctor did not like her symptoms, and urged Adam to send her to specialists in the big city. Eventually, unwillingly, penurious Adam agreed. The specialists examined her, declared that she had cancer of the uterus, and sent her home to die.

She took to her bed, feeling depressed and desperate. But then Effie came home with Virginia, and Effie was ripe with child. Effie—Eva's daughter, and her darling—needed help. She needed seeing to. And so Eva got out of bed and—telling the stories and singing the hymns which warmed her soul—she saw to Effie, to Adam, to Virginia, and to the boy child who was born on February 4, 1904. She saw to them, looked after them as best she could, for twenty-six years. Then she died: of cancer of the uterus.

And so my father was born into a household filled with both a sense of defeat, and an awareness of the possibility of miracles. I think that, encouraged by his mother, he feasted most upon the latter.

Chicago was a miracle, also: so vast, so bright, so shining, so filled with gullible fools. Or so it seemed to John Kantor, in the bold light of that October morning in 1911. There were politicians to be bribed, real estate investors to be cozened, monies to be gained. And now that he had learned his trade he spent less time in jail. In fact, he had not been inside a jail in several years. He had learned how to dance around the edges of the law, and that was a smart, a clever, a pretty dance to do.

His taxicab came to a stop in front of the Chicago & Northwestern railroad station. It was a fine new building, all glittering and white; its facade, and all the interior walls as well, were lined with marble. It was magnificent, it was sumptuous—yes, that was the word which should be used, which he must use: sumptuous. He paid the fare and overtipped, receiving in return a servile gratitude which pleased him greatly, and walked, sedate and slightly ponderous—a procession of one—into the terminal, carrying his cane.

Once inside he paused to glance at his large gold watch, then nodded gravely in approval. He was just late enough to remind Effie, the children, and himself of his own importance, and so he proceeded up the stairs to greet them.

5

One Solid Week

Chicago, seen from the train, was a vast and grimy wonderland. And, in that wonderland, the terminal seemed a palace. The waiting rooms were huge and thronged and, in them, metal gleamed and marble glistened. Also, there was a restaurant! (In the shabby little railway station in Webster City there was only a small, rusty machine, which dispensed moldy bits of chocolate if one had the necessary pennies.)

Dad always remembered in clearest detail the breakfast he consumed while they were waiting for his father: orange halves, "huge and sweet and juicy; the hot chocolate had a creamy, purplish gloss; I soaked my buttered toast in it and ate in a blissful fog."

After breakfast they went to the waiting room, and they waited.

Virginia sat decorously on a bench, beside their mother, but little boy Mack was restless. At last, after long minutes of wriggling and squirming, Effie gave him permission to wait for his father (father he had spoken to only once, and only to be cheated, and had never seen at all) at the head of the stairs. He had not been standing there long when a tall man, richly, soberly dressed, came slowly up them. The tall man paused, and then deliberately he tucked his walking stick under his arm and, again deliberately, bent down—he seemed always to move in slow motion, as though haste was undignified—and asked, "Are you looking for someone?"

A small voice, far away, as though it did not belong to Mack at all: "I'm looking for Mr. Kantor."

And the man smiled the most wonderful smile, and he reached out his hands, and he lifted him high. He said, "I am John Kantor, and you are my son," and his words hung, golden, in the air.

46

* * *

Chicago was a big red taxicab, it was a laughing, booming, overriding voice, it was a rich purple box of candy filled with nougats and chocolate creams, the most wonderful box of candy Mack had ever owned. Chicago was a *suite* in the Saratoga Hotel, wonderful clothes purchased in expensive stores for Mack, for Virginia, and for Effie, rich dinners and suppers (only here dinner was called lunch, supper was called dinner) with expansive, alien men seated at the table where John Kantor presided—men introduced as partners, politicians, lawyers, and one who wore an impressive uniform and was the Chief of Police. And always the men had high-pitched, glittering women in tow. Chicago was a surfeit of relatives with exotic names: Uncle Herman, Uncle Arvid, Aunt Besse. Chicago was the bright glow of electric lights on signs and in streetlamps, in stores and hotel lobbies; and the equally electric sparkle of John Kantor's enticing bombast, his presence, and his money.

Doormen hastened, headwaiters bowed low, and waiters fawned whenever he came near.

There were also late-night banquets and after-the-theater parties to which their mother was bidden after the children were in bed. One of the gifts Effie had received was a black satin dinner dress with a white silk yoke, and when she put it on Mack thought that she looked more beautiful than ever—to him she looked like an angel—and he did not wish her to go. (Their father had paid for that dress with a hundred-dollar bill. Virginia had seen him do so, and, when they considered this incredible fact, both children were overcome with wonder.) After a few such nights, spending hours with people whose dress, whose accents and actions, whose apparent sophistication and evident insincerity were so different from the more homely ways of Webster City, Effie did not wish to go herself.

She shouldn't have come. She knew that before four days were out. She had made a terrible error.

Back home she had finally achieved a certain meager independence. No longer did she, as in the first years after Mack was born, have to play the piano at parties or lodge functions, clerk in stores when a substitute was needed, take in sewing, take in personal laundry from her friends, do embroidery, take pictures of families or social clubs with her little Kodak Brownie, bake cakes, do *anything* to earn a few pennies, to earn a few dollars. No longer did she have to do the demanding, sometimes demeaning, work of a practical nurse, either in homes which made her own seem bare and primitive, or in homes which *were* bare and primitive. Now she was the cashier at Scriven's grocery store on a regular basis, and she earned enough to buy her children and herself the basic—oh, the most painfully basic—necessities, and to contribute something to the household budget as well. She was proud of this hard-won independence, but she had dreamed eagerly, blissfully, of surrendering it; she had imagined that she might once again cleave to John Kantor, once more be his wife and consort, with all the fervor with which she had clung to her children—nurtured them, sparked them, almost smothered them with a passion which had no other outlet—during all the difficult years.

But now she felt that she'd been wrong to dream.

She did not like his friends, she did not feel comfortable with them, she felt—in her prairie naïveté—that they condescended whenever she came near. And, despite all the evidence he displayed of honest financial success, despite the obvious respect and admiration of those he drew to him, and the deference with which they treated him, despite his own protestations, she did not fully trust him. There was something false about all his ostentation, especially when she compared it to his lack of support through the years, especially when she thought of that single lower berth in which they'd come to Chicago.

Yet the sound of his voice, the wonderful way he used words, the heat of his glance, the quickness of his mind, the slightest touch of his hand, set her thighs aquiver, and made moistness come in that secret, central place which only he had known and entered. When he looked at her, and she felt that feeling come upon her, she remembered the joy he had given her—physical joy so intense as to make her shudder—and she wanted to be the third Mrs. Kantor, just as she had been the first. (He had remarried after divorcing Effie—charging her with desertion—but now he was separated, and suing, or being sued, for divorce again.) But she did not, could not—despite all urgings of desire—trust him.

"Yithgadel ve'yithkadash sh'mei rabbo." John Kantor lowered his eyes from the ceiling toward which they had been straining with such intensity, and smiled fondly upon his children. "Which is to say, 'Magnificent and sanctified be the name of the One on high.' Those words are from the kaddish, which is part of our daily prayer." Virginia and Mack stared, their own eyes wide open—both in admiration of the rich sound of their

father's voice, and in amazement at the strange sound of the words he had uttered.

The role of The Converted Jew had been discarded, and also that of the Reverend Mr. Kantor—though the latter, or else the part of the Reverend *Dr*. Kantor, would be enacted again in later years, whenever circumstances demanded. He was once again professedly Jewish, though it is unlikely that he ever sullied any synagogue with regularity.

The apostate, twice-converted, turned to Effie. (And she *was* troubled by his apostasy; he had seemed so fervent in the pursuit of his newly found vocation, when they first met at Drake.) "And do my dear children go to church every Sunday?"

Effie smiled. It was hard for her not to smile when he looked at her like that, and when he treated Virginia and Mack with the generosity he had displayed during all that week. "Of course, John. Every Sunday."

"That is good." He still had a small accent, he always would: either Swedish, or Swedish influenced by Yiddish. *Th* came out sounding more like *d*. "That is as it should be. There are many paths to the Almighty, and the children should be nurtured in the religion of their mother. It is so in Judaism." Slowly he nodded his head in approval of his own words, and he beamed upon them all. "It is good that little ones should be raised in the ways of righteousness. 'Just as the twig is bent the tree's inclined.'"

So kind and caring he seemed: so evidently impressed with Virginia's beauty and the quickness of her mind, so obviously proud of handsome young Mack's ability to read anything he encountered. Effie allowed herself to dream. She accepted, as though acceptance had come fresh to her for the very first time (and it would come afresh, afresh, in later times as well), that she could not build a future with this man. But surely, now that he had come to know the children, now that he had so proudly paraded them before the approving gaze of both relatives and friends, he would help her to raise them, help her to clothe and feed them well. Surely he would. Surely.

But far below the level of conscious dreams, she knew that he would never do so. Somewhere deep within her mind that secret knowledge writhed and twisted, distasteful as a worm, elusive as a snake.

From an immense height he bent down, and his smile was warm, his big voice gentle. John Kantor said, "Now I will take you to see the most lovely woman in Chicago."

It was their final day in the city, and Aunt Besse had taken Effie and Virginia on a final family visit, or on some other errand. Mack, perhaps as the result of an attempt by Effie to ensure fulfillment of her dream of closeness and support, was spending these final hours with his father.

"Where is she?" Mack asked. In his mind that loveliest woman could only be his mother.

"She is living at the Sherman House, and her name is Miss Tucker. She knows that I am bringing you, and has some lovely toys for you."

A big red taxicab again and, as they drove through the thrilling clamor of crowded city streets—a clamor which would soon be reduced to a murmur in memory of an unreal place, an unreal time—Mack wondered if the promise of toys would prove as false as the promise of that half-forgotten bicycle. But no! His father sat beside him in the cab, erect and dignified. It was not like a promise made on the telephone, for Mack could actually touch him. And there had been that box of candy, there had been those clothes, there had been the hotel suite and all those restaurants; in such a fantastical world there would be toys as well.

Soon they were entering a crowded, noisy parlor at the hotel and Mack was being presented to a big blond woman who was wearing a dress covered with sequins—and the sequins glittered so that he was sure they must be diamonds. Sophie Tucker bore herself like a queen, and her face was kindly. And there were toys, wonderful toys, including a papier-mâché cornet with keys that worked, which made a wonderful sound. There was also food to eat, and Miss Tucker took Mack to a table a little aside from all the grown-up talk and laughter. She left him there to stuff himself, to play with his toys, and to treasure this moment of glory, but every so often she would return to talk with him, and to make certain he was happy.

Sophie Tucker was no more than twenty-three, and she had just begun to enjoy the success and acclaim she would know for over fifty years. Later on she would take the title of "The Last of the Red Hot Mamas," but in 1911 she was young, glamorous—a fine singer with a powerful, pleasing voice—and she was very handsome, though her features were far too strong to be described as pretty. At this time she was "a very, very dear friend" of John Kantor's, and they would remain "very dear friends" for a number of years. During the same period he stole five thousand dollars from her in the form of some fraudulent investments. Five thousand dollars then was the equivalent of fifty or a hundred thousand today; but Sophie either forgave him or, more likely, and in company with so many others, simply could never accept the fact that he had deceived her. Over fifty years later her face grew brighter, younger, whenever his name was mentioned.

When it was time to go Mack thanked Miss Tucker with all his ardent, seven-year-old sincerity. He cherished her gifts, especially the cornet, as long as they lasted.

That evening John Kantor led them in grand procession to the railway terminal, for he had invited some friends and business associates, and perhaps a relative or two, to serve as an audience when he bade farewell to Effie and his children. This time they were not crammed into a lower berth, all three together; rather, since there were others to observe, others he wished to impress, they were provided with a drawing room, and everyone applauded his consideration and his generosity.

After the last good-bye had been said, after John Kantor and his retinue had left, Mack looked around for the crayons and pencils and paper he expected to find in a drawing room, but there were none. And so he settled down in his seat, watched as the bright lights of the city outside the window diminished slowly in their numbers, and contemplated the presents he had received, the people he had met. He thought that he'd liked the box of candy best, the candy and Miss Tucker.

The empty box was taken back to Webster City with us; perhaps handkerchiefs or toys were packed in it. We kept it down in the lower section of the sideboard, and that delicious chocolate smell persisted...year after year, but growing fainter. I would open the box and push Virginia's paper dolls aside in order to sniff the perfumed comfort of the past—a comfort which I felt for one solid week in 1911, but which never came to me again until I had built it with my own hands and beneath my own feet.

Through the train window the next morning Mack could see stubbled fields stretching to the horizon, and occasional farm houses, and even more occasional villages and towns. The train wheels passing over the rails made a different sound: no longer did they seem to chant "Chi-ca-go" or "My fa-ther"; now they intoned "Web-ster Ci-ty!" Now they spoke of a familiar compound of meagerness and warmth.

Now they sang of home.

6

A Bag of Buttons

At home there was a bag of buttons which Grandma kept tucked away in one of the sideboard drawers. In it there was treasure: the glint of gold, the sound of bugles, the crack of a Sharp's rifle, the silver echo of the past. In it there were stored the large gold buttons which Lieutenant Joseph Bone had worn on the front of his blue jacket, the smaller buttons from the jacket sleeves, and also his gilded shoulder straps, each with a tarnished golden bar. When he was very small, Mack, under Effie's or Eva's supervision, was allowed to take out that bag and spill the buttons on the floor. Then he would sit or stretch out beside them, and play with them for many long minutes at a time. By the time he was five he no longer played with them; rather, he held them in his hands, caressing them, imagining the stories they might tell. They seemed to speak of the past, and the past was real, it was certain, it had happened. There was so much uncertainty in his young life, so many whispered discussions about money, so many things he could not have, and always the mystery which enshrouded that strange being— his father in Chicago. But Joseph Bone was real, he had existed, and— after Mack's great-grandmother Rachel had put away his coat of blue and stored its buttons in this bag—he had run Bone's Mill, and then Bell's Mill; later, Grandpa had run Bell's Mill, and Mother had been born there, and Bell's Mill was real also, it had solidity and form. Mack knew that was so, for they had gone to the Mill for picnics, and it was just as real as the buttons he clutched so firmly in his hand.

*   *   *

52

Soon after they got back to Webster City he went to the sideboard, took out the bag and opened it, seeking for the certainty within. For in Chicago there had been no certainty at all, only wonder and confusion, and what little sense of self he owned had flickered in the shadow of that big, booming, beaming, glowering presence which was John Kantor.

But a sense of certainty was not the only illusion offered by shoulder straps and buttons. They also offered a sense of masculine achievement, of masculine strength and glory, and, in a household where femininity flourished rife, young Mack treasured any symbol of masculinity he could find, just as he treasured—just as he absorbed and took for himself—the tales the old soldiers told.

He fought his first battle, and suffered his first wound, when he was five. The grape arbor in the back yard was his redan, his shelter from Minié balls and cannon shot, and the outhouse some twenty feet away, to which he laid such ardent siege, was Vicksburg. (Ah, Vicksburg, Petersburg, Chickamauga, The Wilderness—the names of those and other battles of the Civil War made a wild music in his head whenever the Old Soldiers spoke, and wove misty, thrilling names into their yarning.) For hours on end he sniped from shelter, he feinted, charged, retreated, rallied, until at last the awful moment came and he screamed and dropped onto the grass. It seemed forever that he lay there, with imagined blood seeping from his breast and the bright sun burning through his eyelids, crying out for water, until Eva or Virginia came to succor him.

A few days later he announced to startled neighbors that he, too, was an Old Soldier, and that he'd been wounded at Vicksburg. The more sensible among them reacted in appropriate fashion, with looks of wonder and words of sympathetic admiration, but a few of the more foolish told Effie or Eva in shocked voices that little Mack was telling lies. Just like his father! They all had heard of the doings of John Kantor.

With puzzled amusement Eva said, "Mack. Now, you know you weren't *really* in the Civil War."

"Yes, I was!"

"And you know that you weren't *really* wounded."

"But I was! And you came and you gave me water."

"But, honey, that was just a game that you were playing. It wasn't real-life true. It was just a game."

"But..." It had seemed so very real indeed.

*   *   *

Always Mack remembered her striding through bright fields or exploring sun-dappled woodland trails with an eagerness scarce hampered by the long skirts she wore. Particularly she loved the timber, and all the feathered or gossamer-winged wonder which sheltered there. She had done so ever since she was very small and first tried to catch a mote of dust, floating in a sunbeam which pierced a window, or heard the call of a meadowlark, or chased a butterfly. She had done so since she lived with her parents at Bell's Mill, on the banks of the Boone, and first became aware of the river's easy somnolence in the summer or the fall, and of the quick, silver anger it might display in the late winter or early spring, when the ice began to thaw. Since first awareness came, Effie Kantor had loved a thing called Nature with all her eager soul.

She taught her son to love it also.

Often, during the long, hot days of summer, she'd come home from work, walking swiftly with that sense of barely contained energy with which she always moved, and as she came through the door cry out, "Mother! Virginia! Mack! It's such a glorious evening. Let's go on a picnic!"

Mack would be the first to respond, and his agreement would be loud. Virginia might mope for a minute, and her response would be more tepid. She did not share her mother's passion for the out-of-doors; she was afraid that something might bite her, and therefore something often did. Eva would stand in the kitchen door, her hands twisting the apron she wore, her face at once bright with anticipation and clouded by uncertainty. "Effie, I'd love to go, but... it would take so long to *fix* everything."

"Oh, Scotland! Mother, we'll have things ready in no time, no time at all." And, marching briskly past Eva into the kitchen, Effie would snatch her own apron from its hook and set to work. She loved to cook; it was another passion which she owned, and, as with most passions, the work attendant to it came easy to her hands.

Eva was different, and thus her hesitation. She was a very good cook, but hers was a skill born of necessity, not ardor. She enjoyed the smiles on the faces of her dear ones, gathered around the dining table, far more than she liked the tasks which brought those smiles to be. So she labored, while Effie played, and so on such occasions Effie took command.

"Now, Mother, here's some ham. We'll take the skillet, and Mack can build a fire, and we'll fry it there. And there are some potatoes in the larder, and a few ears of corn; we can roast them in the coals. And there's that jar of beet pickles in the icebox, and some tomato pickles too. We can take them. Virginia, you make some iced tea, and help Grandma to fill the hamper, while I change my dress."

And soon, with the hamper placed in a little green wagon, and the wagon trundling along behind them as Mack pulled, they walked through the warm gold of early evening down to the end of Willson Avenue and beyond: to Huddleston's Hill, or Frank's Pasture, or some other field of summer glory, star-sprinkled with wild flowers and teased by the wind.

Sometimes there would be friends along, sometimes the picnic would be a neighborhood affair, but for Effie and Mack both food and friends were only excuses for the journey, never the reason.

"Hush! Do you hear that?" They stood and listened.

Where-where, the soft call came. *Here-here*.

"It's an indigo bunting! But where is it?"

Sweet-sweet, the clear piping rang. *See-it, see-it*.

"I see it. There!"

A rich, liquid blue when caught by the sun, but almost black when seen against the sky or hidden in shadow. *See-it, see-it*.

They saw the bunting, they heard it, and to them it was soul's delight. At the very edge of winter they saw the wild geese fly, in their unending squadrons, and the deep *ah-honnnk, ah-honnnk* they uttered suggested whole packs of Missouri coon hounds set to run and bay across the sky. In April they would vie to be the first to spot a meadowlark, with its yellow throat and chest and the soft black necklace it wore, and then be lured farther away, further into the day, by its sweet pronouncement: *Spring-o'-the-year! Spring-o'-the-year!*

There were butterflies to name and wonder at, the ephemeral beauty of moths to be praised. And Mack did more than praise. He had a need, like others raised in a welter of emotional perplexity, to thoroughly know, and thus command, small portions of the world around him. Thus he absorbed words, thus he absorbed, not just the names of presidents and battles, but the smallest details of the American past, and thus he absorbed the lore of Lepidoptera. By the time he was thirteen he had a huge collection of moths which he had caught, which he had preserved, which he had placed and pinned in homemade display cases. He could describe with confidence the brown and rose and black of the Sphinx Moth's patterning, the soft russet colors of the cecropia's intricate design.

So he imposed order upon a disorderly world.

And, the more freely he wandered through fields and through timber, the more he shared his mother's love of nature, the more he felt bound to

her. The sight of a red admiral flashing from puddle to puddle, the sweetness of a meadowlark's song: these brought him close to her, just as did the
sound of her laughter, the warmth of her touch, the feel and smell of the
clothes in her closet when she was not near.

And so, with dreams in his head of bullets and butterflies, with an odd
mixture of yearning and of fear locked tight within a dark, untidy closet in
his mind, the days passed full and fast for Mack, and the years. And, just
as in fact she strode through the fields and timber which surrounded the
town, delighting in wonder of the natural world, so in metaphor did Effie
Kantor stride through those years, exulting in the pride of real accomplishment. She no longer labored as cashier at Scriven's grocery, or Shipley's
dry goods store. A good fairy had touched her with his wand; a kindly ge-
nie, reversing tradition, had liberated her from the bottle of frustration in
which she'd long been pent. The editor of the Webster City *Freeman-Tribune*,
impressed perhaps by a chapter she had contributed to a history of Hamilton
County, impressed certainly by her quickness of spirit and of intellect, had
hired her as a reporter. As the only reporter the paper could afford. She
had long resented the need for menial or trivial occupation, and now she
was free. Free to ride the country roads, free to walk the streets of the
town, free to talk and free to listen, free to write and write, free to record
the doings and the humors of her community, of her small, exciting world.
   She did well at this new, this wonderful trade. Already she dreamed of
being editor herself. Within months her salary had grown from nine to ten
to eleven dollars a week. And eleven dollars a week was almost enough to
support, in the sparest fashion, her parents, her children, and herself.
   Money! It did not rule, it did not dominate in that house, where Eva
sang her simple songs of Glory, where Effie praised bird song and summer-
winter delight, and where all joined in paying reverence to a wondrous,
fabled Past. And yet pennies, nickles, dimes, dollars: their presence or
their absence were forces to be felt. To be felt and dealt with not out of
avarice, but of necessity. Twice there had started a rillet of checks from
Chicago, signed in John Kantor's stately hand; both times the rillet had run
dry. Sporadically there came checks for ten or twenty dollars, in micro-
scopic repayment of Adam McKinlay's loan to Joseph Bone. Adam himself
was now reduced to the sort of menial labor from which Effie had escaped:
he had lost his last job as manager of a grain elevator, and now served as
night watchman in a local factory.
   After school and on Saturday afternoons Mack worked too, and found

pride and a certain glamour in his task. After his tenth birthday he had been given a regular delivery route for the *Freeman-Tribune*, and if it was his mother's job on the paper, her friendly relationship with both editor and business manager, which led to such early preferment—for he was the youngest paper carrier of all—he did not care a bit. His route was the shortest and the fattest, it led through the central business district, and he delighted in the adult busyness he found there. Also, he had a position of responsibility. He could help Grandma and Grandpa, he could help his mother—even the thought of helping his older sister sometimes gave him pleasure. Each week he was paid one dollar, and each week he gave his mother seventy-five of those one hundred cents to help with the family budget, and each week he had twenty-five cents left over, to squander as he would: a nickel for the Saturday movie, a few pennies on this bit of candy or that bag of popcorn, and, in late spring, sometimes a dime to put aside for the purchase of firecrackers for the Fourth of July. He felt he had entered the world of almost-manhood, and he relished being there.

The days passed, full and fast, and the seasons, full of the pepper of challenge, the salt of labor, the sugar of accomplishment. And a few of those years carried also another flavor, rich and unaccustomed. For a few of those years Mack almost, truly, had a father.

I am nine, I am ten, and the gun is light, it is relatively small and feels comfortable in my hands. A .22-caliber Winchester repeating rifle, redolent with the sweet aroma of gun oil; the burnished stock is silken smooth against my cheek. I fire, and the tin-can target jumps into the air.

"Good shot, Timmy!" Again I fire, again the tin can jumps, and then goes spinning, rolling down the beach to rest at the water's edge. "God damn it, that's real shooting!" His big hand musses my hair. "You shoot better than a lot of grown men I know." No matter that the hand resting on my head is heavy, pulling at my hair, for his praise is food and drink to me: his words are meat for my ego, wine for my soul.

He takes the rifle and handles it fondly, then puts another bullet into the target. "Do you know where I got this gun?" I do. It is, like so many of his stories, a twice-, a thrice-, a dozen-times-told tale, and yet to bask in his company, to relax in the heat of his voice, is so comforting to me that I offer the expected denial. "Dr. Von Krog gave it to me. Dr. Heinrich Von Krog."

"Who was he?"

Like tenor and baritone, fondness and anger are mixed in his reply.

"He was a pharmacist, back in Webster City. He wasn't a real doctor, but in those days, if a pharmacist was respected, everyone called him that. Oh, he was a German, he was a real Prussian—stiff and formal—but he was also a very nice man. He bought this gun in Nicaragua, where he used it to defend himself from bandits, when he wasn't healing them."

The pressure of his hand grows heavier, and I feel myself constricted. "My mother almost married him."

"Run, Sheep, run!" The clear voice rang through the long, deep dusk, and the Sheep all ran to hide. Mack was a Sheep, and he ran with the others; first to hide within close shadows of the Marvels' yard, and then to other refuge at the Neels' or Sterlings'. No Sheep was more fleet than he that evening, no spy more daring, for a certain Knowledge itched inside him, making him aggressive and uncertain all at once. Warm breeze off the prairie, promising summer yet to come, sweet scent from flower beds and new leaves of the trees, familiar thrill of tension when the "enemy" came near: it was a typical end to a typical weekend day in May, and yet not typical at all.

His mother had company. A gentleman had come to call.

The fire whistle groaned the curfew at nine, but Virginia and Mack went on playing with the rest and, remarkably, their mother did not come out to call them. Half an hour passed before another parent summoned his own children home, and thus broke up the game.

Virginia's soft voice was filled with eager curiosity. "I wonder what he's like." Starlight filtered through the branches of elms and maples as they walked toward home.

Mack asked, "What's his name?" His eyes focused on the familiar yellow warmth which came from the living room windows. But, on this night, that lamplight seemed no longer familiar, no longer homely, no longer comforting. His mother was inside their house, alone with a strange man. (Eva had gone to a missionary society meeting, and Adam was working.) His mother was alone with a strange man, and maybe she was kissing him.

"Dr. Von Krog. Dr. Heinrich Von Krog." Virginia pronounced the alien syllables as though she savored them.

"You mean the man at the drugstore?" A tall man, slim and soldier-straight, who presided over the prescription counter with stiff formality.

"Yes. Shhh." They were home now. Mack rushed to open the door, and they went in. They found their mother in the summer kitchen. She was standing there alone, holding a plate of cookies in one hand, and a plate of little sandwiches in the other.

"Where is he?"

"Where?"

Effie Kantor was wearing a white dress. Her hair was up, her eyes were shining; never had she seemed more beautiful to Mack. "Hush! He's outside, in the yard. We've been enjoying the evening."

Suddenly loud steps sounded on the back stoop, and then louder still, in martial tread, resounded on the porch. The door opened, and Dr. Heinrich Von Krog strode into the room. He stood there, beaming, with the lamplight bouncing off his glasses. "Ah! I thought I heard voices. Now, Mrs. Kantor, I want to meet these fine children I have heard so much about!"

Confounded by a crazy quilt of feelings, Mack stammered as he made his manners. Dr. Von Krog, towering over him, seemed like an amiable giant; my father always remembered the strength of his handshake, and the force and warmth of his manner.

He was five years the junior of our mother, but he did not look it. The man's hair was russet-brown; he kept it chopped to a short stiff fuzz all over his scalp. His green eyes shone gimlet-sharp, and even the watery depth of those lenses could not take the laughter and steel from their shine.

Effie loved the exotic. If some earnest soul who had served in foreign parts came to town to address the missionary society, and that soul owned a leaven of humor, she would bring the soul to supper. The family would sit around the table, entranced, listening to tales of strange doings in China or in Africa. When Chautauqua was in season, Effie was transported. Not only were there singers, comics, and actors drifting on, or dreaming of, their reputations, but also there were the lecturers: people of apparent sophistication she interviewed for the *Freeman-Tribune*. Just as with the butterflies she fancied, the birds she adored, she liked their color.

And so it was with suitors.

It was not just John Kantor's flamboyance and his smoldering fire which had drawn her to him; his alien manner, his scent of foreignness, had enchanted her as well. She regarded as a drab and dreary lot the young business or professional men in Webster City who were likely escorts for her; she had thought so even before she was a grass widow and the mother of two children. Professionally her world embraced the entire community, as well as exotic visitors; intellectually it was as broad as her considerable curiosity allowed; but socially it was limited, almost claustrophobic. There were family friends and her own friends from childhood, both spinsters and couples; there were neighbor families, with whom the McKinlays and the Kantors often picnicked; and there were her parents.

And there were her children.

Her relationship with Virginia was warm and easy but, like many other single mothers who are deprived by taste or circumstance of a lover, her closeness to her son had a rare intensity. There was a hothouse warmth to their connection which no prairie winter could ever chill. Mack was her confidant, the target of unconscious coquetry; for years he had been the one male constant in Effie's world. (John Kantor remained a distant dream or shadow. There had been another brief attempt at reconciliation during August 1912, when Mack was eight—the year before Effie met Heinrich Von Krog—but from that trip to Chicago she had returned sad and silent.) In the privacy of the bedroom he shared with Effie and Virginia until he was six, Mack was the only male to admire her fine legs, Mack was the only male to cuddle close.

But now Effie's world opened wide, and her senses quickened once again. Under its stern and stolid Prussian cloak, Dr. Von Krog's nature sparkled with warmth and lusty humor. And he was European; and he had Traveled.

Shards of memory again, or shreds: He had been born to wealthy parents, in the city of Bromberg, in West Prussia. He was raised to be an officer, but, to young Heinrich's delight, nearsightedness disqualified him, and he was allowed to study medicine instead. I do not think that he finished his studies; certainly he was not qualified to practice medicine when he came to Webster City. Wanderlust had driven him to travel. Wanderlust, and a young woman named Gertrude, whose unwelcome passion not only pursued him by mail to Central America, where he wandered for several years, but then followed him to Webster City. Just as Gertrude in person would pursue him, follow him, and track him down in a later season, to his embarrassment, Effie's delight, and the amusement of her children.

So Dr. Von Krog (always he was Dr. Von Krog, or simply "Doctor," to my father, and so I think of him now) entered their world and, for several years, they prospered from his presence. There had been a void in their lives—a lack of masculine warmth and force—which now he filled. He had in common with John Kantor only height, a rich voice, foreignness, and a strong desire to preside over the doings of those near to him. "I will be Boss!" he said, and he meant it. But he had also a true sense of humor, and only rarely was it cruel. If he had a Teutonic thirst for order and propriety—his favorite phrase of disapproval was, "In Germany, it would not be so!"—he also had a Teutonic love of custom and of festival. He did not approve of Halloween as it was celebrated in small-town America, with trick-or-treating and the overturning of outhouses, but Thanksgiving and Christmas he adored. Those holidays were celebrated with greater glee and warmth than the household had ever known before, in the years when Dr. Von Krog was courting Effie. (Still I remember my father singing, his fierce voice gentled to croon the words, "Stille Nacht, Heilige Nacht" when I was as young as he was then.)

Doctor also loved to cook. His cuffs off, his sleeves rolled back, his hands and forearms scrubbed as clean as any clinician's, he would make the stuffing for the turkey, and all the family loved the savory result. And he translated his Germanic liking for hare into a fondness for rabbit, rabbit he prepared and cooked himself. Rabbits he and Mack had hunted together.

"There is one, Mack. Shoot him!"

Sky as big as all of Iowa, with a cold wind moving clouds across it, and a rabbit bounding across the hillside, running for cover. Mack was nine, he was ten, he was eleven. He lifted to his shoulder the little single-shot Stevens Favorite he carried—the rifle had been his grandfather's, until Mack had proved he could outshoot Adam, and hit a rabbit on the run—and he fired. The rabbit took two convulsive leaps, and then it fell. Its legs kicked only once before Mack ran to pick it up.

As he came back, his shoes rustling through dry weeds and grasses, he saw Dr. Von Krog smiling on him. "That is good, Mack. That is very good! You shoot better than even some grown men I have known."

Mack blushed. He reveled in this masculine praise: praise from a man, and about a manly doing. Neither his grandfather nor his father was free with honest praise. Even when Adam McKinlay had presented his gun to Mack he had only mumbled, taut and taciturn, "Here, Mack. I don't use this much any more. It's yours." But Doctor offered freely both criticism and praise, and my father was glad to bear the one, if only he could receive the other.

He thought he might shoot even better with Doctor's rifle—purchased, Doctor said, for protection against bandits when he was in Nicaragua—and he longed to try it. But that, as were so many things, was *verboten*. Someday, perhaps, when Mack was older.

Another tawny form went fleeing, and Dr. Von Krog raised the Winchester repeater, holding it firm and sure. "Now it is my turn. Now I will shoot one."

And he did.

Effie was casual about allowing Mack to see her in states of undress (oh, black stockings on lovely legs, and black slips and petticoats which whispered in his mind for years!), casual to a degree her mother thought immodest, but in other ways she was as prudish as most women of her time and place.

Surely she had had no lover since her marriage, and just as surely she regarded sex outside of marriage as improper, perhaps even downright wicked. But when she was almost engaged to Doctor and, later, when she *was* engaged to him, I think it seemed to her almost like being married. He was almost a father to the children, too, and she loved him dearly. And Heinrich Von Krog was a pharmacist, and he had had medical training; certainly he knew about sponges and condoms. And the importance of prayer.

He was a vital man, and her every act and utterance was marked by a high, fine passion. I think that, when awkward circumstances permitted, they sinned together joyfully, and then forgave themselves the sinning.

Mack and Virginia looked at each other and giggled. "Careful, Doctor! Gertrude's hiding down there!" Dr. Von Krog, on his way to fetch some coal, had just opened the cellar door. He paused and scowled, then made a rueful smile, raised his eyes as though imploring relief from both unfeeling children and a baneful woman, and proceeded down the stairs.

With customary openness, Effie had told Mack and Virginia about Doctor's bane: a blond Valkyrie and would-be opera singer whose love for him had led her to pursue and pester him in medical school, and who, even now, after several years and across thousands of miles, still pursued, still pestered, with letters bearing German stamps and Germanic handwriting which caused much wonder at the post office. It tickled their fancy that the man they knew and had almost come to love had triggered such extravagant passion. When they first teased him about Gertrude, Doctor had been mortified, but also he had been amused—such teasing seemed to add a note of intimacy to their relationship—and now Gertrude had become a household ogress who might be found anywhere, in closets, under beds, in the cellar, lurking and waiting to pounce.

One day, after Effie and Doctor's engagement had been made formal, the ogress pounced indeed. She emerged, incarnate, from the noonday train. She embarrassed Doctor in public, once she had tracked him down, and she railed at him in private. It was with sweaty hands and reddened cheeks that he persuaded, almost pushed her into the eastbound train that evening. Effie was smugly pleased, and the children were enchanted, when they heard about it.

If there was an ogress laired in the cellar, or brooding in Bromberg, there was also laughter in the kitchen, and every corner of that house seemed to hide a song. As he drifted into sleep at night, Mack would listen, comforted, to the hearty masculine rumble which came echoing up the stairs.

Dawn, and bird song, and a soft mist steaming off the lake. Ten-year-old Mack slipped out of bed, pulled on some clothes, and went foraging in Eden. Quiet there, and peaceful, with only birdcall and squirrel chatter in his ears, and all the other human folk asleep. So new the air, and clean. He found a patch of wild strawberries and, sprawling on the ground, gorged himself with sweetness. And then his dog—half hound and half terrier, wholly eager and wholly ridiculous, whom he had named Trix but who knew no tricks—Trixy came to frolic. Trixy came to play.

Soon the sun had risen high enough to burn the mist from off the lake, and the cottage stirred to life. Mack abandoned Trixy and went to plague and play with Doctor instead. He slipped in the front door and went quietly to the little curtained-off alcove where Doctor slept.

He would lie in bed with the covers drawn up to his chin, and make a grimace as I came in. I crept under the quilt at the foot of his bed; then he would try to seize my wrist with prehensile toes, while I giggled; and failing that, he would burrow under the covers and reach for me, his long arms seeking out.

Once I gasped, "Your arm, Doctor—it looks like a great big German eel!" and from then on that was the name for his arm.

"*Bow!* Look out, Mack, that German eel is going to get you. *Bow!* That German eel is getting you!" and I would shriek as he seized me...I wallowed in an ecstasy of male camraderie. That kind of play I had never known before. I would never know it again until I had a son.

Berries, a vacation home, an almost-father, a dog: the year 1914 brought a glory of unexpected riches, just as surely as it brought sadness traveling after. In partial payment of Joseph Bone's debt to Adam, the family had received a modest summer cottage on the shore of Clear Lake, in the southern part of the county. It was crude, it was rustic, it was wonderful, and they went there for the month of June. Effie and Dr. Von Krog had connived to take their vacations at the same time, Eva and the children went with them, Adam was able to come for two of those four weeks, and so were Aunt Grace and Uncle Jack Sheldon. The last were Uncle and Aunt in name only, after the homely custom of the time, for they were close friends of Effie's and had introduced her to Doctor. I remember Aunt Grace, with her ample body and more than ample smile. She lived well into her seventies, until she succumbed to Christian Science.

There was a rowboat moored at a dock in front of the cottage, and Doctor taught Mack to handle it well. There were woods to wander through, and happily they wandered, though, if they went as a family group, Trixy was left behind for, "I will be Boss!", and Doctor did not approve of Trixy's clownish ways. He would have preferred a dog of nobler breed and more solemn disposition. There were word games to be played, jokes and songs to be shared. In the evenings they made popcorn or fudge, pulled taffy, told tales.

It began with a jarring mix of sounds. First Trix howling like the hound he almost was as he caught the scent of a bitch on the other side of the road that ran behind the cottage, then Trix yowling as he set off in pursuit, with Mack calling after him, "Here, Trixy, here, Trixy, here!" And then there came the loud, mechanical stutter of the touring car. There was a thud, and a yelp, and the car slowed for a moment, and then went on. Trixy was on his feet again and, *Yi-yi-yi!* (oh, broken bone and mangled sinew, an Indian caroling in the wilderness), careened away into the trees.

Mack looked and looked, but Trixy wasn't found until later in the day. He had gone to cover, as injured beasts will do. Two neighbor children came upon him at last, cowering and whimpering under a bush, far, far down the road. Doctor carried him home, with the whole disconsolate family trailing after. In between moans Trixy tried to lick Doctor's face, but Doctor kept his face averted and found his way by looking through the very edge of his thick glasses.

They took an empty box and softened it with rags, and placed Trixy in it, and then Doctor examined him. His clean, strong hands pressed and probed quite gently. A fore shoulder was broken, a leg was crushed, he thought there were internal injuries. "This dog should be shot."

"Oh, no!" A long, long wail from Mack. "Not Trixy!"

They had no car. There was no veterinarian nearby and, if there were, a veterinarian would cost a lot of money. They had a cottage, but they had very little money. "I will be Boss! This dog should be shot."

Foolishly, Effie said, "But, Heinrich..." Mack loved the dog. Perhaps something could be done. She could not stand the grief which flickered, the outrage which flared, from Mack's eyes. The dispute lasted long into the night, and Doctor's stern voice mixed with Effie's sobs and Trixy's moanings in Mack's dreams.

The next morning he heard a shot.

Doctor confronted him as he lay weeping on his bed. "Now, Mack, you be a man or a mouse!"

But Mack was neither. He was a grieving, embittered ten-year-old boy. Material luxury had been wanting throughout his life, but, emotionally, Effie had spoiled him rotten. Like many other young boys raised in a houseful of women, particularly one where the mother cherishes guilt, however irrational, about the absence of the father, he had early learned that his tears could make him tyrant. Often, when he was small, and she was looking forward to a respite from work, and from domestic demands as well, looking forward to an outing with the maiden Wickware sisters or with the Greenwood "girls," Effie had been confronted with noisy, damp disaster. Mack crying, Mack writhing in a tantrum, Mack screaming, "I want to go too!" All too often she had surrendered to his wilfulness, indulged her love for him, catered to her sense of guilt. She had sown hysteria with her mistaken compassion, and now it blossomed.

Mack stood and faced Dr. Von Krog. "You killed Trixy! You wanted to kill him! You're glad he's dead! You were *glad to kill him!*"

"Mack, you must be reasonable. You must be a little man."

"I hate you!"

"Heinrich please! He's all upset." Effie came to solace Mack, to appease Doctor. "He doesn't know what he's saying."

"I do, too!" Mack was crying, the tears were oozing, but still his words came clear. "I hate you, you goddamn old German!"

Dr. Von Krog flung up his hands, punishing the air—never, ever, did he strike my father—and then he marched off to pack. He declared, his accent thickened by his anger, that he would no longer stay in such a madhouse. What he had done had not only been sensible, it had been kind. Which was true. Effie followed him, cajoling.

But Virginia remained behind. She had been silent witness to the entire scene. She had loved Trix, she loved Doctor, she loved Mack, she loved her mother—she loved the entire world. And now her cheeks were damp, her brown eyes sorrowful. "What are you doing?"

In his pocket, my father had a knife. A Barlow knife, none too sharp, but still... He took it out and forced it open. "I'm going to kill Doctor. He killed Trixy. He made Mother cry last night. I'm going to kill him." The blade shivered, shimmered in the morning light as he started moving.

It took Virginia's scream, Effie's words, and Eva's hugs to quiet him. And when at last he made a muttered apology, Doctor hugged him as well. But there was something present between the two of them which had been missing, something missing which had been present.

Twilight again, in the spring of 1916, and there had come a letter.

Dr. Von Krog had gone off to medical school in St. Louis over a year before. He lived frugally; he had saved money, and he had found a part-time job as a pharmacist. It was understood that in three years, when he was established in practice, he and Effie would marry. "Then our names will all be Von Krog," she said happily, and even Mack was partly enchanted with that prospect, and even Mack missed Doctor, and welcomed him warmly when he visited on rare vacations.

But Dr. Von Krog would not be visiting any more, and now their names would not be changed.

In the letter Doctor had insisted that Effie come to marry and live with him right away. But he could not yet afford a home for all of them, so Effie must leave the children with their grandparents, and he would send what help he could. Effie sobbed, and Effie clenched her teeth. "If that man thinks," she cried, "that I would leave my children..." She lay abed weeping, Virginia sat sadly in the living room, and, half glad and half forlorn, Mack wandered through the gloom. There would be no more criticism of his heathen Iowa ways; there would be no more hearty masculine praise, when he shot well with a gun.

But at that thought he brightened. Doctor had left his rifle behind. The little Winchester repeater stood now in a closet off the living room. Now the gun was Mack's. He went inside and looked at it—cold blue metal and warm brown stock—and touched it lovingly.

He swore that he would learn to use it well and, through the years, that rifle remained in fine condition. Doctor had taught him how to clean the bore, Doctor had taught him how to tend to it. But, almost without his willing it, his use of the gun did change.

Winter, spring, summer, fall: there came a season when he had shot one too many squirrels, gutted one too many rabbits. After that he shot for pleasure and not for plunder. Perhaps Effie's pantheism, her increasing substitution of a picnic in a meadow for blathering in a church, had something to do with it. Life was glorious and not to be marred, save of necessity. After that he substituted paper targets, tin cans, and the gnarled knots of trees for warm flesh, alive, aquiver. Squirrels, rabbits, and larger game were safe from him. By the time he fathered me he shot only poisonous snakes, or gigged frogs, caught fish.

Save for occasional sparrows and pestering jays, he killed no other warm-blooded creature until that Messerschmitt came in, and he caught it in the stream of bullets from a larger, fiercer gun; until, as the bombardier screamed "Bombs away!" Mack pressed a lever and then, through Plexiglas, watched little crimson flowers blossom far below.

7

Telling Tales

July 1918.

He stood outside the recruiting office, and his knees were shaking inside his new long trousers. Heat struck him in the face, blasted from the pavement, and a strange caduceus of twisted shame and pride was lodged within his soul.

Chicago steamed about him, vast and drab under a heavy sun, and the wind which blew through the streets carried no trace of sweetness from the prairie, just the scorch of city heat, the scent of city closeness, city dirt. Mack hated the place, and he hated the circumstances which had brought him there.

The telegram had come to them in Webster City two weeks earlier. At the moment they read that telegram, Mack had missed Dr. Von Krog more than ever. He would, almost gladly, have given up that Winchester to have Doctor's voice once more booming jovially underneath their roof. Doctor had been stiff in utterance, but honest and kindly by nature, and he had not been pompous.

The telegram was addressed to Virginia.

You and Mack are to take the noon train to Chicago on next Monday and Daddy will meet you. I am very lonely for my darlings and shall take this opportunity to express the great affection for my children and try to make up for unhappy years which have passed. Give your mother my love. Tell her my sins have been sins of omission and not sins of commission. Kiss your wonderful grandmother for me.

Concrete evidence of my devotion accompanies this message. All my love to my dearest daughter and son.

Daddy.

"Concrete evidence" was railway fare.

A similar telegram had arrived the summer before, and they had done its bidding then. The result had been new clothes, wonderful restaurants, and enormous misery. ("Mack, do not embarrass me in front of my friends.... Tell them what you would do to save another Charley.") And yet...the children needed a father! And perhaps this time John Kantor would actually fulfill a promise.

Effie had moved to another newspaper in the town, responding to offers of greater pay and greater responsibility. She had become a figure of importance in the community, a figure of renown, but the paper was underfinanced and it failed. She worked now as copy editor for an agricultural journal, for far less pay. Perhaps John would help to support the—*their*—children.

Certainly he could afford to do so. It had been reported in the Chicago papers that John Kantor received sixty thousand dollars a year from the City of Chicago as a "real estate consultant." Also he was a crony not only of the Chief of Police but of the Mayor as well. (Mayor "Big Bill" Thompson was already notorious for the corruption over which he was said to preside. How Effie could have failed to smell the taint of his friendship with John Kantor I do not understand. Perhaps she was blinded by love, by dreams, by wishfulness.) And John was now "chief fiscal agent" of the Consumers Packing Company.

If only he got to know the children better! Effie insisted that they go.

And so, reluctantly, they went. The consequence was much as they hoped, much as they feared. An impressive hotel, shops (for the first time Mack was allowed to wear long pants, and he wore them proudly), impressive restaurants, impressive friends and eager toadies.

And bombast, always bombast.

Virginia still hungered for the Daddy who once had swung her high, but Mack wanted out, he wanted away. He did not want to accept gifts from a father who made all his gifts seem like acts of charity. And this temporary luxury seemed to make bleaker still their circumstances at home. He felt that he was a burden on his mother, and never, ever, in his life did he wish to be a burden.

He wanted out.

Always he had loved uniforms. When on Memorial Day the Old Soldiers donned their mothy Blue and trooped out to the cemetery, Mack thrilled to see them pass. When he was eight he, with Herbert Arthur, Bob Richardson, and three or four other boys, had formed a private army which they called The Company (Mack was Captain of Scouts) and, dressed in whatever khaki oddments they could find, they had waged weekend war in yards throughout the neighborhood and in fields outside the town. When Mack turned twelve he joined the Boy Scouts (Herbert was almost two years older but, because he was fond of Mack, he had waited until Mack was also old enough to join), and wore khaki of a more official kind.

So, always he had loved uniforms, and—oh, laying siege to Vicksburg beneath a burning sun!—always he had dreamed of combat and of glory. A cousin by marriage, Nate Lieberman, one of the few Kantor relatives for whom Mack felt any true affection and respect, had just won the Distinguished Service Cross for heroism in France, at a place called Chipilly Ridge. Perhaps Mack might also go to France, and fight there gloriously. Perhaps he might be killed; he thought he did not care. In that season the juice of life had a bitter savor for him, just as it would again in certain later years.

He was only fourteen, but he looked old for his age: he was a lanky boy, and tall, almost tall enough to look his father in the eye, if he had had the will to do so. He thought he could pass for sixteen, at least, or maybe seventeen. He knew that the American Army would never accept him without proper proof of age, but the Canadian Expeditionary Forces had been in France far longer than the Americans, and they were hungry for troops: troops to lose to rifle, machine gun, mortar fire; to rotted feet; to poison gas. They had a recruiting office in Chicago, and they were known to accept almost any man, or almost-man, who declared that he was a British or Canadian citizen. Perhaps Mack could enlist in the 48th Highlanders, the Canadian Black Watch. He thought of his MacKinlay forebears and longed to wear a kilt, even if it was only a khaki one.

He mopped his sweaty face with his sleeve, then wiped his palms against his trousers. He lit an illicit cigarette, a Sweet Caporal, to make himself seem older, and marched into the recruiting office. The sergeant on duty was a kindly man, and hardly laughed at all when he rejected him.

As Mack stalked out of the building with what little gangling dignity he still retained, his face was flushed and his eyes were wet.

Breakfast the next day was awful; dinner would be worse.

Their father greeted them in the lobby of the hotel where they were staying, for he was to breakfast with them, and his deep, rich voice seemed to penetrate every corner of the room. "Good morning, my dear daughter. Good morning, son. I hope you both slept well."

"Yes, Daddy."

"We did, Daddy."

There was a pause, and then a sigh, and John Kantor raised his handsome face heavenward and rolled his eyes, as though seeking comfort from the God he had betrayed before and would betray again.

Virginia cried, "Daddy, what's the matter?"

Another sigh, then he sadly shook his head, and looked at them reproachfully. "I was just thinking how nice it would be if a father were greeted by two children who smiled happily and said, 'Daddy, we love you very much.'"

Mack stood mute. He remembered a bicycle which had never come, he remembered—just the day before—receiving, in front of an admiring audience of John Kantor's relatives and followers, the immense sum of five dollars as weekly allowance from a man who seemed to have a lot of money, however it had been gained, yet who had never made any sustained effort to put food in his children's bellies, or warmth in their hearts.

But Virginia ("Oh, lift me high, Daddy, lift me high!") ran to her father and hugged him. "But Daddy, we *do* love you."

"You did not say so."

Glumly they went in to breakfast, glumly they ate, and, after John Kantor had allowed himself to be placated by a chorus of thanks and praise, Mack eagerly went off to wander through the city. The heat and clamor which awaited him were far less oppressive than his father's false and demanding presence.

He thought of going to Lincoln Park, but he had been there before, and its seared grass and other struggling growth seemed a pathetic reminder, a mockery, of the woods and fields he knew at home. If his dog had been with him he might have gone, and the two of them could have run and romped together, but Rex was back in Webster City. (Rex, a dignified clown of a dog, had come into Mack's life as a replacement for poor Trix. Half collie and half setter, he was a mongrel too: just like Trixy; just like Mack.) He missed Rex, he missed his friends, he missed his mother, he missed sugaring for moths, chasing after butterflies.

That last thought caught him, as surely as ever he had netted a red admiral or a monarch, or other winged wonder in the grass. He was used to work; he was used to employment. He hungered after independence as fiercely as did his mother. At home he no longer had his paper route; now he worked, after school and on Saturdays, as janitor and errand boy for Mr. Seymour Eichman, in his clothing store on Second Street, for three dollars and fifty cents a week. But here in Chicago there was no job for him, and the money his father gave him was money grandly given, as though to a beggar, not money honestly earned. But Mack knew a lot about moths, a lot about butterflies. He had not only collected them, he had studied them well. Perhaps...

He took a trolley out to the Field Museum and wandered through its cool, dim halls, past stuffed lions and zebras in their display cases, past collections of arrowheads and other Indian gear (ah, at home! at home Mack himself had found arrowheads along the banks of Brewer's Creek, and in the rich loam of cornfields, where they'd been turned over in the plowing). At last he found his way to the entomology department and declared himself to its head, a respected scholar named Dr. Gerhard. No, said Dr. Gerhard, they had no work, not even part-time or temporary, but he was impressed with the extent of Mack's insect lore. He talked with him for hours, and made it clear that Mack would be welcome to come and talk and study in the future. Mack was thrilled with the chance to talk with a real entomologist, he was pleased by that offer, but still he went back to the hotel feeling depressed; still he felt the weight of the city all around him.

And he was going back to face a father he was impressed by, overwhelmed by, embarrassed by, ashamed of, resentful of. In later years a feeling of scorn would be added to that list. Scorn and contempt.

And yet he tried to be honest.

[That] night Daddy took Virginia and me to the La Salle roof for dinner, along with my father's brother, Herman Kantor, and his wife and two little daughters. Virginia and I walked in a trance, as always on such occasions. She was older and a lot wiser and more adjustable, so she could pretend to enjoy herself. But I was cruelly aware of the way other diners turned and stared at Daddy "showing off." His bell-like voice aroused people many tables away as he instructed the fawning head-waiter:

"De quicker de service, de bigger de tip!"

"Uncle John always says that," remarked my cousin Thyra with a chuckle.

Indeed he did, and Cousin Mack always shuddered when he said it.

Through this evening he was in one of his self-pitying moods. He sighed heavily and did a lot of brooding. At last, when he was stirring his coffee, he raised heavy-lidded eyes to meet mine.

"Son, you are not happy here."

I said limply, "Yes, I am."

"You are wid your sister, who adores you. You are wid your uncle and aunt and cousins, all of whom love you. You are wid me, your fadder, who gave you de gift of life. I have lavished every care, every tenderness upon you: I have spent large sums of money to dress you properly so dat you may appear before de world as you should. But still you are not happy. Why?"

I sat with blazing face, tortured at being subjected to this tongue-lashing in front of my father's relatives. They were kindly people, but forever they let my father bully them, just as he was bullying me now.

"I will answer dat question myself. I will tell you why. You are unhappy because you are lonely for—a dog."

He made it sound as if being lonely for a dog was the most vile emotion any boy could hold.

I burst out, "Yes, I am! I miss Rex. And I miss my mother, and the kids, and I miss—" Tears were coming, and I didn't want to be seen crying—not in front of all those people. I got up and hurried to the washroom.

My father came in, some time later, and found me mopping at my face. He was a little alarmed at my reaction, and this was one of the rare moments when he showed an honest understanding.

"Son. Forget all about it. Come out and enjoy yourself wid de folks. Do you want to go back to Iowa? Well, you can go. You can take de train tomorrow night. Tomorrow!"

I shall never insist that he was always cruel, always a bully, always an eloquent swindler. He had flashes of kindliness and whole-heartedness. When he commanded us to come to Chicago, I believe that sincerely he thought he wanted his children near him—where he could see them frequently, where they would be well taken care of, with no danger of ever lacking proper comfort. Out of Sight, Out of Mind...this was true, on the whole. But he had a heart in his breast; sometimes it was warm.

His way of life was not mine, and never would be. He was false to the core—false to his family, to partners, to employees, to the whole abused world. Auburn Prison was waiting for him down the years ahead; and the Cook County Jail, and the Tombs prison, and Sing Sing penitentiary itself. Worse than these well-earned disgraces would be the voices of those he had wounded repeatedly, whose spirits he had tried to kill.

Three days later it was Sunday, and Mother and I were prancing away toward hills below Millard's Bridge, with Rex ranging ahead of us, and hamburgers and a frying-pan in my knapsack, and meadowlarks rising from the long grass.

"He was false to the core—false to his family..." Those words were written in the late forties or early fifties, when his father was still alive, still busily engaged in thievery; but always Dad referred to John Kantor in the past tense when he wrote about him, and usually when he spoke of him as well.

"I remember when that bastard, your grandfather..."

...*and meadowlarks rising from the long grass.* But meadowlarks would not rise before them again, not for a long time to come.

A few weeks later Virginia came home, looking as lovely as ever, but there was tension in her manner. She had a letter for her mother in her purse, and two hundred dollars pinned inside her dress. "Daddy wants us to come to Chicago. He wants all three of us to live there, so he can be near." Her soft brown eyes had never been bigger, and elation and uncertainty were at war within her mind. "He said he'd pay for an apartment, and give Mother an allowance of two hundred dollars a month."

"But, lovey..." Eva hurt at the thought of losing these she loved so dear. She felt that the children were hers almost as much as they were Effie's. And yet, if John really would take care of them...

Two hundred dollars a month, plus an apartment! Effie opened the envelope and read the letter. It was full of promises: things that John Kantor *could do*, things that he *would do*, for his children. "Oh, lud! I'm not certain that we should go, but...Why, with the money you brought, Virginia, we could pay off most of our debts. Let's see. There's twelve dollars and forty cents due to Mr. Scriven, and we owe the doctor, and..." Effie had lived with debt and want and uncertainty ever since she had retreated to the lean security of her parents' home, with a three-year-old girl in hand and an unknown being restive in her womb. Now that she had lost her job as reporter and editor it seemed that the independence she had earned in recent years was slipping away once again. This seemed the fulfillment of all her hopes, of all her contrivance through the years. They could have a home. Though she loved her mother dearly, and her sad, courageous father, she had always longed for a home of her own; not a home, a living room, a kitchen in which she felt herself to be a guest, however welcome. "We could pay the others in a few months' time, and then, Mother, we could help you and Dad. And I wouldn't have to worry about finding a job in Chicago, I could just take care of you children, and our home. *Our home,*" she said again, as taut Virginia started preparing supper in the kitchen, and Mack sat, moping, on the couch.

"I won't go,"—his voice was whiny with the harsh changes of adolescence—"unless I can take Rex!"

Virginia came back into the room. "I asked Daddy. He laughed. He said Rex can come."

They left Webster City on August 26, with Rex crated in the baggage car, miserable and moaning. It seemed to Mack that he was leaving Eden: a harsh Eden, perhaps, and demanding, but Eden nonetheless.

And he was leaving it.

...Leaving the river and the sweet corn, and the walnuts to come, and the crushed smell of leaves when we walked in them. Leaving the winter which would bluster with its farmer's bobsleds lurching and jingling over icy ruts and under sheeted trees; leaving the unseen spring ahead. Uncle Jas Bell could stroll to the gate with his pipe and dog, with his flowing beard and crinkly laughing eyes, and his stories of elk and Sioux—and never see me coming across the bridge to wave at him.

And there was the holy beauty of our cemetery where now the old pioneers were going fast. In early May, lilacs hung forever wet and scented above the graves; I could not walk that way in later May to put a branch of lilac on the mound where Charley lay. Nor could I see the crowds forming, nor hear the distant rumble of drums and high-pitched yodel of fifes, as the long file of old soldiers came trailing in at the gate.

He was leaving so much, and the future was uncertain. He hated cities. He would come to love them, but that would be in a future he could not yet imagine, even dream of. He wondered if his father would be forever posturing in their lives. He thought of recruiting offices, and of the Field Museum.

Chicago, that fall and that winter, was full of surprise: surprise both fond and nasty. Oh, recruiting offices held no surprise for Mack, nor did the Field Museum. The former turned him down; the latter welcomed him. And school was just as painful, just as dreary, as he had expected. There were three thousand students at Nicholas Senn High School, a number that equaled half the population of Webster City. In that number, Mack felt himself to be a cipher. His mind was a greedy sponge which absorbed everything he chose to hear and retained everything he experienced, but he was willful in his choosing. He was a poor scholar unless he chose to be otherwise. The lore of Lepidoptera, the lure of history, the lust for words: these for him were important. Other subjects did not matter. And so, in school, he did abominably. Hated, studious Virginia ranked high in the senior class; Mack ranked low, stubbornly low, in the class which followed after. And that was to be expected. That was according to custom. But there was surprise tingling in their veins through all the long, slow fall, jangling in their hearts through most of the winter.

The surprise came from John Kantor. For the first time in Mack's life, and for the second time in Virginia's, he gained a portion of their love, and also their respect, unmixed with awe. As always, he claimed the title of "Daddy," and now the two of them accorded it happily.

With the help of their father's chauffeur they had found an apartment quickly. It was in the Fernwood apartment hotel, on Sheridan Road, and though it was small, it was clean and bright and welcoming. Effie and Virginia shared the bedroom, a little sun parlor was made into a bedroom for Mack, and there was a davenport sofa in the living room, which could be made into a bed if they had company. But the most frequent and most welcome visitor to that apartment during the fall and early winter was John Kantor, although he did not sleep over.

He was still married to his second wife at the time, but he lived apart from her and with another "very dear friend" instead. The motive for his frequent visits was domestic, not romantic. Despite all his wantonness, there persisted in his nature a stunted growth of humanity, of human warmth and kindness. And, for a few months, he allowed that growth to flourish.

He would often come by in the evenings, unannounced, and they would rush to greet him. Sometimes he would just chat for a few minutes (it was unusual, in the children's experience, for their father to chat), and sometimes, particularly if there were other guests before whom he could perform, he would enter into the word games, and charades and forfeits they loved to play, with barely a hint of his usual pomposity. He would join them in telling ghost stories, and they particularly delighted in one he claimed he had heard from a guide on a hunting trip in Canada with Mayor Thompson. Upon occasion he was invited to dinner, and often he accepted; Effie would offer, after scrimping throughout the week, more impressive food than the simple country fare she and the children were content with, and he would revel in the children's attention and compliment her cooking. One night he came by when both Mack and Virginia were out, and talked with Effie for hours, reminiscing about the happier periods of their married life while enjoying a favorite dish: cold boiled potatoes and sour cream.

In telling the children about it later Effie said, "You know, he seemed just like a boy again. Just like the young man I married."

When they said grace at meals there may have been confusion in their minds about the object of their prayer, but it was with no sense of irony at all that they chanted, "Father, we thank Thee for this food; help us to be kind and good. Amen."

It was cold for March. There was a feeling of snow in the air, and the rent was overdue.

Their father's visits had tapered off during the course of the winter, and it was now at least a month since he had come by. Effie still kept boiled potatoes in the icebox, and the sour cream to accompany them. Eventually the potatoes would oxidize and blacken; eventually the sour cream would turn runny and rancid. Then she would boil potatoes anew, set fresh cream to sour, and keep them hopefully, until, in their turn, they also spoiled and had to be replaced.

The rent had been late several times before. Each time Mr. Harrison, the apartment manager, had come knocking at the door. "I'm sorry to bother you, Mrs. Kantor, but I haven't received the check for the rent."

Effie's face would tighten, whiten, and her voice would be strained.

"Oh, Mr. Harrison, I'm certain there's been some mistake. I'll have Mack telephone, and..." Mack would telephone and John Kantor, with a sugar-coated nastiness concocted of patience, condescension, and outrage, would say that the check had of course been sent.

And each time, after a week or so, Mr. Harrison had come round once more. "Mrs. Kantor, I really am sorry, but it's a month and a half now." Mr. Harrison was a nice man, and he liked them, but he only managed the building, and he had owners to satisfy.

Again the tightening, whitening, and the strain. And again, "There must be some mistake." But this time she would add, "As soon as Mack gets back from school I'll send him down to Mr. Kantor's office." Neither Virginia nor Effie could bring themselves to go on such an errand, for fear of embarrassment—though in Effie's case perhaps the fear was more of embarrassing John Kantor than herself.

In the late afternoon, in the falling light, Mack would take the el down to the Loop and then trot toward the Otis Building, where the Consumers Packing Company maintained its impressive offices.

I trotted toward a miserable experience.

"Daddy—"

"Hello, my son. How are you?"

"I'm fine. Daddy, Mr. Harrison was—"

"Do you not venture to ask how I am?"

"I'm sorry. Dad—how are you?"

The creaking of the leather swivel chair, the cigar smoke puffed out, the sigh and eye-rolling. "Son, I have been very, very busy. Also I have not been well. I was dangerously sick, in bed, for more den a week."

"Dad, why didn't you let—?"

The smile which said, "I am patient, I am forgiving. I do not wish to annoy others with my troubles." Cigar smoke again... a secretary coming in with a sheaf of papers. "Oh, I did not wish to worry you. One night de doctor told me sincerely dat he feared for my life. Dat was only last Monday. But—you see—here I am, hard at work!"

The rich laugh, the smile turned toward the secretary. "Am I not speaking honest facts, Miss Melnitz? Am I not working hard?"

"Gee—yes, you sure are, Mr. Kantor—"

"Dad, I didn't want to bother you, but Mr. Harrison asked me to come down here. He said the rent had not been paid for a month and a half. He said he just had to have a check right away and—"

Silence. A long, bitter, stony silence—a silence fit to reprimand a son for daring to intrude with such an accusation. "Surely dere is some mistake. Miss Melnitz, did I not give instructions dat de rent for my daughter's and son's apartment should be paid promptly on de first of every month?"

"Why, yes, you did, Mr. Kantor. I'm sure I sent it. Gee, I think I remember when you signed the check."

"Dat also is according to my recollection of de facts. However, I wish you to look it up. If de check has not been sent—and I am confident dat it *has* been sent—please take care of de oversight immediately. Son, you have heard me give de necessary instructions. Now—*if* you will excuse me—I have a great many people to see before I leave dis office tonight. Last night I could not leave before nearly eight o'clock, and I was very, very tired. Goodbye, son. Give my love to de folks. I shall come to see you very soon."

And though John Kantor never came again to chat and visit with Effie and their children, soon a check would come to Mr. Harrison.

But on this bitter day in March, things were very different. Once more Mack boarded the Jackson Park Express, once more he trotted, shivering, toward the Otis Building but, when he opened the door to the Consumers Packing Company's showy suite, he entered a brutal bedlam such as he had never known before. The office was jammed with photographers, reporters, and grim young men in shiny suits. A cacophony of voices dinned in Mack's ears, and flash powder flared, hellfire bright. Gone were the impressive partners, the glittering salesmen. Mack looked through into what he had regarded as the holiest place of all, his father's office, and there some stranger sat in John Kantor's chair, with his feet on John Kantor's desk. A silver badge glittered on his chest.

"What do you want, sonny?"

("I want my life back. I want my world. I...") "I'm looking for Mr. Kantor."

Harsh laughter came from all around him.

"Well, kid, you came to the wrong place. Say, who are you, anyway?"

"I'm Mack Kantor. I'm Mr. Kantor's son."

The man's voice softened, but only a little. "Do you know where the Federal Building is?"

"Yes, sir."

"You'll find your father there. In the U. S. Marshal's office. He's been arrested for fraud." As Mack turned away, the man added, "No need to hurry. I guess he's going to be there quite a while."

And run, run, run through the cold streets. *"Your father's in prison. Your father is in jail!"* Mack reached the Federal Building within five minutes. A court officer, ancient and amiable, passed him through a guarded door. There they were, all the partners and officers of the Consumers Packing Company, seeming shriveled, diminished, by their circumstances and surroundings—all save John Kantor, who loomed above the others, calm and dignified.

He beamed when he saw my father. "My son! How did you come here so quickly?"

"I went to your office, Daddy. The men—the men said you'd been arrested."

"Ah, it is nothing. Merely a few disgruntled stockholders who are trying to cause trouble. We will soon dispose of them."

The room—indeed the world—whirled around Mack, giddy and uncertain. But—"a few disgruntled stockholders." He concentrated upon that comforting phrase.

"And now, my son, since you have come to this strange place"—and John Kantor smiled, his voice laden with grotesque irony—"I wish you to help me."

"Couldn't Mayor Thompson help you, Daddy? He's a friend of yours."

"No, Mack. This is a federal case, and Bill Thompson"—his voice hugged those words—"can have no influence at all. But it is only a temporary inconvenience. Tell the folks that." He scribbled lines upon a sheet of note paper, and then upon others. "I wish you to take these notes—you may try to read them but it will be of no avail, for they are written in Yiddish—to certain men whose names and places of business I will also give you." And he scribbled again, but this time in English. "There! And tell your mother not to worry."

Run, run again through the early darkness, to a jewelry store, a tailor's shop, a bar, a bank. At the tailor's shop a wizened old man read his note and scowled. "Tell him no, no! Not one penny," the tailor said. "Not for *him* would I do it! So like him also I should become a goniff? No! No!" Mack did not know what *goniff* meant, but he heard the scorn in the old man's voice, and cringed accordingly.

At some point in his journey he passed a phone booth. He stopped and called his mother, and stammered out his story. And then he ran on again. Thinking about fathers.

The fathers, the fathers—the thousand good fathers of Webster City—the hundreds of thousands of other good fathers who must be dwelling beyond this Chicago noise and chilliness and evening thunder.... Papers were being sold at every corner now. A bawling man shoved a fresh-inked smear into my hand when I offered pennies. THOMPSON HENCHMAN SEIZED IN PHONY STOCK DEAL. KANTOR HELD IN CONSUMERS CASE.

Mack refused to go to school the next morning. He couldn't face the other children, knowing that scorn would smolder in their eyes. He'd get a job instead, he said. He did, and so did his mother. Virginia was due to graduate in a few months, and perhaps she was braver than her brother. (Though fear of shaming was not Mack's only motive in insisting on dropping out of school and finding work. They had no money, and, "Virginia's *got* to graduate," he'd said when arguing with his mother.) With her lovely face armored shut, her eyes fierce and wary, and her ears as closed to nastiness as she could make them, Virginia continued going to Nicholas Senn. But Mack didn't go back to any school until the following fall. And when he did, he told lies.

"Just like his father."

Night wind, and the stars. Mack lay on top of a stack of straw. The straw rustled beneath him whenever he moved, and individual straws pricked his back, just as fiercely as unpleasant thoughts pricked his mind. He lay there counting the stars, and watching the Dipper pour space upon the Pole. It was a warm night in August, and the scent of new-threshed oats was rich around him, but the stars were so sharp and bright and white that they reminded him of the frost of winter. When he thought of that he shivered, for there was winter—a cold and bitter winter—in his soul.

The world itself, and certainly his own life, seemed made of straws,

straws far less substantial than those on which now he lay. An owl hooted far away, hunting mice. That hoot was real, and so were the stars above him, and the sacred Past, and words in certain books he'd read, but everything else he knew seemed shifting and uncertain. During that black night even his mother seemed a misty being to him, for she had taken part of her love from him and given it to Dr. Von Krog and, before and after that, to his father. His father, free now on bail. His father had *stolen*. He had robbed people; he had hurt them. He had robbed, he had hurt, just as surely as if he'd used a gun. And everybody knew.

Orion swung overhead, and the Pleiades. Mack felt as though he were falling into the stars which hung above him. He felt that he'd been falling his whole life long.

His father was a thief, a bully, and a liar, and, if Mack came from such bad seed, what in turn would he become? Tears threatened, but a fifteen-year-old shouldn't cry. The stars were blurred by moisture in his eyes. He lay there, fists clenched, trembling, and listened to the sounds of night.

Virginia had graduated from high school the previous May, third in her class, filling Effie and Mack with pride, and they had come home—poor Effie, so many of her dreams in tatters, seeking refuge once again—home to Webster City, where the *Chicago Tribune* was widely read. The *Tribune* was bitterly opposed to Mayor Thompson and his cronies, and John Kantor was linked to him; the *Tribune* had played the Consumers Packing story big, with John Kantor's name and heavy, handsome face prominent on the front page for days on end. Good friends were kind and supportive, they ignored that notoriety; but there were jibes again, there were looks, there were sneers. Mack's old job was filled. He wanted a full-time job anyway—and there were none to be had. The young men who had served in the Rainbow Division, in the Navy, the Marines, were back now, and they were also looking for jobs. There were none left over for a gangling fifteen-year-old, no matter how tall he was, no matter how old he looked. Nor was there work for Effie, during those first hot, hard months at home. But John Kantor was out on bail now, and he had made another business deal, found other suckers, or perhaps he had money hidden where Government search could not discover it. He sent a few small checks, which were actually good. The family went on picnics; they went to Chautauqua, when it came to town. Sixty-eight-year-old Adam worked now as fireman in the same factory where he had watched through long nights before. He stoked the boiler fires with chips and shavings, and a few times Mack helped him. Mack was filled with admiration for his grandfather's stubborn courage—his wiry muscles husbanding all the strength that lingered in his scrawny body—and filled with outrage that he must labor so. He was also filled with outrage that there was so little work for himself. He moped around, he scowled, until his mother gave permission for him to go tramping. He put some cooking utensils and a light raincoat in a knapsack which Dr. Von Krog had left behind, slipped a fish knife in its sheath upon his belt, and retreated to the countryside he loved. Away from town and shame and disappointment. He slept in the open, bought food from farms.

Bats swooped and squeaked nearby, and the wind purled in his ears. The world seemed unfair to him, and threatening, and so he dreamed of other lives. *"I was wounded at Vicksburg. I ..."* He wished he were older, old enough to have really been a soldier. Then he would find it easier to get a job; then he too could put ribbons on his chest when he went courting during the long Saturday evenings of summer, talking casually of the Marne and the Argonne offensive. But the War was over, and it had been The War To End All Wars. He had wanted so to fight and be a hero, and now he'd never have the chance.

He had wanted also to impress the people of the town. He wanted to walk tall along the streets where once he'd walked (or run) so small. But still he felt small, poor, incomplete, unaccomplished. He gritted his teeth and moaned with the wind. Someday, by God, someday he'd show them all. He would do great things! *"...when you're a man, you've got to do great things."* He'd be rich and famous, and they'd all admire him. Oh, he knew that sometimes he was loud and bumptious, but someday he would move through crowds of admirers with stately confidence, just like his father. But never would he cheat, and never would he steal. He'd be honest and generous. And never would he lie!

His eyes closed at last, and sleep wrapped his misery around him like a cloak.

Early morning, with a clean, rich blue above him, a prairie mix of gold straw and black earth all around, and the green of windbreaks in the distance. Mack was stiff and a little sore, but dreams had swallowed his sorrows, taken them deep, and he felt almost as fresh and clean as the day itself. He clambered down the stack of straw, some ten feet to the ground, and plodded across uneven loam until he reached the road. Then he stepped out along its dusty surface, singing a song he knew.

Only wisps of those night-thoughts lingered in his mind.

He was hungry and, when he came opposite a farmhouse, he turned in at the lane and walked down it, through the yard, and up to the kitchen door. The farm wife was as old and plump as his grandmother, with a pleasant, windburned face.

"Please, ma'am, could I buy a loaf of bread and some eggs?"

"Where are you from, young man? I don't reckon you're from hereabouts, or I'd know your face and name."

"No, ma'am, I'm from over to Webster City." In ordinary speech he would not have spoken so. He would have said, "I'm *from* Webster City," instead. But mimicry was native to him—mimicry of the chameleon, not the clown. And he liked to absorb and copy the speech of elder days, because it made him feel a part of them.

"Why, my heavens, you've come a long stretch. Where are you bound?"

"Just hiking around, ma'am. I haven't been out in fields like these in over a year. I've been away. So I'm taking a few days to go wandering, sleeping out and buying my food along the way." He reached to bring out money from his pocket.

"Why, mercy! You don't have to buy your breakfast from us! We ain't that poor. You come in, young man. We're just setting down at the table ourselves, and we've got plenty to spare for you." He put the money away. He'd hoped she'd say that; he didn't have very much. And, to her husband in the kitchen behind her, "Mister, we got company."

He was welcomed, he was shown where he could wash up at the pump in the yard, then he was seated at the table and given a farm breakfast fresh from the stove. Thick, browned slices of ham, and eggs, and cornbread still hot on the inside.

Mack was wearing the khaki shirt and moleskin trousers that had been his Junior ROTC uniform at school in Chicago the year before. (Aside from English and Botany, the Cadet Corps had been the only part of school he'd liked.) The farmer eyed his shirt with puzzlement.

"Were you in the Army?"

"I . . . " My father was tempted, and he fell . . . *falling . . . falling his whole life long.* "Yes, sir."

"That's a funny kind of uniform you got."

"I was with the Canadians, sir. The CEF. You see I was kind of young, and they were easier to join."

"Were you Over There?" The grizzled old man with the lean, hard body gestured toward the east. "In France?"

"A little over a year ago I was fighting the Jerries at Amiens."

The farmer settled back in his chair, impressed and interested, while his wife clucked with admiration and sympathy. "Were you wounded?"

"Not badly, ma'am. Just a touch of gas." And Mack went on, telling tales. A few minutes later he remembered to cough into his bandanna. The husband of one of his Chicago cousins had, in fact, served with the Canadians in France and, during the previous winter, Mack had listened, fascinated, to war stories that were true. Certain of those he repeated now, with just an occasional cough to support deception.

When the coffee pot was empty he thanked the couple for his breakfast and walked down the lane with their obvious respect a golden kiss upon his cheek, a golden halo round his head. He felt no sense of guilt at all. They had given him a meal, and he had paid with glamour, with his imagination, in return. He felt quite smug about the whole charade.

"You a vet?"

"Yeah." Mack's voice was as taut and tough as he could make it. He sat at the soda fountain in a drugstore near North High School, in Des Moines. He wore a khaki shirt and overseas cap, as did the young man who had spoken to him. "You?"

"I was with the Forty-Second."

Mack nodded soberly, respectfully. "The Rainbow Division—you must have had some tough duty."

"You can say that again. Château-Thierry, and the Meuse." He was really still a boy, only eighteen or nineteen, but he had the tight-drawn face of a man who has seen bad things, and there was challenge in his voice, challenge in his eyes. "How about you?"

My father produced a shrug—my God! how tense he must have been— and a few laconic words. "I was with the Canadians. Too young for recruiting sergeants here." He sipped his chocolate soda. "We took Mons last November." The other nodded in acceptance, and Mack was filled with false pride and guilty pleasure.

They had moved to Des Moines in September. Two old friends of Effie's, men of consequence in the state government, had found a job for her in the Capitol Building. A minor job, for small money, but still a job. And John Kantor had written to announce that he still felt responsible for the education of his children, and promised to send a check for two hundred dollars every month. He said that he had formed a "business connection" in Indianapolis, and that he expected his "harassment" by the Federal Government to be speedily and happily resolved. And so it was. When the Consumers Packing case finally went to trial the other officers of the company received prison terms, but John Kantor was given only a ten-thousand-dollar fine. It was said that, after receiving that sentence, he took the judge to lunch.

They found a small, cramped, inexpensive apartment in an unhappy part of town. Effie worked for the State, earning one hundred and, later, ninety dollars a month; Virginia went to a secretarial school called the Four C's to learn the skills she could use to put herself through college; Mack, reluctantly, attended North High. The eleventh grade again. He had grown used to treating boys two years older as his equals during most of his years in school, and now his fellow students were almost his own age. He thought of them as children. He had suffered ignominy, he had lived in Chicago, he had seen the world, and they had not.

But there were the veterans: youths of seventeen, eighteen, nineteen, who had dropped out of school and traveled even farther than he, and now had returned from training camp or from the Argonne Forest to finish their schooling. He felt that he belonged with them. They had scars upon their souls, and so did he. He thought of that farm couple's respectful acceptance of the stories he had told, and of the golden glow their respect had given him. And so he lied again.

He could not state, even to himself, the reasons why he did this silly, shameful thing. He flinched from self-analysis then. He would flinch from it always. Surely his status as a "veteran" helped in feminine conquest, and that was already important to him, but I think the prime reason was more, was less, than that. He felt uncertain about himself, he felt in danger of being smothered by his mother's labor and love and self-sacrifice, and he felt stained by his father's infamy. Through a few cheap lies, he could make himself seem a man among other men. Brave and noble, just as they.

Through a few cheap lies, and a lot of studying. He spent hours at the public library, reading books of war reminiscences by Canadian and British veterans. He bought a few campaign ribbons at an Army-Navy store. He remembered to say "*Lef*tenant," rather than "*Loo*tenant" whenever he spun his tales. His mass of invention grew ever higher, like a sand castle built by a clever, careless child, below the mark of high tide.

He slept poorly at night. He tossed and turned in shame and agony, and horrendous nightmares plagued his broken sleep. He daydreamed about having the school principal call a special assembly where Mack could publicly announce his crime and beg forgiveness, for he felt that he *was* committing a crime, and he was disgusted by the sham he played. But each time he strode boldly toward the principal's office his stride became a shuffle before he got there, and he would slink away.

And the tales kept coming to his lips. (Always tales would come to him, or they'd go skittering through the wilderness within until he found them.)

A pretty girl, and blond. Firm breasts promising under cotton of her blouse, wool of her coat; trim ankles alluring below her skirt. Bright eyes alive with wonder and admiration. "You were really wounded?"

"Yes." A stoic shrug. "But it wasn't bad. We'd just reached the first line of German trenches, outside of Mons. We'd only lost a few of our chaps, getting through the barbed wire. Of course our artillery had stopped their barrage, so they wouldn't hit us, and it was dark as hell. Pitch black, in between the glow of the star shells coming down. You know—flares. I'd landed on top of a couple of Jerries, but I thought they were dead and I was just starting along the trench to join up with the others." He made a little grimace, just barely noticeable. Tough and noble. "Then, all of a sudden, I felt this flash of pain down here," and he touched the calf of his right leg. "You see, one of those Germans was only wounded, and he'd got me with his trench knife. But I took care of him."

"Oooh. Can I see?"

He raised his trouser leg briefly to display the scar he'd received when a dog had bitten him two years before.

"Oooh," again. Soft lips opened to him and he liked the taste of her. Liked it just as fiercely as he disdained himself.

In late November or early December the bubble burst, the card-built house fell down, his lies came all undone. He was sick, he had the flu, he couldn't be in school to counter discrepancies in his lies with new invention. And one of his teachers had encountered an old friend from Webster City, and had mentioned Mack "the veteran." The old friend laughed. "Mack Kantor? He can't be more than fifteen. His father's a swindler, you know. A fraud. He must be telling lies just like his father."

But Mack had not lied "just like his father" at all. His father lied, had lied in his twisted past, would lie in his ugly future, out of a compulsive desire to manipulate, to impress, and sometimes out of malice, and often out of greed. My father's schoolboy lies sprang from only one, the second and most innocent, of those four needs.

He went back to school when his body was healed of sickness. He went back to face the angry contempt of the boys and girls he'd conned, whose admiration he had gained with false tales of deeds undone, and to face the kinder, though far more hurtful, amused dismissal of the true veterans he'd also taken in. His body was healed, but his pride was in tatters. With adolescent certainty he felt his soul was dirtied, and never would again be clean.

In later years he claimed that he didn't remember one day of sunshine during all that filthy winter. At night the air was foul, and he couldn't see the stars.

His father's falseness saved Mack in the end. That and his own inborn courage, his native strength and drive.

For four months they had awaited John Kantor's checks with the queasy eagerness of people enduring the first long climb of a roller coaster ride, or lined up for their first flight in a barnstorming airplane at a county fair, but each month the checks had come. In January of 1920, just before Mack's sixteenth birthday, the roller coaster plunged, the airplane crashed. The check was late and, when it came, it would not serve. True, it was signed by John Kantor in his own distinctive hand, but the rest of the check had been made out by another, and made out incorrectly. At the right-hand side, beside the dollar sign, was the figure "200," but on the line below, where the amount should have been written out, there appeared only "Two", followed by a series of dots. The bank refused to honor the check for more than two dollars. Effie sent it back, suggesting there had been a mistake. When eventually John replied, he did not mention money at all.

They did not hear from him again for years.

In those hectic, inflationary times Effie's ninety dollars a month was not enough to house and clothe and feed them all. "Mother, I've got to quit school and get a job."

O glorious release from scorn and shame.

Her kind hands on his cheeks, her sad face composed and grave, nodding in agreement. "Yes, son, I think you must. At least for now." And now was all he cared about. His past seemed filled with misery; he saw his future as a somber mystery, and no bright vision glimmered to lead him out of darkness.

But he could work, and he did. He found a part-time job as an usher in a movie theater for a few weeks, and then a full-time job as a "mosser" in a commercial greenhouse (insulating plants for shipment with bits of moist, soft green). But the job was seasonal. That summer he went back to Webster City to stay with his grandparents, hoping to earn pocket money by doing yard work for older folk who could no longer do their own: mowing grass, trimming trees.

He was lucky and found a real job instead, installing coal-burning furnaces in private homes, working ten hours a day, six days a week. It was hard, hot work in those un-air-conditioned times, but he earned twenty four dollars a week. That was more than his grandfather made, or his mother. There was joy in helping them: pride in the purchase of blue slips of money orders to send to his mother and Virginia, pride in the purchase of groceries for his grandparents, the paying of small bills. Further delight because he could afford small luxuries when he got together with his friends in the evenings, or went courting girls.

The memory of the lies he'd told was etched someplace within, but he had proved himself generous and responsible, and he had earned the little money he had gained, not stolen it. He felt himself redeemed by labor, washed nearly free of sin.

But though he had allayed the past, and through his own effort made the present almost pleasant, still the future threatened. The future was forever, but he had no idea of how to reach it, or what to do when he got there.

Knowledge came to him that fall. Dream and certainty all intermixed.

His job installing furnaces had vanished in September with the departure of the man who sold the furnaces. The salesman had admired Mack's industry and efficiency; he had offered to take him with him to the new territory he was going to exploit, and offered to raise his salary as well. Mack was pleased and flattered (perhaps he really had made himself a man among men), but he turned the offer down. He missed his mother too much, missed his sister, missed the warmth and pleasures of domestic intimacy they had shared: popcorn and milk in the evenings, the reading aloud of old books, the retelling of old tales, the singing of treasured hymns and ballads which they loved.

He went back to Des Moines and the brother-in-law of a family friend from Webster City gave him a job with the State Highway Commission, helping to test cement, sand, and gravel for the highways Iowa would someday build.

It was hard work, and physically demanding. There were long hours spent driving over muddy roads, or dusty, in search of quarries, long hours spent digging sand or gravel, long hours testing samples in an overheated laboratory. But, just as in his job of the previous summer, it was work that demanded nothing of *himself*. Once he had dreamed of becoming an entomologist someday, or a curator and student of relics from the Civil War and other regions of the past. But now he understood that it was the bright glory of the butterfly's flight, the mystic shimmer of the moth's, which enchanted him, and not their physical architecture. If the structure of the past enthralled him, it was its human structure which did so, not merely the labeling of relics with their proper dates. The certainty of the past held him captive (it always would), but he must prepare himself to do some grand thing in the future, to achieve, to impress the people who had sneered at him, to make a lot of money, honestly, so that never would he lack for comfort as he had before, nor his mother lack for fine clothes to wear, nor his grandmother the luxury of the store-bought ice cream she loved.

He must use himself in a grand way, not trivially. He must do some thing, but still he wondered what that way, that thing, might be.

It was in October or November when the Knowledge came to him. (Always, in later years, he regretted not remembering the exact date on which he Knew.) The other workers were out in the field; he was working in the lab alone, performing dreary tasks and wondering, as so often, what he could do to shape his future, to shape himself. For he was a poor thing, he felt, ill-formed, not properly assembled. He paused and stared through a dirty window. He stood stark still, and he stared. That world out there, where now his fellow workers shoveled sand or gravel, where now his grandfather labored, sweating, old and weary, where now his mother filed and sorted papers in a job beneath her dignity, where now his father connived and lied and disregarded him—that world frightened him.

If he could only better shape that world, better shape himself.

And he could! Suddenly he Knew. He had sung songs in the past both sad and happy, he had told foolish tales and people had believed him. He could use words well. Shimmer in the woods and sorrow in the city, laughter in his home and anguish in the night: he Knew them all, and he could *tell* about them. His body was hot, was cold, from scalp to toes. He felt consumed by a fever which must never end. He loved ballads, stories, books. Maybe he could write them also, and make magic out of words.

He had no satisfactory world, no satisfactory being, of his own. But perhaps he could shape them, out of words.

8

We'll Look Back
and Laugh

Friday, April 2nd, 1926—Went to the Graeme Players, an amateur drama group, for the first time tonight. Met MacKinlay Kantor who writes for the Line O' Type column. I had already cut out "Floyd Collins' Cave" and "Leather Gods." But he ran down to answer my ring wearing an old khaki flannel shirt and a black vest. Ugh.

So my mother-to-be, Irene Layne, had heard of my father before they met, and already admired his writing. And scorned his dress. Apparently Mack wore more suitable clothes when the Graeme Players held rehearsal the following Sunday, with a party afterward. During rehearsal he kept losing his lines, because his eyes and thoughts were all on her; at the party they talked, she shyly, he with an eager blend of sensitivity and bravado. (She sought force and drive; he longed for acquiescence and support. The words he chose, forty-five years later, to describe his vision of her on their first meeting, mean a lot: "Irene Layne with the pliant face, the shapely legs, the shimmering hair and becalming eyes...")

The next Tuesday they had a date.

He limped as they walked along the street, her slim arm tucked in his, toward an Italian restaurant he was fond of, and which was cheap.

"Were you wounded in the war?"

"Hell, no. I was too young for the service. This"—he touched his left thigh—"is from a car wreck I was in. But I wasn't driving!" He smiled at her, tough and noble. He liked her eyes. They were big and soft and grayish green. Someday he might tell those eyes, that mouth, that pert and wistful spirit and sprightly body, about his adolescent lies. But not now. Now he must impress.

They reached the restaurant about eight thirty. Dinner for two was out of the question, which is why he'd made their date for eight P.M. Mack worked for American Flyer, the company that made the toy trains which roared and moaned through so many childhoods. He wrote advertising copy and brochures for twenty-five dollars a week, and a good chunk of that had to go back to Webster City to help support his grandparents and to pay off bills for repeated surgery on his leg. But a bottle of red wine cost only a dollar and a half at La Bohème, the bread was free ("A loaf of bread, a jug of wine / And thou..."—he'd recite that to her later in the evening), and there were candles burning.

They toasted each other, smiling, eager, speculative. Irene said, "I think this place is lovely."

"Glad you like it. I wish this could have been for dinner, but I'm kind of broke right now. I just sold another sketch to *College Humor*, but I haven't got the check yet."

"Oh, you write for magazines too?"

He liked that too. It meant that she must have read his poems in the "Line o' Type" column in the *Chicago Tribune*. "Sure. I've sold a bunch of sketches to *College Humor*, and a few to other magazines. And I'm trying to sell short stories, and I've got a novel with an agent in New York."

"A novel!" The very idea was impressive to her. "What's it called?"

"*Half Jew*. You see, I'm half Jewish myself, and..." He waited for her to flinch at his statement, but she didn't, and so he told her. Told her about his fractured feelings: about growing up Christian in a small town in Iowa, but with a Jewish name which always attracted curiosity and sometimes insults, and with a distant father whose conduct attracted insults also. And a little—oh, just a little more—about his father himself. He told her about his family and friends in Webster City, and about alien relatives there in Chicago, a few of whom he liked and others whom he loathed. He told her about a fifteen-year-old boy crying out of confusion, into the night, "God damn all Gentiles, God damn all Jews! Which am I? I'm neither one!" And how he had been that boy, and that boy was in the novel, and the novel was with an agent in New York.

"Are you an atheist?" Now there was shock, now there was flinching.

"Oh, no. I was just unhappy and confused. I was baptized all right—in a smelly tin tank in our church at home—and when I was little we went to church regularly." He grinned, a young boy peering out of a young man's face. "Why, I bet I could sing you a hundred hymns—two hundred. I was raised on them. My grandmother sings them all the time. But when my sister and I got older, Mother felt that we could get closer to God out in the fields and the timber—on Sundays we'd go for picnics, watch for birds, listen to the wind—rather than by listening to some marshmallow-voiced minister. I don't go to church much any more."

"Well, I don't go to our church—Grace Methodist—as much as I ought to either. But what you told me before explains about your name. I'd wondered, when I saw it in the paper."

"Yeah, but that isn't the name my mother gave me. She called me Benjamin, because it means 'son of the right hand,' or something silly like that. Benjamin McKinlay Kantor. *Mc*, not *Mac*. That's the way her people spell the name. But, when I was a little kid, I hated being called Ben, or Benjy, and my grandfather sometimes called me Mack—just like his father— and I liked that, and I dropped Benjamin altogether. And then, in my teens, I started reading about the clans of Scotland, and I found that the original spelling of the name was *Mac*. So I changed my own to agree with that, and now I'm *Mac*Kinlay Kantor."

"MacKinlay Kantor. It's a nice name." And then she laughed, a little shaky, through a shimmer of candles. "I changed my name, too."

"You're not really Irene?"

"Oh, yes. But originally I was *Florence* Irene Layne. And people would call me Florence, or Flo, or even Flossie, and I hated them all. I couldn't *stand* being Florence."

"I don't blame you." Beauty was facing him—beauty, and eyes, and the promise of warmth. "But Irene's a lovely name."

"Thank you. I like it. My mother used to call me that." And suddenly Irene Layne, she with the small, trim body, she with the lovely face and legs, with alluring breasts and hips beneath her dress—Irene looked to be a tiny girl instead of a tiny woman, and there was sadness evident within her.

"What's wrong?" He reached to take her hand.

"Oh, it's just—mentioning my mother. I loved her so. She died when I was seven. And then I missed her so."

"Of course you did."

"But it was worse than that. You see, just before she got so sick, and died, I'd been guilty of some wicked prank, some bit of childish mischief. I don't even remember what it was. And she'd been very angry, and she scolded me. And I was angry in my turn, and sullen. I told her that I hated her, and I wished that she was dead. At least—I don't know if I really told her that, but certainly I felt it."

"But all kids say things like that, feel things like that."

"I know that now. But after that my mother did get sick, she *did* die, and I felt guilty. I felt that somehow I had killed her. I felt that, thought that, for years and, even now, sometimes when I think of her, speak of her, it makes me sad." She shook her head and then she looked at him. Her eyes sparkled in the candlelight, and he thought their brightness came half from wonder, half from tears. "I don't know why I'm telling you things like this. On our first date."

"I don't know why I told you what I did either. Maybe it's because we like each other's voices. Maybe it's because we like each other." They went on talking, and the minutes turned into hours, and the evening turned into other evenings during the weeks which followed.

"You'd love Webster City. The people are nice there—mostly—and the country is so beautiful. The woods so deep, and filled with magic. And the fields. They're just black earth and stubble in the fall but, toward the end of summer, the corn seems to be growing right up into the sky. And the sky is so blue, with the white clouds marching past. You can see cities in those clouds, and buffalo. Indians. Why, I've seen herds of mustangs ride across that sky!" (Someday those herds would come thundering again, and he'd put them down on paper, in a book called *Spirit Lake:* "... clouds walked with you, they came rolling in at the door, they occupied your mind. You could not forget that they were pillars, that they were a stockade, they were ponies running loose.") "You'd love it. You'd love it all," he said again, as though repetition could make his claim come true.

"I'm sure I would." Then she paused. "But I'm confused. I thought when you were sixteen you were living in Des Moines. How did you get from there to Webster City again, and then to Chicago?"

"Well, the winter I turned seventeen was pretty lousy." He smiled the smile of suffering endured and overcome. "I lost my job in that laboratory, just before Christmas. We were having a depression out in Iowa—in all of the farm states—then, and I couldn't find anything else. And then, two months later, Mother lost her job with the State government. And she couldn't find anything either. My sister, Virginia, was the only one working, and she could just work part-time, because she was going to college. The landlord was unhappy, and there were times when we lived on bread crusts and beans and soup bones, and not much else. Mother was playing the piano for a dancing class, and for church socials a few times a week, and I did odd jobs when I could find them, but things were pretty tough. And then"—his face changed as he said "then"; it had been somber, but now it sparked with gaiety—"then we got lucky."

"What happened?"

"An old family friend—did you ever notice how often miracles come from friends?—decided that he wanted to get into politics back home. And he thought the best way to do that was to start another local paper. The *Webster City News*. He didn't know anything about newspapering, but he knew that Mother did. And so he asked her to run it for him. He'd be listed on the masthead as editor, but she'd *really* be the editor. And he'd pay her forty dollars a week! That seemed like a fortune to us."

He shrugged his shoulders in boyish wonder at that miracle—that transformation. "I'll never forget the evening when I heard about it. I'd been wandering around town, hunting for girls and not finding them, looking for friends and missing them." He laughed. "There wasn't much I could do with only twenty-five cents in my pocket. I got home about ten o'clock, and the apartment was brighter than I'd seen it in months. We'd been very careful about saving money on electricity, but now every single light was on. Virginia was sitting on the couch with her fiancé, Jim Sours—he's a nice guy and you'd like him, even though he is a preacher—and they were both laughing and smiling. And Mother was standing in the middle of the room, just beaming, just *radiant*." His voice softened, as always it did when he spoke of Effie. "She told me that she'd just received this offer. Well, I hooted along with the others. Salvation! But then she said, 'Mack, I want you to come with me. I won't take the job if you don't. I want you to come home with me and work on the paper.'"

He sipped his tea. Another poem had been published in the "Line O' Type" column—that meant no money, but it did mean a certain amount of glory—and he'd just received a check, eleven dollars, fifteen dollars, for the sale of another sketch to *College Humor*. They were celebrating with dinner in a cheap Chinese restaurant—a "Chop Suey," they called it—on Lincoln Avenue. I think, and I know my mother thought, that all the room brightened with his warm and wicked smile. ("He's so young," she thought, "so young. Just a year older than I am. But he's so strong and brave.")

"You see, I'd been hanging out with some pretty rough guys. Mother was worried, probably with reason, that I'd end up in trouble. And also, I had told her that I wanted to write. I'd already written a few bad short stories, and she'd admired them, encouraged me. She said, 'I don't think

I can get you a salary at first, but forty dollars is enough for all of us if we stay with the folks, and you'll be helping me with the paper. And you'll be writing. *Writing*, Mack, and that's the only way anyone ever learned to write.' And I knew that she was right." He laughed at that echo of words, the unintended pun, and then he reached across the table and took Irene's hand. That was rare, for him. Always he was bothered by public display of affection. But he brought the tiny hand up to his mouth and kissed her fingers, one by one.

This was their third week, and already she felt that she loved him. He had long hair for that time, and there was something vulnerable, appealing, in his eyes, and he was so handsome. She thought him almost beautiful.

She kissed his fingers in her turn. She wondered about his mother.

His eighteenth summer lived forever brilliant in his memory. That summer was an artist, a painter highly skilled, and many colors were mixed upon its palette. Gold of sun, of course, gold of wheat and corn, green of corn ears swelling full, green as well of elm and maple, of oak and hickory in the timber, and willows along the Boone, scarlet of tanagers, red of robins and prismatic wonder of the butterflies, dull silver of the printers' font, and stark black of letters on the typewriter keys. Orange fire in the dawn, and purple glory of the dusk, with painted Indians riding high across the west when sunlight failed at last.

And words. "The Order of the Eastern Star held a meeting Tuesday night. The first order of business was to..." Words. "Frank Bonebright, one of the foremost of our early settlers, was hospitalized yesterday. We understand the illness is not serious." Words. "A Committee of Concerned Citizens has been formed to..." Words. Hundreds of them. Thousands of them every week.

The use of so many words sharpened his ear for them, trained his fingers as they hunted on the keyboard (he was a two-finger typist then; he was a two-finger typist always). And the observation of people, as he roamed about the town in search of news, fed his human understanding.

The dentist with his passion for wild ducks; the barber who won rifle and pistol titles in the shooting matches at Camp Perry, Ohio; the politician who published his own little volumes of verse—unoriginal, ponderous, in weightiest classical tradition, and yet toiled over with love each night while the rest of the town lay sleeping...the termagant in the lopsided hat who came screaming into our office

with so-called Temperance screeds which she desired us to print...
the plaintive quarter-witted county constable who brought self-com-
posed eulogies whenever some National figure died....

We saw them not as futile little people in an agricultural county
seat, but as monsters or heroes of a panoramic legend in which we
should dramatize our own roles, secretly and to ourselves.

The drawling uninspired sheriff, the cashier who stole, and would
be tried and slapped upon the wrist; the county official who would
steal, and would be sentenced and make a heartbreak for those who
had loved his mother and his brothers... the fat-faced sadistic ditcher
who would beat his sons until one ended up as a felon, one as a
killer. The few surviving pioneers with their old metallic faces, their
whiskers and canes... ministers with their extra-clerical generosi-
ties or reiterated dreams or not-too-secret loves... the town drunk
who scuffled along, his little tweed hat nodding on his matted head,
and it was told by old-timers that his father had been a count, a
political fugitive from Poland....

In the evenings, and often on Sundays, he put this new learning to good
use. Under the wild grape arbor in the back yard of the old McKinlay home,
where once he had found cover when he laid siege to the outhouse which
was Vicksburg (acting tales before he told them), he set an old wash bench
and placed a typewriter on it. There he would sit, as the sun fell below the
maples, seeking words to describe the world he knew, and others which he
dreamed of.

It was a foreign-looking motor car to appear in an Iowa lane, but it
purred steadily along, as if accustomed to such surroundings. It was
piloted by a chauffeur who seemed rather soiled by the heavy dust
that hung over the highway they had just left behind them. The au-
to's only occupant beside the driver was a lithe, dark man who
glanced from side to side as if hunting something. Fields stretched
away on every hand—corn with stalks beginning to grow crisp and
tough, oats piled in golden stacks as far as the eye could see; the
early morning sun glistened on freshly clipped stubble, and a tiny
warbler in the grasses at the roadside invited the world to come and
share his store of seeds.

Mack thought of himself as a warbler, uncertain perhaps, but long and
tough and driven, and he also had a store—a store of words—and he wished

to share them. He had been infected by his mother with an addiction to cliché, and what his high school teachers labeled "rhetoric." He hadn't yet learned the importance of simplicity. (He would learn that virtue from a lady, and then forget it in sad, distant years to come). But he had tales to tell, and he told them. He wrote two stories that summer, and his mother praised them and helped to type the final copies. The *Des Moines Register*, for which he'd already written several minor items, ran an annual short story contest—open to any unpublished would-be fiction writer in the State of Iowa—and Effie insisted that he enter it.

He dithered and delayed. He didn't think the stories were good enough. "Oh, yes, they are, darling. Yes, they are! That story called 'Purple,' about the photographer in the car, is just wonderful. It's so touching!" Her faith heartened him, and he sent the stories off. A pen name was required, and Mack came up with "Sheridan Rhodes." As ever after, he was sentimental and sought for omens; they had lived on Sheridan Road in Chicago, perhaps that name would bring him luck. He dreamed of glory—of maybe winning an Honorable Mention—during the night; sometimes he anticipated disaster during the day.

But he went on writing for the paper and, at Effie's urging, he went back to finish school, where he was either scorned or envied by many, both teachers and students, and liked—even loved—by a few. The days, the weeks, the months passed by in busyness, and thought of the contest faded into murmur in his mind.

It was a Saturday, and so he could spend full time working for the paper. The twenty-fifth of February, 1922. The mail came in during the morning, and with it the *Register*, but there were interviews to make, articles to be written. It wasn't until late in the afternoon that he had a chance to really look at the *Register*'s front page.

There was a box at the bottom, about five inches square, and Mack found it hard to read the black, italicized letters through his tears.

PURPLE
by Sheridan Rhodes

First Prize Winner in the Register's Annual Short Story Contest will be published in tomorrow's Register.

What is the author's real name?

That was such an easy question to answer, even though there was confusion, shouting, glee, in that office when he read those words aloud. The author's real name was MacKinlay Kantor, and MacKinlay Kantor could tell tales. He could seize them out of air and make them come true on the page.

He was a writer.

Counting stars again, but in another season, and this time there was no sense of loneliness. Instead, there was a sense of sharing. It was late April, early May, and they were on the north shore of Lake Michigan. Lights of the city behind them dimmed the stars, but could not hide them all. Mack had spread his jacket on the sand and they were lying on it. Looking up. Holding hands.

Irene said, "It seemed the house just reeked of death that year. We held four funerals from that house in one single year."

His hand tightened around hers. "Oh, my God! There was your mother, and...?"

"And my baby sister. You see, there were already six of us. And Mother had lost one baby years before. Before I was born. The doctor had told her that she mustn't have another, but..." He felt the shiver of her body, next to his, and longed to comfort her. (And with that longing he felt increase of force, as though her weakness strengthened him.) "She got pregnant again, and I guess there were complications—such things simply weren't talked about at home—and Mother died a few days after giving birth. There was someone, a wet nurse, but the baby died a few weeks later. I remember my father taking me into the room. He led me to the crib and said, 'This was your baby sister.' And I was sure she was just asleep—she *looked* asleep—and I couldn't understand why he said 'was.'"

Childhood loss which would haunt her all her life. Her voice quavered, and she cried. (Again he felt that rush of strength.) In the darkness he traced her face with his mouth. He tried to kiss away her tears, but they kept coming.

"And then?"

"And then Grandmother Lawrence, my mother's mother, and my father's brother, Uncle Harry. But, of course, Mother's death hurt the most. Hurt all of us the most. I shared a room with my older sister, Ruth, and our room was next to Dad's—to what had been theirs. For months and months, at night we'd go to sleep and hear him pacing back and forth, and in the morning we'd wake up and hear him pacing still. He'd been, oh, I don't know the word—*vivid*. Vital. And the life seemed to go out of him when Mother died. Pacing. We heard that sound for months. I think for years."

Waves moaned on the shore. "Lie closer to me." He did, and Irene went on talking while still the surf came in. "We were fortunate in a way. My father had two spinster sisters and, one after the other, they came to live with us, and tend to us. And Ruth," her voice softened, as Mack's did when he spoke of Effie, "she's six years older, and almost she became another mother."

She spoke then of her schooling—she'd done well—and of art school afterward. The ripening progression of her years. "I like to paint. I think— oh, I hope—I could be good." At that time she labored in the dreary work of painting designs on lamp shades. He pitied her accordingly, but the dreams which danced inside her head enchanted him.

"I bet you'll be wonderful," he said, and *wonderful* meant several very different things to him when he said it. "I'd like to see your paintings."

The next evening she showed him some. They were good indeed, and filled with promise. My sister and I—drowning in relics from so many lives— still have a sketchbook from that time which proves the statement true. Our mother had a good eye, and a sure sense of color. Our father, who had neither, praised those paintings to the skies.

Later, when they left her home to wander through the dusk, he liked the swing of her hips as she walked before him down the stairs.

Despite all early loss, Irene lived wrapped in domesticity. Her father, Charles W. Layne—his Elgin watch, inexpensive, gold-plated, carefully engraved, is in my pocket now, but the name for which that *W* stood is lost to family memory—was a caring man, however much his grieving led him to retreat. Her sister owned a valiant, vibrant soul, and had sheltered, buoyed Irene when she was young. Now Ruth was married, but she lived not far away. Their father had remarried, several years before, and their stepmother was an amiable, placid woman who was kind to Charles Layne, and kind to his children also. Two of Irene's brothers still lived at home: Lawrence, who was older, and Kenny—who was fifteen, and the baby of the family. Kenny was bright and quick. He was Irene's favorite, Irene's special joy. They lived in a pleasant apartment on Wilson Avenue (and that was strange, that was remarkable, that was an omen—for Mack's own home was on *Will*son Avenue, back in Webster City), and warmth and laughter flourished there, with the other brothers, and uncles and aunts and distant cousins, coming and going.

Charles Layne made my father feel welcome in that place, and I think that is why—though I cannot remember him, for I saw him only rarely and he died before I was five—I find such pleasure when I touch his watch.

Kenny died that May. (Just over twenty years later, and one year younger than Kenny was then, I also suffered a sudden attack of acute appendicitis, with no symptoms at all until the last few hours. The doctor said that my appendix was "red hot" by the time he got it out. Kenny had been less fortunate, and medicine was more primitive then. When I awoke after the operation my mother was there, and she was crying, but I did not understand her tears.) Mack loved Irene. He had also become fond of Kenny during the short, bright time he'd known him, and he wished to share her grief. Hidden in his little office at American Flyer, stealing company time, he tried to comfort her with words.

> . . .
>
> *I saw a wingéd colt learning how to fly:*
> *He in a box? He never came to die.*
>
> *All of you tell me the smooth wheels roll*
> *Out to that plain with its deep, square hole.*
> *Hark . . . how the night-hawks scream in their chases*
> *High in the dusk past those platted-out places . . .*
>
> *I saw a pinto where the ranges lie—*
> *Never in a box, never come to die.*

It wasn't poetry of the first order. There was too much dum-de-dum of obvious rhythm, too much of that damned "rhetoric" which plagued him for years, but the emotion was simple and sure. A young voice trying to find itself. All of the Laynes were touched when the poem appeared in the "Line O' Type" column in the *Tribune*. Irene cried when first Mack read it to her. Partly out of grief; partly out of pride.

"The last time *I* cried? That's easy. When I wrote that poem about Kenny." They were enjoying illicit privacy in Mack's quarters in a rooming house on Cambridge Avenue.

"And before that?"

"When I sat in a day coach on the train to Chicago, and opened an envelope."

"What happened?"

"It was one year ago last March, just two weeks after Dick Little ran my poem about Floyd Collins in the 'Line O' Type' column."

"I remember," said Irene, dreamily. She liked to comb his coarse, dark hair with her fingers. "That was the first time I ever saw your name. MacKinlay Kantor." She lingered over syllables. "I loved that poem. I cut it out to keep. 'Floyd Collins's Cave.'"

Floyd Collins was a young Kentucky hillbilly who loved exploring caves, and had got himself trapped in one, and Richard Henry Little was "R.H.L.," the editor of one of the most popular features in the *Chicago Tribune*, the "Line O' Type" column. They had affected Mack's life in odd and wonderful conjunction. The attempt to rescue Collins from the crevice in which he'd snared himself, deep within the ground, had been a national sensation for days on end. The attempts to pass him food, the attempts to reach and extricate him, had been reported by every paper in the country. When the news came to Webster City on February 17, 1925, that Floyd Collins was dead, that his body could not be retrieved and must be left to molder in his dark and distant tomb, Mack limped home to his wash bench and his typewriter and pecked out words. The next day he sent his offering, his elegy, to Dick Little in Chicago. Little, who had already run a few of his poems, placed it at the head of his column on Friday the twentieth, and Mack's world changed forever.

> *Down in the earth thar was fairies and elves,*
> *And they told him secrets that he wouldn't tell....*
> *What's jest beyond, in the turn of the slide—*
> *Thar in the damp whar the cave crickets hide?*
> *Less' go and see, Floyd, less' go and see—*
> *And they left him to sleep in the tomb whar he died.*

Mack was only just turned twenty-one. He was addicted to dialect and sentimentality, but so was the audience for which he had written, and that audience went wild. Newspapers across the nation, from the *Daily News* in New York to the *Daily Oregonian* in Portland, picked up the poem and ran it on their editorial pages. Richard Henry Little called Mack on the telephone and said, "Well, well, well, you're raising Ned all over the country." He asked him to come to Chicago and read the poem on several radio shows. The *Tribune* would even pay for his hotel room.

And thar's moaning—a moaning
Back in the cave,
Floyd Collins' palace is Floyd Collins' grave.

Irene loved to hear him recite his poems, almost as much as he himself loved reciting them. Something wicked, something warm and wonderful, stirred inside. "So beautiful," she said.

"So are you." To live always with her loveliness, her sustaining praise! "But, about that time I cried. I had to scrape together money for the train fare to Chicago, and that wasn't easy, but I did it. I had to hobble over to the station—I'd had another useless operation on my leg—to catch the noon-day train, and, while I was waiting in the station, a woman came up to me. A woman who was a clerk in one of the local banks. And just the sight of her made me feel nervous, made me feel guilty. My grandparents owed money to the banks, and I owed so much for my hospital bills. She smiled, and gave me an envelope, and said it was from my friends at the bank. That made me more nervous still. I hadn't made any money from the poem, but I figured maybe they thought I had. And then the train came in, and she said good-bye. Grandma had fixed me a big picnic lunch—deviled eggs, and pickles, and such—but I couldn't eat much, and the train was halfway across the State of Iowa before I found the courage to open that envelope." His voice was shaky, wondering as it wandered. "There was money in it. Greenbacks, and even a gold certificate! And a note that said, 'Dear Mack: Please do have a good time in Chicago. We're proud of you.' I sat there, and I cried. I tried to look out of the window but I couldn't see anything. The tears kept coming, and they wouldn't stop. Not for the longest time."

Both sympathetic and adoring, she kissed his lips, his eyes.

"Well, I liked Dick Little and he liked me, and the broadcasts went well—I read the *hell* out of that poem—and Dick said he wanted me to come to Chicago and live here. Contribute more to the column. He thought maybe he could get me a job with the *Tribune*. I was still working on *Half Jew*, so I went home for a few months and kept on working at the paper, with Mother, until I finished it. I entered it in a contest sponsored by a publisher, a magazine, and a movie company. The first prize was ten thousand dollars! Someday I'm going to make money like that. Someday! I didn't win the contest, but I did get an agent in New York who liked the book and is trying to sell it. And then I came back to Chicago and there was no job on the *Tribune*—they thought I didn't have enough experience, God damn them—but Dick made some phone calls and got me a job as rod man on the Cook County surveying team. That lasted until my leg acted up, and then I got the job at American Flyer. I've found kind of a hidey-hole where sometimes I can write on the job, really write—like that poem about Kenny—and they never know it."

He turned to her and held her close. "Oh, Irene, I want to write! I want to write and write, and write. There are so many stories to tell." He listened to the sound of his words as he spoke, hoping they were affecting her. "Stories about people back home in Webster City, stories about the people here in Chicago, stories about people everywhere. Stories out of your life, out of mine. Stories! I'm going to be a great writer someday. I know I *can* be. There are all those tales to tell, and words are always buzzing in my mind."

He was lean as a beggar, fey as an elf, but his strong voice warmed her, filled her with his certainty. It was as though that voice supported her, carried her along, and she could ride forever on its cadence. "I'm going to be a great writer!" His dream, his goal, was so grand, so thrilling, and Irene wanted to share in it. And, if she helped him—through her support and adoration—to make his dream come true, perhaps he could help her to achieve the shifting, uncertain dreams which filled her own mind in the nights, and ruled her days. Fine artist, mother, mistress, consort to greatness, witness to a golden world which seemed to glisten far beyond her reach: she could not name all those dreams, but they were there.

She was moth to his candle, and he to her flame. They made love for the first time that evening. Mack thought that Irene was wonderful indeed, and she—oh first, oh first, of first-ever time—thought that he was grand. "What is this lovely thing, this strong and vital being, that has come to lie here in my arms?" He-she wondered, as they lay there in the dark.

"But what would your mother say?"

It was late in the afternoon—5:15 on a hot and muggy Friday—and they stood on a street corner in downtown Chicago, outside the department store where Irene now worked, selling picture frames and wishing that she could fill them with paintings of her own.

"We wouldn't tell her right away. As I've told you, she hasn't been well." Effie had suffered rheumatic fever as a child, and her great heart was great indeed now. Grossly enlarged. There had been dizzy spells, and shortness of breath. If she died he'd be so alone. Irene *must* marry him. Now. "And," he shrugged his shoulders, young, engaging, overwhelmed, "she thinks I damn near walk on water. No girl on earth could possibly be good enough for me. But, when she meets *you*,"—all his need, his urgency, were burning in that word (uncertainty hidden far within; hidden even from himself)—"she'll love you just as much as I do now. She'll think, she'll know, you're wonderful."

They moved through busy, sweating crowds to one of their favorite restaurants. Cheap. Chow mein and tea. Mack could afford it once a week, and this was, to his mind, a day of good omen. July 2, 1926. Three months to the day after they had met.

"But—my father. He'd be crushed if we eloped. So soon after Kenny dying."

"We won't elope. We won't tell him either. You'll still live at home. No one will know that we're married. No one but us. But that will make a big difference. You feel guilty about our making love now, but you wouldn't if we were married. I love you. And I—I *need* you, Irene. I'll need you always. I don't have any money now, and I owe a lot, because of this damned leg. And without you, maybe I never will make any money. Never really succeed at what I want to do." Both of them, in their minds, saw words, words, words, covering page after page after page. "But *with* you, I can do anything, write everything. With you to work for, care for, you to love me, I can't fail."

Mack already had a marriage license—in those days only the man needed to apply. It had been burning in his pocket for the last three days, as fiery as his words were now. "I love you, Irene!" And, holding hands across the table, "Reno, I love you."

She freed one hand and touched his cheek. "And I love you." That night was romance, comedy, farce. Churches were closed, or preachers gone home. It was after eight o'clock when, at the Moody Bible Institute, they found a minister who could marry them.

"...to love, to honor, and to cherish..."

"...to love, to honor, and obey..."

Mack so tall beside her. Rigid. For a moment Irene swayed, and the room went almost black. They were two hours late for rehearsals at the Graeme Players. He had given the minister three dollars, and Mack had to ask Irene for trolley fare, after he'd taken her home.

Late September perhaps, or early October. (Dates and details get lost as they filter through the years.) The evening was chilly, but his hand was damp with sweat, clammy, as he grasped the receiver. Mack stood in the phone booth of a cigar store a few blocks from the rooming house on Cambridge Avenue. There were public phones on every landing of that rooming house, but they were far too public for such a call as this.

The connection wasn't very good. "Hello. Mother?"

"Mack? Son! What's wrong?" His voice was strained, but there was more to alarm her than that. Long distance calls were a luxury. They didn't often indulge in them; they wrote, instead.

"Nothing's wrong, Mother. I've got something wonderful to tell you!" The receiver was slippery in his hand, and the mouthpiece seemed hostile and threatening as he spoke into it. A big, black funnel which swallowed words. "Mother, I've met the most wonderful girl. I met her last April."

"Yes?" The voice at the other end of the phone was taut, distant, filled with worry and suspicion.

"You'll love her when you meet her. You really will, and I know that she'll love you." A half-truth, only. He was certain, of course, that Irene would love his mother. Anybody would. But he wondered if his mother would accept, even love, in return. He'd *make* that all come true. "She's wonderful," he said again.

It had been Mack who had insisted on secrecy, even more than Irene. (Oh, what would Mother say? Mother, Mother...) But three months of sneaking, of this state of hemi-demi-semi-matrimony, had wearied and frustrated them both and, jointly, timorously, they had agreed to Tell. Tell the world, their world, and live together openly, and rejoice. Through love, together, they would slay the dragons which they feared.

"Yes, son?" Effie's voice came whispering down the line, sounding more distant than Iowa, more distant even than Alaska.

"Mother, we're married." There was silence on the line. Only static, which crackled like pine logs in a fireplace, whistled like prairie wind blowing lonely through miles and miles of corn. "We're married," he repeated, and the words seemed both wonderful and frightening to him as he uttered them.

Already they had told Irene's father and stepmother, and both had been mildly outraged, and gently, warmly accepting, as had her brothers. Her sister, her almost-mother, Ruth, had wept when she heard the news. Just that noon. She had wailed, "I always wanted Irene to have nice things!"

But Irene had cried, "And Mack will give them to me!" Her eyes had been so bright, her soft voice so intense, her obvious faith so strong. Soon Ruth's sobs had stopped, her tears had dried, and she and her husband had taken Irene and Mack out to celebrate, with ice cream.

This was different. Still the squeak of static in his ears. He blared again, louder, "Mother!" But still that harsh, electric silence seemed to grow.

At last he heard her voice: thin and taut, made unnatural by loss. "Well, son, I'm sure she's a lovely girl, but... I don't know what else to say. I had so wanted you not to be burdened down. Not now, when you're just beginning to fly."

"But Irene won't burden me, Mother. She'll support me, help me. She *believes* in me, just as you do."

A long, hurt silence, then, "Well I certainly hope she does!" The rest of the conversation was unsatisfactory also. Mack started to walk home slowly, despite the cold. He felt confused, almost defeated. And his leg ached. But then his pace picked up and he limped eagerly through the chilly streets. His mother was a sensible woman, and kind. She'd see reason. She would come to love Irene! And he knew that there was fire awaiting him in his room. Their room. Irene's love, to warm his soul and ease his mind, and a real fire in the tiny fireplace, to warm his body.

When he got home Irene was there to welcome and caress him, and flames flickered from twigs and fallen branches they had gathered in the park.

The next day, hiding in the stock room of the store where she worked, stealing company time, Irene wrote a letter in her prim and dainty longhand.

You are part of me—the sweetest and most thoughtful lover and husband a girl could ever have.—And what does it matter that we're a bit poverty stricken now. Some day we'll look back at now, and laugh and be happy over it all—and never think that I shall slave and save for you and be unable to keep up with you when the time comes—Ah, no, Adorable! you are saddled with me for life!...

They are gone now, only ashes underground, the same ground, Iowa ground, where Effie lies, and sprightly Eva, and grim, sad Adam. But they were young then, and vigorous, and not to be defeated.

9

Long Remember

The first consecutive words I ever said were, "Daddy, Daddy, Daddy!" When I cried them out I was almost two years old. I was slow to talk, reluctant to eat, cautious about using my body. I had found the world a hurtful, threatening place when I entered it; the spastic pyloric valve with which I was born had made the digestion of food an agony for the first three or four months of my life. The pain which followed nursing had served to keep me more distant from my mother than is common, just as my father's awkward attempts to comfort me during long, unhappy nights had made us uncommonly close. He had been gone for over a month, the longest time we had ever been apart, vanished to some distant place called California, and all that morning I had been sitting on the front steps of our house, waiting for the sight of him. At last he came, and I rushed down the front walk.

He was so tall and strong. "Daddy, Daddy, Daddy!" He lifted me high into the air, and smiled the warmest smile in all the world.

It must have been earlier in that same summer, or in the spring before. The air was warm and soft and clean, and smelled of new-cut grass, and of secrets hidden in the trunks of trees. I think the trees were maples, though perhaps there were chestnut trees as well, and elms. The light of the sun was golden where it found ways through dark green leaves above and, higher still, it turned thin leaves at the very tops of branches to a shimmering yellow. I lay flat in my baby carriage, gazing up at the wonder of the world: gold and darkness spangled with yellow and with green. A butterfly flickered past, and once I heard the hum of bees. We were on our way to the park near our home, and the park had a pond in it, a big pond. Later we would feed the swans. All the world was peaceful there, serene, and it would last as long as each day lasted then: forever.

This first memory of mine is sharp and brilliant in my mind. There is only one detail missing. I know that my mother was there, pushing the carriage, and I can summon up the thought of her, bending over to talk to me, and to make sure I was comfortable. I see the trees, the leaves, the light, and I know that my mother was there.

But I cannot see her face.

And what does it matter that we're a bit poverty stricken now. Some day we'll look back at now, and laugh and be happy over it all...

I was born on the sixth of October 1932, in a hospital near Westfield, New Jersey, six years to the month after my mother wrote that note to my father. On the stormy Thursday morning when, laggard, I emerged into a world loud with thunder and ripped by lightning, my parents found it hard to look back and laugh at anything. Those six years had been rough and harsh and often bitter, though sweetened by love and the gain of just enough success, the receipt of more than enough generosity, to sustain their dream of a golden future—a flame of uncertain brightness which forever flickered in their minds.

The storm that raged outside the hospital at the time of my birth—so fierce that my mother half feared that the angry force of wind, rain, and lightning might shatter the windows of the room where she lay straining—seemed to my father no greater than the economic storm which tortured him, and the nation, in those days. The world he had known seemed wiped away. The preceding month *Fortune* magazine had reported that 34 million men, women, and children—nearly twenty-eight percent of the population—were without any income at all, save for what could be begged, borrowed, or bartered, and that figure omitted the eleven million farm families, most of them hurting badly. Just when he had begun to be recognized and respected among editors and critics, more and more magazines were dying for lack of advertising, and fewer books were being sold. And he had so many debts to pay. And yet, and yet—Mack could write and he knew it, and so did others, and lightning flashed and Irene cried out one last time and I was born.

*   *   *

"Before you were born, when we were living out in Iowa..."

Before you were born—there was wonder implicit in those words whenever I heard them. Wonder, and awe at the thought of the almost unimaginable: a world which had existed before I was here to bear it witness. Scraps of memory, fragments of event, all these acquired the coloring of myth when my parents spoke of them in later years.

Sitting in the back seat of the car, trees going by and distant houses, listening to them talk, and the world outside the windows seemed far less real than that vision of another world summoned by their voices.

"...when I had that job as a feature writer on the *Cedar Rapids Republican*. You know, you kids, that's where we first met Grant Wood. You remember Grant, kind of a gnomish little man. He's a great painter—he *knows* America."

"Yes, and he's such a lovely man."

"He is." And, for a moment, the vibrancy of his voice lingered in the silence it had left behind, and those syllables, "Grant Wood," mingled with the engine's noise. "Remember, Irene? We had a *big* furnished room, and a real kitchenette..."

"With not just a gas ring, but a stove and oven!"

"Your mother made the most wonderful casseroles." His enthusiasm made me hungry, even though I wasn't certain what a casserole was. "And, at night, I'd work at my own stories, and send them out to the magazines."

"And they'd send them back, and then your father would revise them, and send them out again."

"That's right. Again, and again, and again! If you're going to do great things in this world, Timmy, Layne-o—and you will—you've got to work, and then if you're *good* at what you want to do, why, you'll succeed.

"Anyway, there we were, my first newspaper job that really paid money, the first time I'd supported us by just words alone. And those bastards, the owners, sold the damn thing to a rival paper, who just bought it to shut it down. God, do I hate businessmen. And there we were, the middle of nowhere, and the depression had already started out in Iowa. Oh, I tried the Des Moines papers, and the *Tribune* back in Chicago, and even Webster City. Nobody had any room. So we went to ground, crept back home to my grandparents' place, with everyone in town saying, 'Well, well, the Town Poet's back again, and looking kind of sad. Thought he was going to make it big in Chicago, and then in Cedar Rapids, but now he's back in town with a wife and no money, hiding out at his grandfolks' place. Never did think he'd make it.' God, how I hated that."

"Mack, not everybody! So many people were good to us."

"Yeah, but I remember the others too. The nasty, small-town minds who couldn't believe that I'd ever amount to a damn. Well, by God, I showed them."

"That's when I first really got to know Mother Kantor, your grandmother, children." And her voice had the color of an autumn afternoon, with sun and shade all mixed together. She squeezed words out, thinner, tighter. "Such a wonderful, vibrant woman."

"Indeed she was. And so generous to us. I don't know how I ever would have written *Diversey*—you know, my first published book—without her support."

"Oh, darling, you would have done it some day."

"Yes, but I wanted to do it then. I'll never forget, kids—it was in April of '27 and we'd only been home a few weeks. The man who'd been publisher of the *Republican* had promised me a job on a paper he was buying out in California, but he wouldn't be in business for two or three more months. And even then, while he could offer me a job, he couldn't come up with the train fare. So we puttered around the house, doing some little chores. My grandparents were staying with your Aunt Virginia and Uncle Jim down in Corydon, and Mother had a new job, editing the *Community Magazine* in Boone. Oh, it was a wonderful job, and I'd never seen her so happy, but that meant she had to live there and only come back on weekends. I wrote a bunch of little sketches, and some poems, and sent them off, but the most I could hope for from any one of them was fifteen or twenty dollars, and we just didn't know what to do for money. And your mother said, 'Mack, why don't you start on that novel you've been talking about? You know, Chicago and the gangs.' It had been growing in my mind for a long time." And his strong voice wrapped us in its smile. "So I sat down at the typewriter and started in. Every night I'd make up a batch of popcorn, you know the way I do—with butter and salt and pepper, and bowls of milk to put it in—and I'd read what I'd done that day to your mother, and she thought it was wonderful. Well, after a couple of weeks, on a weekend when Mother was there, and your Aunt Virginia and Uncle Jim were visiting, I read what I'd done to them. I had about twelve thousand words. And they were impressed. They thought it was just great! Virginia hugged your mother, I guess she knew where the credit went, then Mother said, 'I've been calculating while you've been reading those last pages, Mack, I've been reworking my budget, and I find that I can give you and Irene four dollars a week. You've *got* to finish this book, Mack. It's wonderful.' And Virginia and Jim offered five dollars from every ten-dollar wedding they had, and then your Uncle Jim said, 'No, honey, no! We'll give them ten dollars from every ten-dollar wedding!' Well, I kicked and screamed. I've always hated taking things from people. But we all agreed that this was a chance that I shouldn't pass up..."

"He worked so hard. Every day, and on into the night."

"Damn right I did. I had to make it work. I was laid up for a little while with my game leg, toward the end of it, but I went on working. I had to finish the damn thing, and I did, early in August. And then I had to type up a clean copy before I could get it off. You've seen me work, you know I'm just a two-finger typist like the old newspapermen, and my right index finger really took a bruising. In the end, the tip of the finger split just below the nail, and I started getting blood on the typewriter keys. Blood and pus. Well, I bandaged it up with gauze, and a little pad of cotton and some tape, and went on typing..." His words hung heavy in the air, and he shook his head in wonder at his own determination. "Of course, I had a lot of support. Your mother was just wonderful, and so were family friends like Aunt Grace and Uncle Jack Sheldon. And Virginia and Jim wrote a lot, and so did Mother, during the week."

Indeed she did.

Boone, Iowa
August 12, 1927

My dearest Son:

Your little note this morning makes me sorry that you were blue so I am writing you just a line of type or two, to tell you to cheer up. You know that we cannot put hard honest work into things, without a return sometime. It may be slow in arriving, but it *will* arrive, so do not forget it. It is harder to wait, than just to work hard. You have the job of typing to do and are doing all you can do. Just keep up a brave heart, and your ship will come sailing in. It may be only a little boat at first—those things have a way of never giving warning... But again... it may be a big sailing vessel or an ocean liner.

The hardest part of life is waiting... don't I know?... waiting for letters that never come. For money that never comes... Waiting for people who wait and wait and wait... and then sometimes come. But women have most of that sort of thing to do. Men, even when they wait long, never have the waiting part as hard as women. If only in your life my dearest son, you can keep your *spirit serene*, you will have learned the secret of life. To do that, I think one has to dwell a little apart from the crowd, who press too much on the spirit. I know you get what I mean.

I am glad you went up to Uncle Jack's and Aunt Grace's. I knew you would have a good time. Plan to go some evening to Cook's, too. You will have another satisfying time. These tolerant, jolly folks are surely life savers in a hard and barren world. The folks who like to laugh and like to hear what you think about things, while at the same time disagreeing with you, are just as rare as white-breasted robins, and a thousand times more welcome. I am thankful for Aunt Grace almost every day. She has been to me more than a sister, I know.

. . .

Well, darling boy. Cheer up. Things will soon be clearing and right now—just this week—old dear—you have not a thing in the world to worry about, have you now, honestly? When once you can get all well again, things will look brighter to you. You are the bravest young man I have *ever known*, that is all I can say, and every time I think of you I am just as proud as I can be. Not only of your talents, but of you for what you are. I seem always to see you lying in bed, pale and wan, but trying to smile—the finest and bravest boy I ever knew... Yes indeedy. That from mother, who knows you well and who cannot think of the years when we became so very well acquainted, without a few tears of my own unworthiness and complete failure to be the exalted being you should have for a mother. I succumb too easily to worries over common things and lose sight of the only big issues of life... I know I do.

But I believe in you as I believe in a Supreme Being, and trust you also, as I do Him. I could do no more.

Your always loving
Mother

At that time my mother was three months pregnant, but there is no mention of her at all in that letter, nor of her pregnancy.

"...Then, when I got the manuscript in shape, I took it to an editor in Chicago, riding in a cattle car..."

"And remember, before that—I think it was in June..."

I see their voices as notes on a scale: my mother's higher, softer, my father's lower and louder.

"No, honey, it was in May! You mean the time we hitchhiked to Chicago, so that I could do some research for the book, and we ran into all those muddy roads—you kids have no idea what the roads were like in those days, when it had been raining. Most of them hadn't been paved at all. So we ended up riding in a boxcar all the way from eastern Iowa into Chicago, your mother dressed as a boy, with her hair stuffed into a cap."

"Yes, and there was that old bum, and I was so frightened."

"Yeah, but it turned out he was a tramp printer." His warm, tough laughter filled the car. "Anyway, I had that jackknife in my pocket..."

"And we hitchhiked coming back. One truck driver wouldn't believe that we were married—he said we had too much fun together. And one night it looked like it might rain, so we took shelter in an abandoned farmhouse. And I woke up in the middle of the night, the moonlight was so bright, and I saw a man standing there..."

"The ghost of some unhappy soul... And then, in late September," and his voice became softer, but even more important than usual, *"McClure's* bought "The Biggest Liar in Eagle Falls." And *McClure's* was an important magazine in those days. It had been over six years since I won that newspaper contest with "Purple." I'd sold poems, I'd sold little sketches to *College Humor* and other magazines, and I'd earned our bread and butter on the *Republican,* but for over six years I hadn't sold a short story, or a short short story. I'd written over fifty of them, and sent them out, and they'd all come back. Again, and again, and again. And then I got a letter saying that *McClure's* was buying "The Biggest Liar" and, oh, we were so excited. But it was only a short short story, and we wondered how much they might pay."

"I guessed that it would be twenty dollars."

"And I said, 'Oh, phooey, I bet they'll pay at least twenty-five.' And then"—a portentous pause—"we got the check, and it was for one hundred dollars. We figured there must be something to this writing business after all... But the weeks went by, and the months, and I didn't sell any others.

"...It was Mother's idea, I didn't want to do it, but she insisted. She was always dreaming that some day the man would display some common decency. So, once that story was published, I sent a copy of the magazine to my father. Mother had heard from Aunt Besse recently that John Kantor"—and, oh, his voice went deep and low and dreadful—"was engaged in *legitimate* enterprise in Montreal."

"Yes! Selling blue-sky stocks."

"No, Irene, not that time. Don't you remember? That time he had an absolutely legitimate deal. He was selling perfectly good stock in gold mines.

Of course, your grandfather never could be honest, even if he tried, and so he took those perfectly good shares of stock and sold them two times over, or three or four times over! But we didn't know that then, that particular bubble didn't burst until months later, and he wrote back saying what a fine story I'd written, how impressed he was—hell, implying that it was almost as good as *he* could have done, if he'd tried—and offering me a job with his company in Montreal. The Gold-Copper Trove. Said they needed some brochures written, and had other public-relations work. Well, I didn't want to go..."

"But we had no money."

"We were flat broke, and didn't know what to do. You see"—and a rough hand came back to touch my sister's cheek—"your mother was carrying Layne-o at that time. The editor in Chicago had turned down *Diversey*, and the manuscript was off with an agent in New York, and I had sold a few more sketches but no other stories. And so, well, hell, we went... He had offered to send us one-way tickets, but I told him that we wouldn't come unless he sent us return tickets too. He was reluctant—his next letter sounded pompous and abused—but he did send the tickets, and so we went. And had the most hellacious time..."

"I'll never forget the first time I met him—the way he kissed me. I couldn't stand it. It was as if—"

"As if what?"

"As if he were giving a dime to a beggar.... And he had no job for your father at all. He did put us up in a good hotel, and then in a nice apartment..."

"And he gave us walking-around money."

"And he showed me off, with all his oily ooze, to all his 'associates.' How he loved that word. What he meant was toadies."

"Yeah. And I kept asking, but he had no job for me at all. He'd gotten us up there to be baby-sitters for my half sister. A dreadful time, but your mother was so very pregnant, and we were stuck."

"At least he had gotten me a good doctor. Such a lovely man."

"He was. And then we got the news, late in January. *Diversey* was sold!...I took the train to New York, night coach of course, and met the publisher, Tim Coward—your godfather, Timmy."

I stir at this mention of my name, and listen, fascinated.

"God, what it was like—being in New York and meeting agents and a publisher. *My* publisher. I was just a young man from the sticks. Felt like I was dead and gone to Heaven, that I was walking the golden streets of Paradise."

"And I was so glad that you *weren't* dead, darling, because Layne was almost due."

"Yes, and the Saturday before she was born my dear father gave a party for himself in my honor. His sycophants said to him how wonderful it was that his son had sold a novel and, to give the devil his due, he agreed with them that it was wonderful indeed, and then added that he, himself, on the other hand, did not just write stories, he *lived* them. God, the gall..."

"Presumption!"

"...pomposity of that man..."

"And the people he gathered around him! Hanging on his every word..."

"And then one of them said—oh, inevitably—'John, recite that poem you told us about the other day.' And all the others said, 'Oh, John, please do!' And so, after enough prompting and pleading to satisfy his ego, he did. Told how when he was a messenger boy for Western Union, shortly after he first came to Chicago, he'd been given a 'very important telegram' to deliver to an address in a fancy part of town. Lake Shore Drive, Goethe Street, Schiller Street, sometimes Division Street: the address varied through the years, through his many tellings of the tale. But the basic story was always the same. How he, the brave little messenger boy, had knocked on the door of a mansion, and been ushered inside by a butler and taken into a large room where a handsome, weary man—and he would describe the man in great detail, that was one of his gifts, and the detail would be accurate—was sitting at a big desk, surrounded by a bunch of other distinguished men who were pleading with him to stop Drinking. And the man asked, 'Do you wish to know why I Drink?' And he gestured—your grandfather was a great one for gestures—toward a shelf near the desk where there stood, in dramatic isolation, a little toy dog and a little tin soldier. And the men asked, 'But, Gene, what do such childish toys have to do with your Drinking?' And the man stood up and, facing the room, he spoke these words—and so my father stood up and, facing the fools he'd gathered to him, let his deep voice roll, thickened by his accent, his 'dese' and 'dat's and 'dose.'

> De little toy dog is covered wid dust,
> But sturdy and stanch he stands;
> And de little toy soldier is red wid rust,
> And his musket molds in his hands.
> Time was when de little toy dog was new,
> And de soldier was passing fair;
> And dat was de time when our Little Boy Blue

Kissed dem and put dem dere.
"Now don't you go till I come," he said . . .

"And he recited the whole damn poem. The women were weeping, the men had tears in their eyes—Christ, he did have a magnificent voice. And then he went on, 'And dat was de first time he ever spoke dose words, and I have remembered dem ever since.' And then came the idiot question: 'But who was he, John?' And his deep and solemn answer. 'It was Eugene Field, one of our greatest poets.' God, how could they have listened to such shit, and believed it, been moved by it?"

"Mack!"

"Well, honey, the kids have to learn to recognize shit when they encounter it. . . . And then there was that time when I went to see him, to tell him off after he'd been so horrible to you in the hospital—after Layne was born. I asked to speak to him privately, but he insisted on keeping some of his cronies around as an audience while I ranted and raved. And then he turned to them and smirked, and said, 'I could wish that my son had a voice as rich and deep as mine, but he does not. He has the nasal, Iowa twang of his maternal grandfather.' And I said, 'Yes, and I'm glad I do. Adam McKinlay is a poor old man, and he's weak and crippled. But he's got one thing left to him, beside his pioneer memories—a reputation for honesty. And back home, tucked away in a box, are some letters he received in 1901, and '02, and '03. And there are receipts as well, for money which he paid out in bail, or in making good on bad checks signed by another man.' He sat there leering, his face contorted, the soft jowls scrolled in anger, and his voice contracted in ugly mimicry: 'A reputation for honesty . . . bad checks, signed by another man . . .' 'That's right,' I said, and turned to go, but my father made a loud sound and I looked back, to see him bursting into glee. His face was demoniacal, and he beat his fist on the desk. 'By God,' he cried, 'how I love to burn him up!'"

There was silence for a minute. "Well, six weeks later—as soon as Irene was fit to travel—we were out of there."

And my mother made a squeaky sound, half giggle and half sob. "Yes! Carrying Layne-o and smuggling hidden booty."

"You see, my father had given us a set of silverware as a belated wedding present. Of course, he'd made certain to do it when all his hangers-on were around, and how they praised his generosity! Well, we were afraid that he'd be so furious at our taking off, though he'd lured us up there with the promise of a job and there'd been none—oh, he didn't mind *giving* us money as long as it kept us dependent on him, and God knows he was making enough of it, stealing enough, but by leaving we were defying him— anyway, we were afraid that he might tell the police that we had stolen that silver. So we put it in the bottom of the wicker basket we'd fixed up to carry Layne-o in—right underneath your bedclothes, Layne—and we kept it there until we got across the border..."

It is late and I am tired, half asleep. Only fragments of their speech now lodge in memory.

"...in that tenement in Chicago. And the gangsters' molls who lived in the place above us had the lovely habit of getting drunk and then taking their leaks out on the fire escape, and they pissed all over the diapers which had been left hanging on *our* fire escape to dry. Pathetic creatures. I chewed them out, and then—for fear of their friends—I carried a gun every time I left our room for the next two weeks...and we had to dry the diapers inside. Seemed like I was always writing with a forest of diapers dripping overhead."

"Oh, Lord, yes. But you kept writing, and good things did happen."

"Two, at any rate. I broke into *Real Detective Weekly,* and they were buying so many stories that they started using a pseudonym for some of my stuff. One cent a word. And we got to know my other grandfather, John's father, Joseph Kantor."

"He was such a lovely man, so neat and trim and proud. And I think that you, Layne-o, were the first of his great-grandchildren he had seen."

"He'd come to visit us, a trim old man, but tired, walking for blocks and blocks because he couldn't afford the car fare. He'd sit beside you, Layne, and poke out his finger, and you'd grab it...and he'd croon, 'Ba-by, Ba-by, Ba-by.' Once I walked him home. It was hot, so hot. Imagine, that fine, gentle old man—a Talmudic scholar, and more! Why, he even read Sanskrit and Greek—walking through the heat in his dark, patched clothes, back to a tiny furnished room, while his son rode around in a limousine.... We talked about John Kantor, and my grandfather, Joseph, was filled with scorn for him. Scorn. He had an even heavier accent than his son. 'So,' he said, 'so. You say you hate your fader, you hate Yan. Dat is too bad. It is sad, but no one should blame you. He was always so. Sometimes I dink it was my wife, Tobia. She spoiled him, everyding must wait for him. Yan is great, he does noding wrong, ever...when he is bad I want to beat him. Give him spank, because he talk so bad, and telling lies. No, no. His moder never let me put my hand on him. Never, never spank dear Yan...And so. Like dat. His whole life. Lying always.' And then we talked about *Diversey*, and I could tell that he was proud of me, and pleased *for* me. That meant a lot... Before I left him, in front of his rooming house, I mentioned my father again. And the old man said, 'Who? Yan? Bah!' And he spit on the sidewalk. Later in that year, he died."

"...We went back to Iowa, to Des Moines, because the *Tribune* hired your father as a columnist. We made so many friends there..."

His voice was happy; certain and self-satisfied. "Reno, we make friends wherever we go."

"...Mack, remember the times when we splurged on a baby-sitter for Layne-o, and drove out into the country and parked..."

"And we'd take along that old, hand-cranked phonograph..."

"And dance by the light of the moon. It was about the only time your father would ever dance."

"Well, damn it, my leg hurt, and I felt awkward." He paused. "But not those nights..."

"...So many parties. We'd all bring something, made dishes and bath-tub gin, and your father would take his guitar and sing."

Dreamy Layne spoke up. "I can remember you singing at home too, Daddy. Singing to me. One night, when we were living in that house out in the country, you sang the song that starts, 'Oh, bury me not on the lone prairie' and when you got to the part about, 'And the coyotes will howl o'er my grave,' you howled so mournfully that I expected other coyotes, in the dark outside the windows, to start howling back."

Our father laughed. "Well, I did a lot of singing in those days, and I got good by practice. Just like writing. There is nothing like writing to learn how to write. I had that daily column, and I was writing short stories—I was making regular sales by that time to a lot of the pulp magazines, de-tective stories and horror tales—and I published two more novels during those years. By God, I was learning. And we were actually making a liv-ing. Of course there were always bills from all my operations, though dear Daddy had paid for one useless operation I had up in Montreal, and taxes on my grandparents' house and other bills which they'd incurred, and then, in the end, Mother got ill again and had to give up her job." His voice caved in. "And so, that last year, she came to live with us. Until she died."

Effie died on the day after Christmas 1931, and I was made ten days later, quite deliberately, in an act of loving yet almost desperate affirmation. Made of lust and loss and tenderness, all strangely, in mortal fashion, in-termixed.

As intermixed as the crazy quilt of experience—of feeling, personality, and event—which my parents had pieced together through the years.

We drove east in April, escaping an army of creditors—my parents and sister jammed into an old Chevrolet with all their belongings that could be made to fit, I secure in that warm sea I floated in, in my mother's womb. But if we were fleeing creditors—indeed, the payments on the car itself were overdue; my father broke the law when he took it out of the state—we were also bound on pilgrimage to New York or, at least, as close to the city as we could afford to live. Manhattan was the center of the publishing world. Most of the magazines had their offices there, as did Mack's publisher, Thomas R. Coward—variously known as Tom, or Tim, or Timmy, as I would be known too, in time to come—and Sydney Sanders, who would be Mack's agent for many years. Mack's third novel, *The Jaybird*, had been published recently, and while the early royalties had already been eaten up—Tim Coward had advanced Mack fifty dollars a week during the writing of the book—the reviews had been favorable and Mack thought, he willed, that the future looked bright. He was determined to make his living by writing only fiction now, the constraints of a daily column had drained him terribly, and it made sense to live in the east. To live near New York. To live in Westfield, New Jersey—less than an hour away from the city by train; and so we found quarters there.

Increasingly shabby quarters.

Mack had a lot of cavities. Some were new and others were older, and had been filled, but now the fillings had fallen out. He hadn't been to a dentist in years, hadn't thought he could afford it. And certainly now he couldn't. Sometimes, when the aching got too bad, he'd lock himself into the bathroom so that Irene wouldn't know—she had enough to worry about now, poor darling—and sit on the toilet seat, bending over, with his head between his knees. The rush of blood to his head, and the swelling it caused, seemed to dull the nerves and make the pain more bearable. But usually, as now, the ache was dull, remote, and it was only the foul taste of decay which he allowed to bother him. He would take bits of cotton and tamp them firmly into the cavities with a toothpick, to absorb the rot which festered there. Later he'd pick out the nasty little wads and replace them with fresh cotton.

He was writing a letter to his sister and her husband.

Westfield, N.J.
February 11, 1933

Dearest Folks:

...Today I am writing letters for the first time in many weeks. Did not feel up to it before. We have just passed through the most crucial and devastating period in our history, and once more have a little foot-hold on existence.

Aside from the illness which lurked over us (of course you know about Tom's long siege with the colic...A horrible time. He would cry from noon until midnight, day after day. I was doing all the work, or trying to, and Irene in bed...I think I told you of Irene's two minor operations—Layne was very sick Christmas week, and I had mine sometime before that) we have been the prey of more than one misfortune. Three magazines owed me money, and I could not collect a cent. After October, the income was pitiful. From Christmas until January 30th, we had only sixty-five dollars, and twenty-five of that was borrowed. On January 14th we got an eviction notice, to be effective on February 15th. There were plenty of times when it seemed as if there was nothing to do but turn on the gas. Of course we were marooned here in this house with two children, as I had no money for a license or car repairs, and the car just sat in the garage after December. Finally on January 30th by using the most desperate methods, I managed to get $150 from W. M. Clayton, one of the magazine publishers who owed me money...

Mack took off his thin and shabby coat, and tucked his even shabbier gloves into one of its pockets, before he went inside. The offices of W. M. Clayton Publishing were rich, luxurious, deeply carpeted, with satin wooden paneling on the walls. He went up to the receptionist and asked for Colonel Clayton.

"I'm sorry. The Colonel is in conference. He cannot be disturbed."

"All right, I'll wait here and see him when he comes out." He settled himself, stiff and upright, in a chair.

"You can't wait here. We can't have you sitting around when you have no appointment!"

"Listen. I'm MacKinlay Kantor. My novelette, *The Cannon Kills*, was published in your *Clues* magazine away back in October, and I haven't received a cent for it yet. I'm sitting here until I can talk to Colonel Clayton. He owes me three hundred dollars. When he walks out of his private office he has to come through here to go to the elevator. I'm waiting for him."

The receptionist disappeared for a moment, and then came back and sat at her desk, ignoring him.

Fifteen days until they were out on the street. He just couldn't take it any more. He'd already received small advances from Sanders, and large ones from Coward-McCann; he didn't see how he could ask for more just now. And this money was *owed* to him. Syd Sanders had told him, just an hour ago, "Mack, you're not the only one. I have at least ten other authors to whom Clayton owes money, but I can't do a thing with him. Of course, we could all get together and sue, but it probably would drag on in the courts, and not do anybody any good if he's really going down the drain." So he'd asked Syd if he, Mack, could try himself, and Syd had said, "Certainly."

The minutes passed by, and the hours. Other supplicants came, and sat, and left. Secretaries and young editors passed back and forth, staring at him angrily, or else pretending that they didn't see him. Perhaps many of them were wondering if their own paychecks would keep coming, in the months ahead. And then an older man came up to him, perhaps a senior editor but more likely a company official, a treasurer, a *businessman*. "If you continue to insist on interfering here in our office, we'll call the police."

"Fine," Mack said, and for the first time he relaxed. He almost smiled. "Go ahead and call the cops. I won't move—they'll have to carry me out. That will make a hell of a newspaper story." Which he knew was just what they didn't want.

Finally he was summoned to the Colonel's lair. He was greeted by a ruddy-faced man with a silver mustache, rather handsome, rather leonine. "What's all this nonsense about? I understand you're disrupting the outer office."

"No nonsense at all, Colonel. I just want my money. What you owe me. I'm a very desperate man. And you have owed me three hundred dollars for over three months. I want it. Now."

The Colonel paused, and rested his head in his hand. A small vein twitched in his temple. Certainly he owed many other authors money. Probably he owed illustrators, printers, and the paper company as well. Perhaps salaries were overdue. At last he said, "Look here. I'll tell you. This is the thirtieth. I'll give you a check for a hundred and fifty dollars today, and the other hundred and fifty on February fifteenth. How's that?"

"That will be great, Colonel. That will be just fine. I appreciate it very much."

Two hours later he walked into the apartment in Westfield and said, "Honey, I've got some money. One hundred and fifty dollars." Irene caroled, and then she cried, and then she clung to him.

... Then, on Monday, out of a clear sky, came a telegram from Sanders telling me that *Redbook* was taking a story for six hundred dollars. Of course that saved our lives. We haven't received the money yet but there will be little delay. Thus we are enabled, through a certain amount of manipulation with the building & loan folks who hold a mortgage against our landlord, to remain here at least until April 1st. Pay something on our doctor bills, etc., although the doctors have been very good to us and have waited through all this winter without a cent being paid to them since September.

On top of that, I have been working for some six weeks on a 50,000 word serial for the Munsey people, and they have a spot for that in about five weeks. The tale is not completed yet, but they are very enthusiastic about what they've read, and are sure that it will be satisfactory....

... Of course it's next to impossible to get a job in New York now, though I've been trying hard. Came near a couple of things, but they dribbled out. The radio deal is still hanging fire—no money yet from that. At least this *Redbook* sale is bona fide, so don't think I'm indulging in a further pipe-dream.

Since it seemed that I would never get my Gettysburg novel written unless I took the bull by the horns, I started that, also, on January 1st. Have about 22,000 words done. That would be a third of THE JAYBIRD, but this book will be so much longer that it seems a bare start. Two years ago I wouldn't have been in any way capable of doing what I'm doing now. It is very good. Sometimes I wonder if it's my peak—if I can ever feel anything so tremendously again.

A thousand times I have been grateful to fate that mother didn't have to survive through this last year. There would have been no place for her except with you, and God knows how that could have been managed. She would have been sick with worry over our situation. No, it was so much better the way it happened. Existence means nothing if it is saturated with poverty, pain, discouragement. I have spent hours walking up and down New York, trying to figure some way out of it. Perhaps it was lucky, in view of existing circumstances, that my accident & life insurance lapsed last fall. I would have been tempted to ease matters with those. No overcoat, except an old light topcoat that we bought when we lived in Boone—gloves out at the fingers—a sick wife or sick child at home—I never really knew what poverty was before. One man can't pull a stick-up successfully, or that would have happened long ago. I didn't want to increase Irene's troubles, and couldn't see anything but a successful job if I attempted it. Consequently—well, I didn't do anything about it. Just hung on, tried to write, waited.

As for our economic system, I think it's all shit. Any formula which, naturally or unnaturally, can bring the ghastly tribulation which has come to this country, ought to be wiped out. Communism, anything would be better. A great city has such a compact mass of misery in its heart that you can very nearly smell it. On Irene's birthday we rode in to town on the train, borrowing the Hoags' (folks upstairs) commutation ticket, and hoped to get a little change. But walking along Broadway or in Union Square, it was all the same. Human misery, a pageant of it. The evening was a complete failure—Irene wasn't up to witnessing anything like that, although constant exposure had made me a little callous.

We have a handful of friends, positively noble people. What we lack here in quantity we make up in quality. Coward, Sanders, Miss Oliver, the Charles Robbins's—they have kept us alive in more ways than one. Each of them has been prosperous or even very wealthy at some time, and all are hit in varying degrees by this catastrophe. We've never got a concrete or figurative turn-down from any of them, and in a dozen ways they've tried to help. Mrs. Thomas as well—the one who runs the school here. A little, dried-up, puny woman of 45, with the greatest heart you ever met.... It was the interval between, the bleak periods when we sat here at home for days at a time without seeing anyone, that made the deepest pain.

...I'll get my Gettysburg novel done this year. Never once I have doubted that it would be a success. There has been nothing like it before. You knew, of course, that we were at Gettysburg in 1930, again last April, and again in June. I don't need to go again, though I would like to. This winter I have read about three hundred books, pamphlets, magazines, monographs, all dealing wholly or in part with the battle. Also the 1863 files of the *Tribune* and the *Record*.... I used to scoff at the professional "debunkers" but only lately have I realized what a mass of lies and misrepresentation American history really is.... In June and July of 1863 I have been able to lose myself for hours and days at a time, so I have that much to be thankful for. You can judge the result when you read it.

Now you know what happened to us. You must tell us at once what has happened to you. We did get Grandpa's letter, in which he stated that he was sublimely happy with you and that he never expected to see Webster City again, nor wanted to. When I have got those stones set up there in the cemetery, I will feel that the last chore is done and I can grow as supremely indifferent, and let it live only in the dim past, which somehow grows more lovely each month, with the rougher edges smoothing away as if by magic. So that is how history is made, American or personal: we forget what we need to forget, and remember only the cherries and the kind, red hands that were good to us, and the bluebells which grew under the lilac bushes, and Sunday evening lunches when a woman played on a piano.... We are all sentimentalists, and cowards as well. Who am I to blame historians?

...I haven't said anything about the things you sent—Irene's dress, my shirt, Layne's things, the baby's—pajamas—all those things. At the time I couldn't write. You shouldn't have done it, at all, but of course you're both like that! I'm glad you had sense enough to let a couple of birthdays go by, as we have let so many of yours.

We all send love. Irene will be writing you within a few days. It seems years since we saw you—it is a year and a half, and more. Can't the church send you east to a convention, or something?

Tim and Layne send their best kisses to you all.

XX

Mack

He reached out for a toothpick and clean cotton and, when he'd done his chore, placed fresh paper in the typewriter and returned once more to thought of those others, tramping along a dusty road to Gettysburg.

Sometimes Irene thought that the sound of typewriter keys striking home made the sweetest music she had ever known. Sweeter even than the sound of Paderewski's piano or Caruso's tenor blaring from the old phonograph they had, and played so often. She would hear the quick, irregular clatter of Mack's two-finger typing as she went about her housework, she would listen to it as she drifted off to sleep, on nights when Mack was working late, and think, "That's the sound of my husband working, writing a wonderful book, telling a beautiful tale. He's pulling words out of the air, or from some hidden place within his mind. Some place I cannot even imagine. My husband. A genius." The next day he would read her what he'd written, and her tongue would almost stumble as she sought proper words of praise.

That was her job, as both of them conceived it: to offer admiration, encouragement, praise. To tend their children, and to keep herself as tidy as the house, and to be forever feminine.

Sometimes it seemed that they were living on dreams alone—his dreams, her dreams—but I believe she seldom doubted them.

"God damn it, Irene! I can't think!" So he had cried out upon occasion in the past, when trying to shape a plot which would drive a story, and thus sell it and bring in money they needed. She would come to him and try to soothe him, and he would go on struggling. So he had cried out in the past, and so he would cry out in the future, but not this time. Oh, no, not now, not even when he shaped the plot for "Mommie Is So Kind" (which Syd Sanders sold to *Redbook* for $250 in April), "A Shot at Seven" (which went to *Dime Detective* magazine for $90 in May), or "The Slough Devil" (which the *Elks* magazine took in November for $400). He wrote at least fifteen short stories during those months and sold thirteen of them, and he finished the Gettysburg novel, which he called *Long Remember*. (Mr. Lincoln speaking, with his shrill voice pinched by an Illinois twang: "The world will little note, nor long remember...")

Mack was not an analytical man, and the thinking which any sound piece of writing demands went on busily under the surface of thought—beneath his awareness, beyond his command. All he knew was that he had a story to tell, and so he told it. Told about common folk maimed by the horror of war, told about passion.

...some of them are in the Emmetsburg road and some in the fields, and some have bulged the very fences aside. And these are cannon and they come helter-skelter, and behind our house I can hear other cannon in the Pike. The village is being possessed by all these Seventy-second Pennsylvanias or heaven knows what you call them.

Well, she told herself, I heard a car of war coming over the hills, and I could have told anybody this would happen. Dan said there were three thousand men here last night. If three thousand men came between us as they did, what will ten times that number do to him, and do to me? Oh, at any time I would have fallen ill to see them coming, but they are a menace of the darkest order, they are poison for all their glistening and in spite of their speed and their banners— they are worse than any cancer which ever ate at flesh. Because I craved him, I quivered and lived my limit inside his arms, and he within mine. Heaven, she cried without a word, I wish you'd send one of those bullets through the window.

No—grief, not that—not to die. I want to live; I want to go away; I want to get out of this. I want to go away from this war and this town which was a quiet town, a stupid and affable place before the rebels and the rest of them came. Let me get out—crash this glass, cut my way through it, run across the field as I did last Friday, be beside him and hide in the wilderness. He said we should do it. Heavenly Father, why didn't I go? Tyler's coming—somewhere within these swarms he will be snarling and hooting at his men before the bullets pare him down.

. . . They dragged him up on the porch; he was about eighteen, Irene thought, and he had a pale skin dotted with tiny orange freckles. His clawing fingers, the nails crammed with shredded skin—they grew from hands which were as slender as a flute player's, and all raw and blistered by harness and guns. The gasping cry which he uttered was changing now, even as they brought him into the kitchen. His green eyes swiveled in raw sockets, and saw nothing of the room or the faces above. Then moisture came up in his throat; he made a trilling sound, and blood coursed across the clean-scrubbed floor, and he wadded the woman's gown in his hand as he died.

At nights Mack dreamed of forbidden love and permitted death. Shot and shell tore the fabric of those dreams, Minié balls split the air within them, and the sickly smell of gangrene fouled his nostrils, just as the moans and screams of the wounded throbbed in his ears. Often he'd wake up crying. But in the mornings he'd smile as he sat down at the typewriter. His hero was a good man—a pacifist, just as every man should be; and brave, just as Mack was—and it was fun, a private tribute, to give the love of that hero's life the name of Mack's own love: Irene.

*   *   *

Shimmer in the woods and sorrow in the city, laughter in his home and anguish in the night...Well, by God, he'd caught shimmer and sorrow, that was for certain. He'd caught laughter and anguish, too. Caught them and fixed them on the page, just as surely as he'd caught butterflies and moths when he was younger, and fixed them, pinned them to cotton in a case.

"...*I believe in you as I believe in a Supreme Being, and trust you also, as I do Him.*" He'd been wrong when he'd written to Virginia and Jim a year and more before. Dead wrong. If only his mother could have lived to see his triumph, vindication, to share in his success. "...Your ship will come sailing in. It may be only a little boat at first..." Hell, he'd been at sea in a dinghy for years! Bailing like mad. "*But again...it may be a big sailing vessel or an ocean liner.*" Or a streamliner! He laughed at the thought as the long train he rode on thundered across the plains, faster far than ever buffalo had done.

And laughed again, just loud and long enough to disturb and interest the solemn faces which sat near him in the observation car. He didn't give a damn. They were ordinary, mundane: businessmen, agents, doctors, lawyers. They were not famous writers such as he, with a book on the best-seller list; they could not understand the joy he felt. Well, some of them perhaps were actors, and they were different. Living on their guts and talent. But, though actors were a charming lot, most of them were shallow: he'd learned that much during his time in Hollywood. The girl across the aisle was attractive, had nice ankles, seemed approachable, but he was headed back to Irene, to Layne-o, and to me. He turned and looked out the window.

They were in Nebraska. Not far from Lexington now. He'd asked the steward a while ago, when he'd ordered his last drink. Out there, beyond the double panes of glass, beyond the rule of air-conditioning—this train was so different from the sooty, smelly, clanking monsters of his childhood— Lieutenant Joseph Bone had suffered in a jouncing covered wagon, with only the hot prairie wind to ease his fever. Out there red men rode, settlers strove to break the sod, and Mack watched them until the dinner chimes had rung for the second time, and the twilight faded.

It was hard to believe that all that had happened to him these past months was true. He felt like a character in the movie he'd been working on in Hollywood. And yet that character was real, and so was he. It was all so certain and so reasonable. He had written an important book, and the world had responded. First, back in February, had come news of *Long Remember*'s selection by the Literary Guild, one of the two important book clubs of the time. And then, in April, had come the reviews. He'd read them so often that he remembered some of the phrases. *The New York Times* had said, on the *front*—by God!—page of the *Book Review,* "a novel that tastes and smells of war till the reader hates the smell and taste of it, and still is above and beyond war with the saving humanity that survives slaughter and does its slight part to prevent a future built on the past." Christ, he hoped so. Make them feel it so they won't forget it, won't repeat it. And God bless Allen Tate. Mack didn't think too much of his poetry, but what a fine reviewer Tate was. "There is no book ever written which creates, so well as this, the look and smell of battle.... As a spectacle of war, the book has no equal." No equal. Let the little folk back home choke on those words. Why, when "Purple" won that short-story contest in the *Register,* the high school paper had never even mentioned it. But now his friends were so proud of him, and people who hadn't believed in him pretended that they had. And the *Chicago Tribune.* "Passion is piled upon passion in his words, and war, naked and flaming, stalks through the pages." That girl did have nice ankles. A nice rear, too. He watched her move, as she left the dining car.

His leg was aching. Carefully, with his cane to steady him, he made his way back to his drawing room and stretched out on the fresh, starched linen of the new-made bed. But first he poured himself a drink. A drawing room! He laughed at himself as, in an act of both self-sympathy and -mockery, he looked around for crayons, remembering the first time he'd experienced such elegance—when he was seven. The first and last time, until his trip out to the Coast. Savoring Scotch—so smooth in the mouth, so heartening the bite—he considered money. He did not worship money. In fact he did not give a damn about money. Let the bank clerks treasure it, or the businessmen, or the thieves—like his father. But he did treasure the comforts which money could obtain, the protection against discomfort which it offered. And he detested the deprivation, the anguish—the constant, dreary calculation, and the thought of not providing properly for others—which the absence of money brought with it, like a dismal shadow.

In compulsive emulation of the clerks whom he despised, he had carefully recorded every dime and dollar, in all truth every cent, he had earned from writing, since he first won that fifty-dollar prize with "Purple." He took out his notebook and recited the figures. In the eleven years that had followed he had earned, from writing words both good and bad, $18,049.26. And now, in the first eight months of 1934 alone, he had earned $12,622 more. Oh, there had been debts to pay, lots of debts. Almost $2,500 to Coward-McCann for unearned advances on his earlier novels, over $1,000 to Tim Coward personally (Timmy had bet on him, bet heavily, and Mack was eternally grateful), and about $2,500 more in other personal debts—to doctors and hospitals in New Jersey and in Iowa, to merchants back home and in Westfield, and to cover small sums his grandparents had owed. But now all those debts were paid. And—oh, how he relished the thought!—in the last eight months he had earned, including $1,200 for his recent four weeks' work for Paramount and $900 more for a story Syd was certain he would sell to *Redbook*, exactly $12,622. It was a nice figure to toy with in his mind—to savor as he savored Scotch. (The dollar was stable then, and strong; in fact, it had grown in value for as long as Mack could remember. He had no way of knowing that it would shrivel through the years—that, a little over fifty years later it would take over $108,000 to equal what he'd earned in those eight months.)

And they hadn't yet sold *Long Remember* to the movies!

He stood up, poured another drink, and then stripped down to his shorts. Carefully, with first his tongue and then his fingers, he explored his teeth. Over half of them were new, and they were paid for, too. He took the bridges out, put them in a glass of water, and made an old-man face at himself in the mirror. Funny way for a thirty-year-old to look, but hell, he hadn't been able to afford such luxury before. And now the damn leg. The hair around the open wound had long since been pulled away, but still the adhesive tape hurt when he jerked it free. With hydrogen peroxide he cleaned off septic ooze, with alcohol he cleaned away adhesive residue, and then he cut fresh tape, fresh gauze, with scissors, and made another bandage for his thigh. He stretched out on the berth again, and listened to the wheels attack the ties.

A century ago when he was small, riding to Chicago, he'd thought he heard the wheels croon out his father's name. "My fa-ther, my fa-ther, my fa-ther," they had sung. But now his father, no longer a figure of awe but only a tired joke—no, that was not right; he was a hurtful, angry ghost instead—did not have the force to occupy Mack's dreams. (No matter that he stole anew, anew, and now used Mack's name in his thieving.) But still the wheels produced their chant, and he felt that he must match its rhythm with other names. "I-rene, I-rene, I-rene"—he'd see Irene in two more days. And "Layne-o, Layne-o, Layne-o"—he'd see her too. And "My son, Tim-my, my son Tom, my son Tim."

"By God," he swore, "I'll be the best damn father in the world, just as *my* father was the worst!" And then he drifted off to sleep.

* * *

Two days later he got out of the car in Westfield, and I ran down the walk to greet him.

"Daddy, Daddy, Daddy!"

He lifted me up and held me high. "Well, Timmy, I'm back from the wars." And then he hugged me close, with my mother calling from the porch, and my sister dancing near. So tall he seemed, so strong and handsome and oh, he cherished me. And I, little boy, I worshiped him.

10

Mack's World

Early dusk in the second week of October 1936, and I have just turned four. I stand at the window of my room, at the rear of the second floor in our house on Broad Street. I like the boom of that name, Broad Street. It sounds solid and secure, just like the house. The light outside is clear and soft, a sort of greenish gray. Occasionally I catch a glimpse of other children, their bodies flashing—blurred—as they run from tree to hedge to tree, and their voices echoing, distant but sharp and shrill, from hiding place to hiding place among all the back yards which face each other along the length of our block. I am sad because I cannot join them, sad and regretful. I feel as grown up as they, but the doctor says that I am weak because I will not eat, and my parents say that I must go to bed at six. I have been tucked in, and kissed good night, and the door has been closed. After many minutes of listening to voices from another world, the real world, I have snuck from my bed, raised the shade, and I watch the games of others, the games I am not strong enough to play.

Sometimes I think, in recollection, that I spent half of those early years peering out at the world through windows, and the other half seizing and savoring it, borne high upon my father's shoulders. The windows were those of trains and cars, and of increasingly comfortable apartments and houses which we rented, as well as of the house my parents built in 1937, in Sarasota, Florida; the glass in those windows seemed both clear and thick, and I felt safe behind it. And my father's shoulders seemed strong indeed to me, and to him, and fit for any game.

*   *   *

It was a glorious day, glorious, with the sun striking sharp on stone and sparkling on glass, the wind free and easy with spring, and the sky clean and blue, if he craned his neck and sought for it in narrow angles above the deep streets of the city. Late April of 1937, and spring had come to town. What were those words? What had Steve Benét written about spring in *The New Yorker*, last year? "It sneaked in on a market truck." That was it. "...It sneaked in / On a market truck, a girl in a yellow hat / With a pinched, live face and a bunch of ten-cent narcissus / And the sky was soft and it was easy to dream." Beautiful words. Stephen Vincent Benét was a fine poet, a famous poet, and he liked Mack's work, and they were friends. Good friends. And Steve's wife Rosemary and Irene liked one another and that was important too, right then, for Irene was a little stiff and shy, and didn't have many friends.

Mack settled back in the cab as it moved up Fifth Avenue through easy traffic, and counted blessings. In the last eight months he'd sold three stories to the movies: two novels and a novelette. One of them alone, *Arouse and Beware*, had brought more money than all he'd earned back in '34, when he'd first thought he was rich. He had finally cracked the *Saturday Evening Post* with "The Romance of Rosy Ridge," for two thousand—count them, and he did—two thousand dollars. And he'd just had a wonderful, laughing, joking, drinking lunch with Tim Coward, and Tim had agreed to publish *Rosy Ridge* in book form in the fall.

God, he loved this world! Always had, and loved it more than ever now that he found himself in control of it. He might have been a starveling creature once, cherished by some but despised or overwhelmed by others, but now he was a man of accomplishment: because of words he wrote, stories he told, his name was known to millions. He thought that name—oh, it had a lovely lilt, MacKinlay Kantor—a household name. And he had made money, would make more—he'd make all the money he needed, his family needed, for as long as he lived. Too bad—no, not too bad, a tragedy!—that Mother hadn't lived. Never, except for one fur coat, and that black satin dress with the white silk trimmings which still shimmered through the years, had she been able to wear fine clothes. Oh, always she had looked both dainty and impressive in the simplest clothes, homemade, but now he'd dress her all in lace, and silk and satin too, if she were here. Well, she wasn't. She'd worn herself out, raising him and Virginia, long before her time. And that devil—wicked devil, selfish devil, uncaring devil—had had the nerve to wire Mack and say "Now she is a saint," when she died.

At least Irene, lovely, adoring Irene, was here and clung to him—too tight she clung to him, but if she didn't cling?—and he'd dressed her in the finest clothes from Bonwit's, Bergdorf's, Saks. And the kids. He didn't like kids, wasn't interested in them, hadn't wanted them, except for that moonlight madness after Mother died. But Layne-o and Timmy were bright kids, wonderful kids, perfect kids, his kids, and he loved them—and never would they lack for anything, as so often he had lacked.

Flowers! The cab had paused at the traffic light at Fifty-seventh Street. Narcissus, by God. "Driver, hold it for a moment. I want to get some flowers." The girl's hat wasn't yellow, she had no hat, but her *hair* was yellow. And her pinched, plain face was filled with life. He'd have to tell Steve Benét about this. He gave the girl five dollars for the biggest bunch of flowers she had, and got back in the cab before tears came to his own eyes to match the tears in hers.

Yeah, the goddamn depression was still here, but the President was doing something about it. Roosevelt would handle it. If people worked as hard as Mack had worked they'd struggle through. In this land, with this President, anything was possible. Mack had proved that. In this land, his land, America. He knew America down to the deepest root groping in its soil, the most secret bone or musket ball—he knew it as no other writer did. Well, maybe Steve. He also knew the way America felt, the real America.

In reverie, words came to him.

"There are those who say I cannot feel. But the flower girl back there, does she think that—with those five dollars warming in her pocket? The idiots say my characters are stereotypes, not real. Well, if they're not real then I'm not either. Remember what Jim Bowers wrote, after *Long Remember*. He said all the characters were 'as flesh-and-blood and real as you are. That's the truest tribute I know.' A sweet man, Jim, and generous. I wonder what he's doing now. So I am real. I sit here in this cab, rich and famous, happy and confused. Cannot feel? That would mean I cannot love. And I loved, love, Mother, love Irene—oh, God, I love her daintiness—love Virginia, love the kids. Love others. I *do* feel. I know I'm not a perfect father. What model ever did I have? Mother told me, years ago, to not be so impatient with Layne-o. I'll try. I'll try. And I love Timmy so. In my image. By God, he does almost everything I want him to, and I'll do everything for him. And I love Layne. Love Irene. Love...
But women, girls, are a mystery to me. The closer I come to them, the further away I feel. Layne-o is so bright and pretty, but she can be so

refractory. She's warm and little-girl—I love the smell of her—but also she is unmalleable, she fights me back. Thank God Irene so seldom does. Not strong like Mother. So lovely. Women, girls, Irene. So demanding. So bewitching. Girls, women."

"With waiting time, that'll be a dollar and ten cents," the cabby said.

Ignore the years now, forget all sense of time and of chronology. Concentrate on feeling and event. Back first to that overcrowded house—hothouse—in which Mack suffered fever even as he flourished. Back to a lonely, overwhelming woman. Back to Effie, clad only in undergarments—black, and neatly mended—standing in their bedroom on a morning in the fall. So lovely and so vital she seems as she stands there, looking out the window to catch the early sun, and reciting her favorite lines from *Hamlet*. "But, look, the morn in russet mantle clad, / Walks o'er the dew of yon high eastward hill." Her voice so warming in that chilly room, so stimulating. Back to little Mack hiding in her closet, caressing her clothes, when she has gone away.

And then: it must have been a Saturday in late May, in the year they sheltered in that house while Mack labored on *Diversey*. Irene has been shopping uptown, or setting out seeds in the garden, or washing Mason jars in the summer kitchen, in preparation for preserving vegetables yet to come. Suddenly, as she enters the main kitchen, she hears laughter, almost hysterical, coming from the front room. She opens the door and stands there, stunned and flushed with shock. Effie is sitting on the sofa, laughing and applauding, while Mack traipses around the room dressed in a black sateen petticoat and camisole belonging to his mother, with lace insets on the sides and along the hems; he wears black cotton stockings and high-heeled shoes.

Effie turns to Irene. "Doesn't he look marvelous?" she exclaims while Mack poses, preens, and simpers. Effie has never heard of Sigmund Freud, and Mack has never read a word he wrote. Neither has Irene, but she knows what is right and what she thinks is wrong, and what is threatening. She is horrified.

"Mack Kantor, you get out of those—those things! You get out of them now. And don't ever let me see you dressed like that again, or I'll walk out of this house forever!"

My father is used to playing masterful lord to my mother's adoring little woman, but she is not adoring now. She is furious. He doesn't say a word, just leaves the room to change, and his cheeks are reddening before he reaches the door. Effie expostulates weakly, as though she feels guilty without knowing why—they have just been playing dress-up games, as they did when Mack was small.

"Mother Kantor, I love you very much, but I can't accept such games. I don't think they are nice!" Effie leaves the room, and Irene is queen of the battlefield. A very shaken, uncertain queen. But she knows he isn't a sissy, he isn't *really* a momma's boy, and he *does* like making love to her, and...

I do not believe that Effie ever allowed herself to think of that afternoon of "games" again. If my father did, it was only rarely, with all the caution he had shown when he was the possessor of a sore tooth, and poked it gently with his tongue to see if it still hurt; then he packed it quickly with the cotton stuffing of masculinity and conquest. My mother may have brooded upon it a few times, when confronted with occasional strange excesses in the future, but I doubt that she mentioned it to anyone, until she spoke of it to me, with a puzzled shake of her lovely head, three years after my father died.

Now compact the years, and crush them all together. I am eighteen, and I am a "man." At last, to my father's great relief and even greater pride, I have been eased of my virginity. To honor me, to formalize my newly acquired maturity, Dad has taken me out for drinks and talk at a local bar. As almost always, he is charming and magnetic; both impressing and abashing me. He is so delighted with reports of my adventures that I half expect him to announce my news to the room at large and, inwardly, I shudder as I thrill. But he does not do so. Instead, thinking it time that I understood the ways of the world, he takes the sun, the moon, the stars, the heavens themselves, and slams them down upon my head. Quite innocently. Oh, boasting, perhaps, but with no evil intent whatsoever.

Just man to man.

"You know," he says, "sex is wonderful. It's a hell of a lot of fun, as you've discovered. And most real men—oh, Grant Wood was an exception; he was a real man, but he wasn't drawn to women, or didn't crave them, didn't *need* them—most real men need women. And no matter how much we love a particular woman, many of us can't be satisfied with just one. Man's a hunting animal. To court a pretty babe, to charm her, win her, and have her laughter and her flesh to comfort you during the empty nights— the times when you're not working—is one of the greatest joys in this world."

He finishes his drink, motions to me to do the same, and orders another round.

"Now, I love your mother. Her walk, her eyes, her tiny voice. I love Irene more than any other woman I have ever found. And she's the most desirable woman I have ever known. The ideal woman." I cannot believe what he is about to tell me. I have always thought that my parents had a perfect marriage, that they were made for each other: my godlike father and my angelic mother, a perfect foil and fuel for his triumphant masculinity. I am not close to my mother—I have not felt truly close to her since I was six years old, and tired, and she lifted me out of the car and carried me into our house, and I felt as safe and comfortable in her arms as I would have in my father's, and more secure—but I am not aware of this. I know that I love her, I know that she is gentle; I have been taught to think that she is not too confident or competent, a little bit laughable but wholly wonderful, and to be protected. She and my father are both fine actors, and neither Layne nor I have ever been conscious of great dissension. I sit there frozen as he beams upon me, reminiscent, and says, "But I've screwed a lot of other babes as well. Hundreds."

I feel groggy, bruised, as though the world has just come up to me and punched me on the nose. I force myself to make a sound. "Oh?" I must, I *must*, be the man of the world my father takes me for, or wishes me to be. Blasé, perhaps; certainly casual and understanding. I will the blood away from my cheeks, as I try to visualize oceans of flesh, of legs and breasts, and buttocks straining in the act. "Hundreds?"

"Well, I haven't kept exact count, but there have been many." And once again he smiles. "Many."

Mostly he called them "babes." In his ears that word had a jaunty nonchalance which deprived the women themselves of all closeness, and all threat. And yet many of those women felt love for him, and he was fond of them. The first was a pretty girl-child he encountered when he went to visit with his mother on a nearby farm in Iowa, perhaps to hear some of those pioneer stories they both delighted in, when he was thirteen. The girl teased him to the barn, they climbed into its loft, went tumbling in the hay, and he came, he came, he came! Had proof of manhood, of independent being. The last was an old friend he encountered some fifty years later. And in between, an almost constant concupiscent striving. Rich girl, poor girl, star and starlet, singer, secretary, family friend or wife of friend, he sought in each for affirmation and, with every thrust, every conquest, he sought to deny the ties which bound him to his mother.

He sought for sex, romance, indulgence, cosseting—for everything except true knowledge of the other, in which I think he had small interest. He offered, in return, the mixed charade and drama of his own being.

He once told me that he'd been faithful to my mother during the first years of their marriage. "For four long years," he said, "I never even looked at another woman, never even touched one. But your mother was so goddamned jealous. After every party we went to Irene would be all over me. 'What did you say to *this* girl? Why were you talking to *that* one?' She'd be cold and silent, you know the way she can get, and then accuse me—in a fury—of wanting to mess around. And nothing I could say would make any difference. Finally I decided that, if she was going to be jealous anyway, she might as well have a good reason." I think there was some truth in that claim—some truth and a lot of self-justification.

He wanted to, needed to, romp among those shoals of flesh.

Long after he died, I spoke to one of the women he had known. For years she had been a family friend, an intimate. "What opened you so?" I asked. "What drew you to him? The genius, or the little boy?"

Her strong face softened, and she answered instantly. "Oh, the little boy."

But there was one, the only intellectually commanding woman he ever allowed to come so near, who was older than he, and wiser, and—though indeed she loved the little boy in him—she loved far more the man he might become. Her name was Peggy Pulitzer and, after Effie and my mother, she was the most important woman ever in his life.

"Now," said Daddy, "I'm going to take you to see one of the loveliest women in New York. And one of the loveliest little girls." The cab we were riding in was not red; it was yellow. There was snow in the streets. It was getting close to Christmas, and the green and red of the traffic lights seemed made to decorate the city. "Mrs. Pulitzer is a very good friend of mine, and I think she may have a present for you. And her daughter, Susan, is very bright and pretty." He sat beside me in the cab: so big, so real, so strong. "I think you'll like each other." Which was sheerest nonsense. I was six, and Susan Pulitzer was a year or two older—a difference which, at such early age, seems enormous. But it pleased my father to think that I might come to feel a childish love for the daughter of his own lover.

I think there was a present indeed, and that Dad brought one for Susan, and I remember Peggy Pulitzer bending over me, seeming very tall and graceful. But most especially I remember Susan. They were decorating their Christmas tree when we arrived, and she was standing on a stepladder, reaching up to hang an ornament. She was wearing a black or dark green dress made of velvet, and I thought that she did have the prettiest face in all that city, and also very pretty ankles. I never saw her again, though I was reminded of her whenever my father spoke of Peggy, as he did so often through the years. She became for me, in strange fashion, a symbol of the unattainable, and it hurt a lot when I heard of her death, untimely, some forty years later.

We stayed only a little while, and then we went home to our house, and to my sister and my mother. I'm sure that Mother knew where we had been, for I thought then that deceit was unknown in our family and, if Dad had asked me not to tell, I would remember.

We both knew that it was a game we were playing, but the tears on her cheeks were real.

That visit to Peggy Pulitzer took place about the same time that I marched off to yardstick wars, with bagpipes chanting, puzzled by my mother's tears. Twelve years later, when my father jarred my brains with his self-description as a great lover, I learned their cause. But, even today, I sometimes find it hard to understand her willingness to suffer them.

Which is foolish, and only happens when I see her through the eyes of that little-child self which is lodged forever in my mind. Glimpses only: they flicker and elude, for almost always my father is standing at center stage, commanding attention. Usually she is hiding behind him in these visions, or else he is deliberately standing in front of her, and she is out of sight. But on occasion I can seize her features, her touch, her presence, and hold them in clear focus. A very lovely woman she was, petite and dainty, with a lively and curious mind. When she was young her hair was a kind of reddish gold. (In later years she dyed her hair, at my father's insistence, in approximation of that shade, though its natural color had turned a soft brown, almost auburn—and remained that way, with no sign of gray, until she died.)

She was a marvelous teller of bedtime stories, sometimes to our father's chagrin. It amused him, but it also upset him—when he was there in the evenings—that we'd rather hear another installment in the saga of "Bruin and Molly" than yet another chapter of *Rolf in the Woods,* or *Penrod,* or *Little Women.* Bruin and Molly were bears, cubs I think, and they had adventures in their native forest, ventured into cities, traveled around the world and, in 1941, worked with the FBI to frustrate Nazi agents.

Night, and my mother lying on the bed beside me. "And then Bruin said..." I loved her closeness even more than I loved the fascinating tale. Her small voice was so warm and tremulous, her imagination so vivid, that I could touch Bruin, touch Molly, and I could also touch my mother as we lay there in the dark.

Her flesh was as soft as her voice, and as warm.

Other glimpses, other memories, I have mentioned, and two of them cling close.

We had been out for a drive in the country. In New Jersey. Perhaps we had been to see old friends in Westfield; perhaps only to see the country green, and breathe the blue-gold air. Just my mother, my sister, and myself. Daddy was elsewhere. Coming back to the city, over the Pulaski Skyway, I had seen the tin and cardboard hovels of the dispossessed in the Jersey Flats. We were too high up to smell any odor, but somehow the place looked *smudged*, and I knew that a stench was there.

"People really live there, Mommy?"

Taut, tight-faced, recalling lesser privation which she, we, had known. "Yes."

And then, with country peace and flatland squalor all mixed together in my mind, I fell asleep on the back seat. When we reached the large, comfortable brownstone we rented on East Eighty-fourth Street, and Layne-o woke me, I was still groggy. (Still I ate too little; still I needed sleep too much.) Mother picked me up and carried me into the house as the dusk came down to hide the garbage cans, the scavengers, the victims of the times. I was safe there, in her arms, cherished and secure.

And on another day, her tears, when I marched off to war. It seemed to me that, with her tears, with her constant, apologetic explanations for his absence, with her compulsive support of his demands whenever he *was* home, no matter how dictatorial they were—"Be quiet, children, your father is working!"—she had betrayed us. Betrayed me. Surrendered to the king, my father, to whom also I owed allegiance. Surrendered to my kindly, generous, overwhelming enemy. He whom I loved most of all. My rival and oppressor.

All this far beyond awareness, for either my mother or for me. Back where the bad things hide.

But in truth, poor darling, she had no choice. She had been badly damaged by the loss of her mother, for which she had predictably, foolishly assumed the guilt. She had been further injured by her father's kind remoteness: *"The life seemed to go out of him when Mother died. Pacing. We heard that sound for months. I think for years."* Those were not traumas finally accepted and tidily tucked into the bottom of the mind, where they could no longer harm, no longer limit, no longer dominate. Whenever she mentioned those calamities her voice throbbed with hurt, as though they had just occurred the day before. She did not dare to experience further loss. She did not dare to do so once again.

She had grown up in a family where infidelity was never mentioned, never dreamed of. But in the strange new world where now she wandered, uncertain—a world filled with famous names and clever people—such adventuring was tolerated, accepted, condoned. She had gained her identity through Mack's success, his very being. Without him she felt she would be nothing. And he did love her. And so she catered to him, so she tolerated the intolerable, so she suffered, and so she rendered up her tears.

And so, it seemed to me, she shunted us aside.

"Row, row, row your boat..." Voices of children and counselors mingled together, and the water was a mirror in which I could see clouds reflected, and trees. But also the water was clear, clearer than crystal when viewed from a certain angle, and then I could see rocks on the lake bottom far below and the full bite of the oars themselves as they sent their eddies drifting slowly past. "...Life is but a dream."

A mixture of sweet dream and nightmare, or so I felt during the summer of 1937. Daddy had gone away from me before, but never Mother—never the two of them together. Not for more than a week or so. And now they had. Brought me and Layne-o to a strange place, and left us there. They were going on a trip to Europe—wherever that was—for over two months, and they had left us behind. I remember sitting in that boat, singing as it drifted over the water, thinking that I lived within an enchanted dream indeed—colors so true, sound so pure. I also remember the dreadful silence of the nights. A forest silence I had never known before.

Camp Owaissa was an excellent summer camp. As excellent as any camp could be for a child who was not yet five. But my sister, upon whom I was almost as dependent as I was upon my parents, was lodged with older children. Only a year or so before, when my enunciation was still uncertain, I had followed her around with a mix of trust and adoration and, whenever I was told of some new fact or possibility, I would turn to her and ask, "Is dat right, Wayne-o?" Now I could pronounce "Layne-o" properly, but she was seldom there to ask.

That was the summer I swallowed a penny. I and another child—a little girl with a swarthy face and dark brown hair—were playing a foolish game: testing to see which of us could hold a penny in the mouth the longest. I won. I swallowed the damn thing and had to spend the next two weeks, whenever I "did my duty," sitting on a potty, embarrassed and ashamed, while a counselor stood by, ready to examine my leavings. Eventually I passed it, and eventually those two months passed as well; but while they endured, I remember feeling largely a sense of loss, and a sense of shame.

And yet: one late afternoon we walked through damp woods, two rows of us children, hand in hand, down to a rocky promontory which thrust into the lake. We had a "wienie-roast," and the scent of burning wood and of grease spattered on the embers, the scent of cooked hot dogs and charred marshmallows, blended with the smell of trees and shrubs and flowers and other living things. The light was sharp, the colors clean and clear, and the voices of children and adults echoed softly in the air.

That was also the summer we met May Greenwell. She was crafts counselor in the camp, and she was kind and clever, and Layne-o and I liked her. When my parents returned, in mid-September, they liked her also. In time she became our governess—almost our surrogate mother—for a number of years, so that Mother might have more time for herself, more time for Mack.

And always I remember that rowboat, moving over water smooth as glass.

The SS *Paris* moved steadily through the mild Atlantic chop, headed home. Mack and Irene were on the promenade deck, watching the sun sink into the sea ahead of them. They were contented, happy, closer to one another than they'd been in a long time. Uncertainty was, at that moment, just a little, caged animal, barely stirring at the back of Irene's mind—for someone so much a prisoner of her past, she had a remarkable ability to live in, and enjoy, the immediate moment. And for Mack uncertainty was, right then, only a vaguely attractive itch, hardly noticed at the edge of consciousness.

"Jesus Christ, this is beautiful!"

"Oh, darling, it is, it is."

During the past two months they had traveled in England, Ireland, Scotland, France. They had watched demonstrators in depression-bound London marching and stamping their feet and chanting their innocent, idle chant: "No! More! War! No! More! War!" They had watched the dead come home to Edinburgh, and seen the glory of the Highlands. In Ireland—armed with a letter of introduction from Tim Coward—they had visited Lord Dunsany, who had just read and much admired Mack's second Civil War novel, *Arouse and Beware*, a fine story newly published in England. And in France they had toured the battlefields of the Great War, such as Amiens: the sites, the names that had sparked teenage Mack to lie about glory, to dream about death.

Irene had wanted to go on the trip, and not wanted to. Mack had proposed it at a time when his relationship with Peggy Pulitzer was most intense, and when Irene was most upset. Irene knew damned well that they had no business sending an uncertain four-year-old off to camp. She also knew that she loved Mack—the center, always, of her being, for she had then none of her own—and that she was in danger of losing him. They both thought that they might regain, in leisure, comfort, and the forced isolation of foreign wandering, the closeness they had shared during their early, hurting years. And they did do so, as they would—again, again, and again—in time to come.

As they were finishing dinner that evening, Mack spotted a face at another table in the dining room—a face familiar from countless photographs he'd seen in the papers, and faintly familiar, also, from childhood memory. He thought of a red taxicab, and his tall, dark father, and a glittering hotel salon with a big handsome woman bending over him. He got up and went to the table where Sophie Tucker was sitting alone, and stood there, looking down. She raised that proud, familiar face, with the ever-challenging eyes.

"Miss Tucker, you don't remember me, but I remember you very well. One time you gave me two revolvers and a cornet."

"Who are you?"

"Does the name Kantor ring a bell for you?"

Memories stirred, and Sophie smiled at him. "Are you John's boy?"

"Yes."

"Sit down. Let's talk." Mack brought Irene to the table and introduced her, and then they did talk for quite a while. Irene sat with them, shy and silent and impressed. He enjoyed Sophie, enjoyed himself, enjoyed the encounter very much indeed. Except for the moment when, reaching across the table, she took his face in her hands and said, "You look just like John."

He was a little upset by that. In fact his only physical resemblance to his father lay in his brown eyes with their heavy lids, his long nose, and his black, curly hair. (Sophie Tucker was a romantic. In 1961 I, who look even less like John Kantor than did my father, also met her. I was a photojournalist then, and—thanks to a telephone introduction from Dad—she gave me permission to shoot a picture story about her. The first time we met we sat on a couch in her ornately furnished apartment on Park Avenue, and we talked. After a few minutes she put her hands to my face and turned it to the light. "You look just like John," she said.)

Later, Mack and Irene went out on deck again and stood at the rail, watching the ship's wake trail away into the past. There was a bit of distance between them. They had remembered that, in the other direction, New York awaited them, and their kids, and success, and uncertainty, and Peggy.

The relationship with Peggy Pulitzer was a spring-summer romance, and Peggy knew it, even more certainly than did Mack.

> It is even an advantage that our birthdays are so disparate, for the high unsuitability of our ages frees our relationship from all idea of an intimate life together, and permits us, without the restless intrusion of hope, to preserve the quality of our love. Does that sound like a lot of words? I mean that it is normal for two people who love each other deeply to look forward to that fulfillment which must be the end of romance. Well, we have our romance, and are permitted to keep it longer than more fortunate lovers do.

Peggy was ten years older than he, and far more sophisticated. During the twenties and early thirties she had published, under her maiden name of Margaret Leech, three well-received novels and a biography of that grim moralist, Anthony Comstock. She was married to Ralph Pulitzer, the elder son of the great publisher. Mack met Peggy in April of 1936. Their intermittent affair, limited by domestic obligation, lasted into '39 or '40, with meetings in New York and rendezvous in Washington. Washington, in particular, for they both had work to do there, research to pursue.

Mack had first become familiar with the dusty, disciplined mysteries of the Library of Congress when he was writing *Long Remember*. He went back to it again in 1936, when he was working on *Arouse and Beware*. And in early 1938, he had other checking, other digging, to pursue, as he finished a lesser book about a fancied resurrection of the passenger pigeon: *The Noise of Their Wings*. (Always he was good at finding titles, just as—almost always—he had difficulty getting into his story.) Mack was a respected fa-

miliar at the Library, and a respected authority on the Civil War, just when
Peggy Pulitzer needed such familiarity and such knowledge most. She had
started work on a book about life in the capital during the 1860s—a book
called *Reveille in Washington,* which would, without any hint of nepotism,
receive the Pulitzer Prize for History in 1942. So there was an area where
Mack could play mentor to Peggy, just as she played mentor to him when
it came to the grooming of his prose and intellect.

In the spring of 1938, the *Saturday Evening Post* published "The Writing in the Sky"—a tender, lazy screed for pacifism, in the form of a novelette. It was the first of four *Post* issues that featured Mack's name on the
cover that year, and he was rightly proud and pleased. He was famous, he
was successful, he was making money to pay for the house he had built in
Florida and the house he planned to rent in New York. He also had great
kids, a wonderful, sexy, compliant wife, and a brilliant, stunning, moth-
ering mistress. It must have been about that time, after a few shared days
in Washington, that Peggy wrote a note, on the stationery of the Carlton
Hotel.

Darling,
  The yellow church on the corner brings back a luminous grey morning, with all the branches wet and black and the girls hurrying on their
  way to work. The writing on the sky says Mack. It's a miracle.

  Peggy

Almost I can feel the raindrops—teardrops—from those trees.

I have her letters to him, or some of them. I wish that I had his to
her—that I could read his thoughts about her and about himself, about his
own becoming, expressed in his tidy, cautious, backward-slanted hand.
Just to touch those letters would be a pleasure, and might bring me closer
to the open, guarded, public, private man he was. But she apparently destroyed them. I think that she was discreet, thoughtful, while Dad was not.
For he kept her letters, and other love letters, in his files.

I wonder if my mother ever, during his absence or in some secret time
of night, went prowling through those drawers and read those letters, and
scratched her soul upon the words.

Sweetheart, you've got the makings of a great person, and I like the
way you're doing.

  My fondest love-Peggy

My father was addicted, from the time he could first afford it, to a hair tonic produced by Frances Fox, which explains the following allusion.

Not the least of the things that have happened in the last year is, for me, the ability to excite your mind a little sometimes. I don't mean, dragging you to *Othello*, or putting on a disk of Beethoven, though they have a relation to what I mean. But I like to strike an occasional spark from those dim recesses, those flinty strata that underlie the fields of Frances Fox. It's not completely different from the excitement of sex, just the same sort of emotion permitted to invade the entire personality.

She called him a "stubborn chrysalis," an "intentional cocoon."

During those years, with Peggy a spur, a goad—sometimes at the center, always at the edge of his awareness—Mack grew: he opened his mind as he never had before, as he never would again. When playing the word games his mother so loved he had learned all manner of Shakespearean quotes, but he had not really read the plays. An inept teacher in high school had, as happens still so often, soured them for him. "Goddamn woman nearly ruined Shakespeare for me!" Now Peggy induced him to read and see them, and he was rewarded, delighted, accordingly. She teased him into reading *War and Peace*, and Tolstoy became his idol, his lodestar. He had liked classical music before; now Peggy helped to widen his knowledge of it, increase his enthusiasm. There were evenings spent in the home of Walter Damrosch, with chamber music twisting through the air.

On those same evenings Irene might attend classes at the American Academy of Dramatic Arts, leaving Layne-o and me with May Greenwell, or else stay home to whisper tales of Bruin and Molly, to read or sew or practice lines for her acting class, and then to lie in bed and cry.

Peggy also tried to introduce Mack to the bright new world of psychiatry, in the person of Dr. Lawrence Kubie, one of the most respected and fashionable analysts of the time. Years later Dad told my sister, "I went to Larry Kubie a couple of times. He was a nice guy, but I thought it was a bunch of crap. All he did was ask me some damn fool questions about my mother."

Aside from music he now listened to, books he now read, Peggy's greatest influence was on his prose, which became leaner, cleaner, during those years. And Mack returned the favor, filling her mind with some of the vast stock of Civil War lore he had lodged in his own.

All that and romance, all that and sometime sex. He allowed her to share the substance of his professional life more freely than any other woman ever did. Perhaps because she was knowledgeable and older—old enough to be an almost-mother, young enough to be a mistress. And yet *mistress* seems the wrong word. Tim Coward once said, in his nasal twang, "God damn it, Mack! I don't understand it. You treat Irene like your mistress, and Peggy like your wife!"

In 1939 Tim Coward and Mack had a falling out, as they did again in 1942 and 1945, before their final break in '47. That first major row came about the same time that Mack and Peggy were also breaking apart. She wrote a final letter, from which he carefully cut, and then destroyed, both the beginning and the end. I assume those had to do with personal, romantic matters. But though the fragment he saved must have hurt or threatened more than those he threw away, he kept it through the years, folded, and folded, and folded—small—in an envelope marked *Peggy,* within a folder marked *Pulitzer.* A chiding which he was too wise to dismiss. Unable to heed.

We talked hard for an hour about you, in almost complete agreement. Timmy is kind-hearted and loyal, and said afterwards, He's a grand fellow, several times, to make himself feel better. The consensus of opinion was, among other things, that you are At the Parting of the Ways, and, though startlingly undeveloped, won't be able to keep on growing up—even you!—much after thirty-five. So unless you take a brace and look about you and associate with people of more background and broadmindedness and procure a modicum of education and get curious and take some cognizance of the great culture of Western Europe, on which everything we have and are is based and which until now you have tossed aside like an old brochure on the wall-paintings of Southern Tibetan lamassaries, as something too esoteric and unrelated to your experience, as well as too complex and formidable, as well as something you don't feel quite up to bothering with, like typhoid fever shots—I say, taking a long breath, unless you do all these things and set about them hard this very afternoon, you are presently going to turn into one of these elderly Pucks, these superannuated Peter Pans, these elfin, quaint, dear old special Characters, who grow old without ever having grown up, and droop your head like a beautiful florist's bud, without ever having had the vitality to unfold your petals.

Any cracks about that Jamesian sentence will in no way affect the importance of its meaning. I've got things to do, and won't re-write it.

(over)

But there is no "over." It was cut away.

11

Great Me, Wonderful Us

"Eat, Timmy, eat, Timmy, eat, Timmy, eat!" That chant—good-humored but persistent—echoed around our dinner table for years, while I pushed food around my plate and ate as little as possible. When I was five a pediatrician declared that I was the finest case of self-induced malnutrition he had ever seen. Gradually, that changed. I don't know if memory of infant anguish retreated further into hidden places in my mind, or if I just got tired of that chant, and of being sent to bed early. By the time I turned eight, I was eating normally and was thriving. Which seemed natural, for we were living most of the year, by then, in a Florida wonderland where it appeared that all things throve.

The wonderland was named Siesta Key, a thin barrier island which stretched for over eight miles along the coast of Sarasota County. Our house was low and sprawling, with whitewashed walls of pecky cypress and many windows, and it sat in the middle of a clearing hacked out of the jungle. The front of the house faced west, toward the sun when it set. A lawn that seemed immense to me ran out to a sandy lane called Shell Road and, beyond that, sea oats waved their tassles in any breeze, with mangroves and sea grape flourishing on either side. And then a wide, white beach, and Big Pass (blue, green, slate gray according to the light and weather), and a sand bar, and the Gulf of Mexico beyond. In all other directions the jungle stood, tall and dark and dense—a mix of vine and cabbage palm, of live oak, jack pine, and occasional red cedar. From my bedroom window I could see a tall pine tree which reached high above the garage. Bald ea- gles nested there.

Now that I was healthy, active, eager, I had entered into my own Eden, and it was green and always growing.

Thump, thump, thump of sneakers striking the hard-packed sand of Shell Road, intermittent pressure of books against my body as my arms moved back and forth, back and forth, and easy feeling of control as muscles guided flesh and bone in necessary patterns, and the morning bright around me. I trotted toward the Out-Of-Door School, which lay south of our house, and toward the rich enthusiasm of Miss Pierce. Just up there, I thought, just to that cottage, and—when I reached the cottage—just as far as the next bend, that's all, and then I'll walk. But when I rounded the bend the road gleamed white before me, challenging me, and I ran on. Past the next bend, and the next, and others after those—I ran all the way to school and wasn't really tired when I got there, though I'd traveled over half a mile.

Miss Pierce was old and plump, white-haired and almost always smil- ing. Just like the grandmothers in stories I had read, or perhaps like the real grandmothers I had never known, though in fact she was *Miss* Pierce and therefore could have had no children of her own. I thought that books— I imagined them large and handsomely bound—must console her loneli- ness when she was not teaching, and I knew, from warmth and caresses and reprimands she delivered, that her pupils served as substitutes for the sons and daughters she had never borne.

"Timmy, there are two errors in this one problem alone. You'll never master arithmetic if you can't remember the multiplication table."

"Yes, ma'am."

"Timmy, this report is thorough, and neatly written, and very well phrased. Perhaps you'll grow up to be a famous writer too, like your fa- ther. I'm sure that he'll be proud of you."

"Thank you, Miss Pierce."

"And now, children, it's time for your rest period. Get your mats, and carry them outside, and spread them under the mulberry tree. Timmy, to- day it's your turn to carry my chair. And when we're all settled down—stop whispering, Carrie—I'll read a few poems."

Slow to talk, I had also been slow to learn to read—just like my father. But—just like my father—once I had learned to decipher the strange sym- bols on a printed page, I made rapid progress. By the end of the second grade I had not only encountered the Hardy Boys and Ted Scott, but adult books—Stewart Edward White's *Daniel Boone* and a biography of Ethan Allen—as well. Still, in evenings, my father read aloud, but rarely poetry of any worth, aside from his own, jouncing, early efforts.

Miss Pierce did.

"Sherwood in the twilight, is Robin Hood awake? / Grey and ghostly shadows are gliding through the brake..." Perhaps a brake was a cool and shaded place, such as the spot where now I lay and sought for shapes of men and deer among the branches arching over me. "Love is in the greenwood, dawn is in the skies, / And Marian is waiting with a glory in her eyes." I thought of a little girl in the class whose brown eyes had occasionally incited me to teasing and other forms of fourth-grade gallantry, and then my attention was recaptured by the sure, sweet power of Miss Pierce's voice, and by the words her lips formed so carefully. "If I were Lord of Tartary, / Myself and me alone, / My bed should be of ivory, / Of beaten gold my throne..." It seemed to me that words such as these must be golden also, and brightly they shimmered in my mind.

And so, in this Eden I inhabited, I encountered further magic still. Poetry. Comfort and challenge, stimulus and delight, teacher wiser even than the woman who led me to this joy. In my early teens I would discover Keats and Cummings, Housman and FitzGerald and Jeffers, and other poets fit to stir an adolescent, and later still the laughing, raging men who mattered most of all: Homer, and Shakespeare, and the aging, bitter, libidinous Yeats. Right then it was enough to lie there under the mulberry tree, and listen to that pleasant voice, and dream of the day when I'd go far wandering and see the world and master words and do some wondrous thing.

"...And pluck till time and times are done," Miss Pierce recited, "The silver apples of the moon, / The golden apples of the sun."

"Bell-bottom trousers, and a coat of navy blue..." The sun was golden indeed, and the strong breeze was warm on my face. It was recess time at the Out-Of-Door School and I was wandering down to the swimming pen and dock which thrust out into Big Pass, singing the first "dirty" song I had ever learned. "...He'll climb the rigging just the way that I climbed you." My acquaintance with bawdry made me the wonder of all my friends, though none of us were certain exactly what all that climbing was about. My father had taught that song to me, and it had made me proud when he did so. I almost felt that I had entered into the world of men.

It was men that I was seeking now. Daddy had said that he and some of his friends would be fishing off the dock. And there they were, four tall figures standing on the planking, with rods in hand and the lines held tight by the outgoing tide.

"Timmy!" Oh, that big voice booming, the strong face beaming. "What the hell are you doing here?"

"It's recess, Daddy."

"Recess? Well, by God, I could do with a little recess myself. We've been here for an hour and a half, and not one of us has caught a damned thing. Take my rod. Maybe it will change my luck." He reeled in the bait and passed his rod to me.

I cast, and felt the tug of tide against the line. And then, almost instantly, a nibble and then a bite. A real bite! I jerked the rod up to set the hook, and then reeled slowly in, with a red fish fighting all the way. A fine one, maybe four pounds or more. There were cries of excitement, shouts of admiration from the men, and Daddy thumped me hard upon the shoulder. "Good going, Timmy!"

Another of the men handed me his rig, for luck, and again I cast, again a bite, again a red fish, fat and fighting. Apparently a school of reds had come near just as I made that first cast. The others were catching fish now, too, but—oh, the wonder of it!—not as many as I. In that one hour, until the bell rang and it was time for class, I caught almost twenty red fish. The men were loud in praise, and none louder than my father. Never had I felt so proud before. Not even when he taught me that song.

"Bell bottom trousers... He'll climb the rigging..." I sang all the way back to school.

I remember mostly bright lights shining on me through their gels, and the fierce strength of the applause.

The chamber of commerce had invented the "Legend of Sara de Soto" to explain the community's name. According to the tale Hernando de Soto, who had, in fact, landed on the coast not far away (before traveling north and then west toward death on the Mississippi), had had with him a daughter named Sara. She had fallen in love with the handsome son of an Indian chief, and... Daddy told us the whole thing was "nothing but bullshit, pure silliness" but Layne-o and I didn't mind because, associated with the Legend, there was a pageant celebrated every February with a parade down Main Street. Colored lights, left over from Christmas, were strung from lamppost to lamppost along the way, and they danced and seemed to flicker whenever the night wind blew.

The pageant included various theatricals at the Municipal Auditorium. In 1941, the Out-Of-Door School was invited to put on a play of its own. The nature of the play—drama, musical—is completely gone from my mind, though I'm sure I didn't sing; I think that I may have been a sort of master of ceremonies, and perhaps I wore a white suit. But I do remember that applause; there was a lot of it. Afterward, people in the audience ruffled my hair and said that I'd been wonderful. Someone said that I had "star quality." Later, driving home in the car with the lights of the pageant left behind, I savored my triumph as I stared into the friendly night outside the windows. My parents and sister had been laughing and chatting gaily while I mused, but when there suddenly came a pause in the conversation, I came out of my dream. I felt impelled to say something. "Great me," I said. "Great me."

They laughed again, louder than ever, but their laughter was tinged with kindness, and with empathy.

Sunday evening. The quick, sharp steps echoed from the dark and empty street which the radio speaker projected into our living room. Then suddenly the footsteps stopped and a harsh voice demanded, "Your money or your life!" The silence lasted long, the longest silence radio ever knew, and already we were laughing. Again that demanding, threatening voice. "Well? I said, 'Your money or your life!'" And then we heard Jack Benny's agonized whine. "I *know*. I'm *thinking*."

We roared, and none louder than Daddy. He was sitting at a small table, cleaning his guns, and the smell of gun oil was mixed with the strange odor of Frances Fox, for Mother was giving Layne-o a "treatment"—working little gobs of ointment into her scalp between carefully parted rows of hair. I was stretched on the floor, unfocused eyes gazing at the ceiling, with Mr. Benny's taut and miserly features sharp in my mind. Later we would listen to Edgar Bergen and Charlie McCarthy, or "Allen's Alley."

Daddy was away quite a bit during those years, either in New York or "on the Coast," and when he was gone our lives seemed to me only half complete. (I'm certain that my mother, frightened of responsibility, worried about his roving, felt the same.) But when he *was* there, unless there was a party to go to, or guests to entertain, in the evenings he eagerly compensated for those weeks of absence.

Some nights we played Monopoly. Our set had wooden men, and I remember that my favorite was a blue milk can and that Daddy favored a purple piece that looked like a cross between a skinny woman with full skirts and a potato masher. More often we played poker, once I'd learned the rules, for white and red and blue chips. And sometimes we played Authors, with cards which had been Daddy's when he was smaller than I. I cannot believe that he enjoyed such childishness, but he laughed a lot, seemed to take the games seriously, and rarely was he angry.

Other nights he read aloud—*Penrod*, perhaps, or *Treasure Island*, *The Peterkin Papers*, *Rip Van Winkle*, or else from his own work in progress. The room would fill with dozens of voices as he gave each of the characters a life of his own. Or *her* own; though Daddy's females, especially the young and pretty, tended to simper.

Occasionally, before lunch or dinner, and particularly on weekends, he would leave his desk and amble into the kitchen. He'd open the icebox (so we usually called it) and stand there, carefully examining the leftovers. "Reno, I think I'm going to make something for lunch."

"Oh, *wonderful*, Mack. Children! Daddy's going to make one of his Famous Stews." And we would exclaim in delight.

Tag end of a roast, a few pork chops, or—all other meats lacking—hot dogs; baked or boiled potatoes, peas or green pepper, onions—he'd set aside his trove, and make a rich farm gravy. "Just like my mother used to make, and Grandma, too." Oh, the smell of bacon grease heating, in which to brown the flour, and then milk carefully added in small amounts, so as not to curdle. And then the meat and vegetables, to sit and simmer. Perhaps Mother might have baked fresh bread that morning, or the day before. We'd break it up and place it on the bottom of our bowls and ladle the savory mess over it.

Each time Daddy's Famous Stew was different, yet each time much the same: rich and flavorsome. We'd praise it to the skies and he'd sit there beaming, nodding his head in agreement with our praise.

And then he'd tell a funny story about his latest trip to Hollywood, or about some wondrous thing which had happened Long Ago.

Our life together in those years was a fiction—as fine as any my father ever wrote, or read aloud. A fiction all the more wonderful because it seemed, and often was, so very real. And we all conspired in its creation.

We were the perfect family, a royal household, superior to all save those special people we allowed into the magic circle of our lives. There was the king, my father, who was brilliant, all-powerful, and could do no wrong. The queen, my mother, who was the ideal mother, ideal wife. The princess, my sister, who was the only one who might stray from perfection, for she was both adolescent and female—a dangerous combination in any place or time. And me, the fair-haired prince: I know that my father so regarded me and, in fact, I was a towhead in those days.

But there was an underside to our bright world which was darker, bleaker, and unknown to Layne and me. For if we were to be the perfect children our parents wished us to be, then we must have a perfect childhood, unmarred by fret or fear. When they had fights, as sometimes they did, they held them behind closed doors.

Most of those rows were about liquor. In those days Mack's prowling, his tomcatting, was conducted elsewhere: Hollywood or New York, or wherever his research might take him. I think that Irene chose to ignore what she could neither see nor mend. When he was away, she lived with a mix of doubt and hurt and anger tucked deep within. Booze was different.

Both of them came from teetotal families, in which any indulgence in alcohol, save perhaps an occasional glass of elderberry wine, was regarded as the first step on a stairway bound straight down to Hell. During their early years together they had discovered the pleasures of sin: bootleg whiskey, bathtub gin, and home-brewed beer. But they were mostly broke, and such wicked indulgence was largely confined to occasional parties with their friends. After *Long Remember*, however, drinking became a regular and welcome part of their lives. Cocktails in the evening, a few drinks on a Sunday afternoon: these they savored. They relaxed, they laughed, they enjoyed, and nothing awful happened.

Irene's small frame limited her tolerance and, after a few unhappy slips— to be suffered at the time; to be laughed at later—she seldom drank more than was pleasant, more than was safe. Mack was different. His long body, his quick mind, seemed to share an infinite capacity. He could drink during the afternoon, though he seldom did so save on holiday; he could drink past twelve, past one at night, and then, after five hours' sleep, bound out of bed ready for breakfast, ready for work. But as the years went by, sometimes in the evening the louder voice, the quicker laugh, would slide into a sullen, misplaced anger. The daytime drinking would increase, and Irene would criticize, and they would fight about it. Eventually he would decide it was time to "cut back," and he would proceed for weeks, for months, at a far more temperate pace.

They both thought of his drinking as a small problem then; they thought of it so for years to come.

Money was different. Mack thought of money as his concern and— though she might fret about this expenditure or that one, and thus cause yet another row—generally Irene agreed with him. She wrote checks on her own account, but he balanced her checkbook and his own as well. Reno was not to worry her pretty little head about money. It was his responsibility. If anybody had to worry about money it would, by God, be him.

Often he did, for often there was reason.

It was his own fault, too. The fault of confusion, self-indulgence, and determined, admirable generosity. He had been deprived, had had to skimp, for so much of his life. Had seen silly, trivial folk do well, while he—with all his talent—struggled to survive. His children had worn hand-me-downs, and Irene thrice-mended dresses. He had received generosity, and rarely been able to offer it in turn. And he remembered, wished to emulate—but with all honesty—his father's glittering ways. *"What model ever did I have?"* And so...

In 1937 he had earned, before Syd Sanders's ten percent, over $35,000 (about $275,000 in today's puny dollars), in 1938 he had earned almost $27,000, and he had spent it all. Spent it on the house in Florida; spent it, during the winter of '38–'39, on the rented town house on East Eighty-fourth Street; spent it on that trip to Europe; spent it on the kids' summer camp; spent it on financing an archaeological dig on Indian burial mounds when he took his family back to Webster City during the summer of '38 and rented the biggest house available in town; spent it on renting an impressive country house in Katonah, New York, during the summer of '39; spent it on servants to staff those houses; spent it on clothes and gifts for the kids and Irene. Spent it.

And given it away. When he was working on *Diversey*, back in Iowa, and he and Irene were almost starving, Virginia and Jim Sours had helped them. They had also taken on the care of Grandpa McKinlay, when Mack and Irene couldn't help. All that on a small city preacher's meager pay. And they had also sent gifts of clothing during the bitter times before *Long Remember* was published; gifts they couldn't afford, but which they offered nonetheless. And there had been, from so many others, so many gifts and loans along the way.

Now Mack could reciprocate, and he did. Did the Sours' youngest child, Mary Virginia, have the misfortune to be born with cerebral palsy? Very well. She was (and is) such a bright and eager soul, so determined and courageous, and there were special boarding schools designed to help children overcome or deal with such affliction. The schools were expensive, even in that day, and Jim Sours couldn't possibly afford them, but... Mary attended such schools for five years.

Was someone Mack had long known and admired sinking deeper into debt? Mack got together with mutual friends and helped to bail him out. And Irene's sister, Ruth: perhaps she needed temporary escape from a rocky marriage; and Irene would love to see her. Mack sent Ruth the train fare, and some money for new clothes. And that family of squatters in the abandoned house nearby on Shell Road, whose roof caught fire, and the father came running—"Mister, you got a fire extinguisher?" Mack did, and he carried it along, half-running as best he could, and it was he who climbed the ladder and helped to put out the fire. Those folks didn't seem to have much in the way of food and clothes, so Mack helped out.

These acts of generosity were not performed for show. Mack might brag about reviews or sales to book clubs or to Hollywood; not only might—he did. But helping others was a private matter, done not to impress others but to satisfy himself.

So he spent, and so he gave, and so he lived at the limit of his income year after year. And sometimes, if sales were disappointing, beyond. Then he'd have to shift and dance among his creditors, just as others he had helped had done.

Nineteen forty had been a slow year. When, in late February of '41, he wrote a business letter to Tim Coward, Mack added the following paragraph.

I have been working as hard as I ever worked in my life, behaving like a gentleman for a change, with one highball before dinner and nothing afterward. All this exemplary conduct has seemed to profit me very little and I am rather past the point where I can fuss about it. The phone company calls up and suggests grimly that a check would be in order and I merely say, "Oh, is that so?" and forget about it.

Eleven months later, early in the afternoon; Pennsylvania Station was filled with gloom, just as Mack was. Fear and uncertainty had been itching at the edge of his mind for months, but now they burrowed deep. Disgruntled and blue, he fidgeted in his seat on the Silver Meteor and watched other passengers hurry along the platform outside the windows. Steam rose in the chilly air and blurred the figures rushing there. He looked at his watch. Almost time for the train to leave. And that would be good riddance to New York, and good riddance as well to all the editors and agents who clustered there to practice their ineptitude. "Christ!" But his lips formed no words, his mouth made no sound. God damn it, couldn't even swear aloud, not in a day coach. He'd thought he'd never have to travel coach again but, just now, he couldn't afford a drawing room, couldn't even afford a roomette.

He'd made over seventeen thousand in '41 but that hadn't been enough, not with all the obligations he'd incurred. And he'd taken off two months during the fall to write a novel, instead of the short stories Sydney Sanders had urged him to write. *Gentle Annie* was a western and a hell of a good story, and Tim Coward liked it, but it wouldn't be published until next fall and the small advance had long since been spent. He'd sent copies of the manuscript to Syd Sanders—Mack had been sure there was a good chance of serialization in the *Post*, or maybe *Collier's*—and to Donald Friede, his new agent out on the Coast. That was the week after Pearl Harbor. Christ, what timing! Syd said all the editors were running around like chickens with their heads cut off. He said they didn't know what to buy, now that we were at war. But whatever they wanted, it sure as hell wasn't *Gentle Annie*. Mack had had the imagination to make the "Black Hats," the train robbers, nice folks the reader could fall in love with, while the "White Hats," the sheriff and the others, were a bunch of bastards. But the editors, the *real* bastards, said the story was too "immoral" for their audiences. God, what nonsense. And he hadn't heard a word from Friede, out in Hollywood. At the end of December he'd had to slap a mortgage on the house in order to raise some money. A couple of weeks later, he'd decided to come up to New York and see if he couldn't do better than Sydney.

He hadn't. He'd booked into the LaFayette, which he liked and which was pretty cheap. He'd made some calls, seen a few people, and achieved no more than Syd. Perhaps the editors were right, and the book was no damned good at all. Nothing for it now but to creep home and bang out a few short stories and a novelette—maybe something about a kid from a town like Webster City, who was drafted. No, volunteered, that was it. The kid would volunteer.

The door of the coach opened, and a young man came slowly down the aisle. He had a piece of paper in his hand and was checking seat numbers, and Mack realized that the young man, more of a boy really, was headed straight for him. He was chanting "Mr. Canton? Mr. Canton?" as he came. God, couldn't even get his name right.

Mack growled, "I'm Mr. Kant*or*. MacKinlay Kantor."

"Well, sir, I have a message for a Mr. Canton, in this seat. You see, 'Car Seven, Seat Twenty,' so I guess that must be you. You're to call a Mr. Coward, and you can use the stationmaster's phone."

Mack stood up, grabbed his bag from the rack, and followed. Why the hell would Timmy get him off the train? He found that he was trembling, and his shirt felt damp. Maybe the kids had drowned in the Gulf, maybe Irene had been bitten by a rattlesnake, maybe the house had burned down, mortgage and all.

The young man looked back at him and smiled. "Mr. Coward said to tell you that he has good news."

Across the cavernous station and into the warmth of the office. He grabbed the phone and dialed. After a moment Tim Coward came on the line. "Thank God I managed to get hold of you. Donald Friede has been on the phone. He's already turned down twenty thousand dollars from Metro. You're to call him back, so come on over to the office."

Mack folded the piece of paper and slipped it into his wallet (he'd carry it there for years). He picked up his bag, he thought he thanked the men, he wasn't sure, he went to find a cab. "Two West Forty-fifth Street, please."

Didn't hear, didn't feel, didn't think. Cotton batting all around him. "Here we are, sir."

Mack glanced at the meter. Eighty-five cents. He stepped onto the sidewalk and pulled out his wallet, and the world came back in focus. Looked at the cabbie and smiled. "I'm not sure yet, but this may be a lucky day for me. So I want it to be a lucky day for you." He held out a ten-dollar bill.

The driver stared, and grinned, and grabbed. "Holy smoke, mister! Thanks! Here, let me carry your bag upstairs."

The receptionist in the Coward-McCann offices smiled at Mack, took charge of his bag, and waved him on to rooms within. Timmy greeted him, his rugged face beaming. They talked, exclaimed for a minute, and then Mack called Donald Friede.

"Yes, Mack, I turned down the twenty thousand from Metro, because I'm positive we can get more. I'm going over to the studio in a few minutes, and I'll report from there, later on. Where can I reach you?"

He thought of the LaFayette: it was comfortable, it was practical—but not for this day, this night. "I'll be at the Algonquin," he said.

Donald Friede laughed. "I can hear you smiling. Talk to you later."

The Algonquin was just around the block but Mack took a cab anyway. He'd stayed there before, whenever he wasn't counting pennies, and the doorman greeted him by name. Crossing the lobby he moved through a flurry of welcome from bellmen, elevator operators, waiters, and the man behind the desk. He had his bag sent up to his room and went into the dim light of the bar. "Why, hello, Mr. Kantor, welcome back. What'll it be?"

"I will have"—he paused for a long moment in happy consideration— "I will have a Manhattan, if you please. A *double*."

"Yes, sir. Right away." As the bartender poured and stirred and strained he said, "You sure look on top of the world, Mr. Kantor. Get some good news?"

"That I did, Jimmy, and I'm waiting for more. Which reminds me—I'm expecting a phone call. Make sure the people on the desk know where I am."

"Will do." He brought the drink and left. By God, they gave good service here, and they were all so wonderful to him. Of course, he did tip well... He had a sudden vision, sharp and clear, of waiters fawning on his father in hotels in Chicago, long ago. *"De quicker de service, de bigger de tip!"* But that wasn't right at all. That was foolishness. These folks didn't fawn on him. They traded dirty stories with him, told him about their kids. And he listened always, and remembered.

He looked around the bar. Not too many uniforms yet, but there'd be more in months to come. He shook his head in self-distaste. He'd been a damned selfish fool, earlier in the day, when he'd thought of Pearl Harbor only in terms of what it had done to the magazine business. What about the poor guys on the *Arizona,* and the other ships at Pearl? And Manila gone now, and Wake and Guam. But thank God we were *in,* at last. Almost too late for the British, but Churchill would hold on. And Dr. Bennett, at Johns Hopkins, had this new method of surgery—maybe he could patch Mack's leg for good. And then...

"Mr. Kantor, there's a call for you."

Sweet rush of adrenalin as he limped to the phone. "Hello. Donald?"

"Yes, Mack. I'm at the studio now. I know I can get them up to twenty-five thousand, at least, for the book. But see here, would you be willing to do some screenwriting, too? On other projects. I think I can get you maybe a fifteen-week guarantee at a very good price, in a package deal."

And then, if Bennett did fix the leg, he could *afford* to go to war. "Hell, yes!"

"Great, kid! That's just great. Now, look, I think I'll have final word by five-thirty—eight-thirty, your time—and I'll call you either way."

"I'll be here. Waiting in the bar!"

"A grand place to wait. Talk to you later."

He should call Irene. No, better wait until everything was certain. He should eat. Didn't want much; his stomach was knotted tight. Talk about rags to riches, and all in a matter of hours. He ordered a roast beef sandwich, rare, and thought about Donald.

Mack had liked him from the start, and that was kind of strange, for they were complete opposites in so many ways. Donald had grown up all over Europe. He was cosmopolitan. He'd inherited a fortune and lost it in publishing. He'd made another fortune, and lost that too. Now he was agenting in Hollywood. He couldn't comprehend Mack's tall-corn, small-town background any more than Mack could understand his. But they shared a taste for bawdry and for puns, they respected one another, and—damn it, Mack liked the man. Just as he had liked Timmy, and Syd Sanders, right from the start. There was a lot to be said for instinct.

He ordered another double, his fourth. Better be a little careful now. Didn't want his speech slurred when he spoke to Reno. But still...what a hell of a day, what a hell of a world. He'd been so nervous, and now...

"Mr. Kantor. You're wanted on the phone, by an awfully happy guy."

He floated to the booth. "Yes?"

"Kid, what would you say to twenty-five thousand dollars for the movie rights to *Gentle Annie*, and a twenty-six-week contract, spread over two years, at a thousand per week?"

"My God! You really did it, Donald—kid—I guess you're my lucky penny."

"Guess I am." His pleased, smug voice came preening out of the phone. "Congratulations, Mack. Call me tomorrow, and I'll have the details."

Mack jiggled the receiver. "Front desk."

"This is MacKinlay Kantor. Room 302. I'd like to place a call to Sarasota, Florida. The number there is 7-0518."

"Yes, sir." Three-fifths of the country lived for a year on less than he'd be making every three weeks.

He imagined energy passing across the long, lonely miles. *Ring. Ring.* "Yes?"

"Reno!"

"Mack! Where are you? I thought you'd be on the train."

"Well, honey, it's like this," and he spent fifteen minutes telling her, incident by incident, event by glorious event, the happenings of the past few hours.

"Oh, darling, I can't believe it. It's so wonderful! I've been so worried for you, and so scared."

"Scared?" His big voice blasted down the line, all ease and blissful confidence. "I told you not to worry! I *knew* this would work. Hell, I was never scared at all."

After they'd said good-bye he went back to the bar and ordered another drink. "Never scared at all." His image was reflected in the mirror behind the bar. He shook his head and grinned at himself. Well, he had Irene convinced of that. Tomorrow he'd believe it too.

He had a nightcap and then he went to bed.

*   *   *

Imagine a gigantic kaleidoscope, held in an enormous hand, with my young self at the center of it, peering out at the world through rosy, golden, shifting panes of glass. So existence seemed to me, that year and the next. Daddy went out to Los Angeles, to start his studio work, late in February or early in March. Mother took us out of school early and we followed him, near the end of April. Children still heeded school bells in Louisiana, I saw them—eager or laggard—from the windows of the train. Tiny figures of cowboys mended fence on the Great Plains, and the vastness of the land was measured out, not in hours, but in days. (Three times at least we crossed the continent by train during those years; we also traveled north and south and, once, Daddy and I drove from Oklahoma back to Florida.)

Daddy had rented a huge house on Beverly Glen Drive in West Los Angeles, complete with a full-size pool, a patio bar and changing rooms, and thirty feet of landscaped hillside below it, covered with tubular, succulent vines. I could swim the length of the pool and back underwater; Daddy was very proud of me, and so was I. A boy named Bobby Myers lived close by and we became good friends, although he was a year older. We swam in the pool, we rode our bicycles up and down steep and winding roads, we played baseball with other kids (Bobby always picked me for his side, even though I wasn't very good). We defended the California coast against Japanese invaders, or seized islands in the far Pacific, before we were hit, and fell, and died beneath the burning sun. And then went home for supper.

Our parents acquired new friends in this new setting, new at least to Layne-o and to me and, I think, to Mother. Actors and agents, mostly, a few screenwriters, and young officers passing through on their way to war. Often, in the evenings and on weekends, there were parties. Donald Friede was there a lot, and he was carefully, effusively charming. Joseph Cotten and his wife were often there, and some times Harry Morgan, Gregory Peck, Dana Andrews. My sister and I were not awed by the fact that they were "famous actors" (after all, Daddy was a "famous writer"); we treasured their presence because they were interesting, and nice to us, and fun to be with.

Daddy presided over everyone and everything, and I was very happy.

Shake the kaleidoscope.

I think that Daddy already had dreams of going overseas, and that he wanted to show us as much—stoke his own memory with knowledge of as much—of the wonder of our country as he could. In case he didn't come back. At the very end of spring we went up to Sequoia National Park, in the high Sierras, and rented a cabin for a couple of weeks. We saw that gentled wilderness as none could see it now, for our country had barely half its current population then, and gas rationing limited travel for the few who could afford it. Even some of the few cabins existing then were empty. There was a mountain meadow nearby where the snow still lay deep and almost crisp, the water in the streams was clean but made my teeth ache with its cold. We saw deer and they ignored us, unless we came too close. In the forest the big trees grew outside of time and God was in them. A tribe of chipmunks came to beg, and we named them after the Seven Dwarfs—Grumpy, Doc, and the others. Crackling logs in the fireplace warmed the cabin, shimmering flame from kerosene lamps gave light at night. We took turns reading aloud good tales from the past, told ghost stories, played poker for safety matches, sang songs. In the dining room at the lodge they served cupcakes for dessert, with chocolate, vanilla, or strawberry icing.

Shake again. The shifting colors, the shifting panes of time, once more are rearranged.

It was late at night, far past my bedtime, and I was sitting on the living room floor with my back against the couch and my head resting on my mother's knee. It was February of 1943 and, after spending the fall and earliest winter in Florida, we were back in California. This time we were in a smaller house, in Beverly Hills. The room was filled with family friends, and a number of the men were in uniform. Daddy was not. Once, he said, he'd dressed in khaki oddments when he belonged to The Company long ago, when he was no older than I, or else in just a khaki shirt and ragged trousers when he'd been in the Scouts, but now he'd have his war correspondent's uniform custom-made by Brooks Brothers, when he got to New York. I tossed that thought aside—I did not like its flavor—and concentrated on beauty and on wonder.

Burl Ives was there, and Burl had brought his guitar.

Oh, do not cross the hay field, when sets the blood-red sun . . .
For ghosts glide in the hayrick, the hayrick, the hayrick,
For ghosts glide in the hayrick, in the eerie gloom . . .

Daddy's face was stern and closed. (Perhaps he thought of that rick of straw on which he'd slept and twisted, long years before.)

The time it is short, there is none I can spare,
And the nightingale's song will soon die in the air...
Down in the valley, valley so low...

Applause came at the end of each song, and oohs and aahs of appreciation. At last Burl put down the guitar and wrapped the room within his smile. "Singing and playing," he said, "make thirsty work." Every statement he made seemed to me a golden saying, and I resolved—as he picked up the brandy bottle from its place on the floor beside his chair, and poured another drink—to remember that one, the next time I'd been busy at my own kind of play and wanted a Coke.

Burl saw me watching him and winked.

I thought that he was properly named, for he was big and broad and *burly*. His body spilled out of his clothes—his khaki clothes. He was of the earth, earthy. Homely earth of the Middle West, in which seed of the Old World had been sown and grown to ripeness. I sensed great power within him—he was the only man I had ever met who seemed to match my father's force and magnetism. As he picked up his guitar again and strummed, hunting for another song to sing, I thought of the first time we'd heard the honey of his voice.

Three months before, we'd been back in Sarasota. It was my sister who first heard Burl—though in later years our father denied that fact, and took the golden discovery for his own. Our mother had helped Layne wash her hair the night before, and treated her to an excess of Frances Fox ointment, and something had gone wrong. Layne announced that she simply *could not* go to school. What would her friends say? And think of all the boys. And so I'd been dispatched alone down our long driveway, to wait for the bus. (We had switched to public schools on the mainland that year.) Sulky Layne-o had stayed behind, to glower at the world and listen to the radio. And she *heard*. A song she'd learned at school up north three years before.

Tam Pierce, Tam Pierce, lend me your grey mare...
For us wants to go to Witheycombe Fair...

The song sounded truer, purer, than ever she could have imagined. "Daddy!"

Our driveway led back to a blacktopped road. On our side, the gulfward side, the road was fringed with jungle; on the other side the roadbed dropped sharply to meet brackish wetlands covered with a great tangle of mangroves.

The dawn came late at that time of year, and the red sun had barely cleared low clouds along the horizon. I remember that it was cold for Florida. Mourning doves were busy among the trees, and I heard the pile-driver knocking of a woodpecker nearby. And then another sound, a bellowing from behind me and, turning, I saw Daddy standing in the drive. "Hey! Timmy! Come back to the house. I want you to hear something."

"Daddy, I can't! I'll miss the bus."

"To hell with the bus! This is a damn sight more important. Now, come on and get back here. I'll drive you to school later." I started back to the house. He had already disappeared inside, but still I heard him roaring. "Run, damn it, run! I want you to hear this."

I found him standing in the middle of the living room, beaming (already the discovery was becoming his), with Mother and Layne-o sitting, rapt, upon the couch. A voice was coming from the radio. It filled the room with glory. A rich, golden voice.

> *I wooed her in the wintertime, part of the summer too,*
> *And the only, only thing I ever did wrong*
> *Was to hold her from the foggy, foggy dew.*

I dropped my books and stood still, transfixed by the overwhelming truth of tone and feeling.

> *Prison bars all around me, guard a-walking by the door,*

Daddy was looking at me closely, watching the expression on my face.

> *I feel sad and lonely, 'cause I'll never see my love no more.*

"Who is it, Daddy? Who is it?"

"His name is Burl Ives, and he is the greatest ballad singer I have ever heard. And yet, I've never heard of him before at all. No concerts, no records. Your sister was listening to the radio, and she called me." (Layne-o's sulkiness had long given way to wonder.) "And I heard—him. He's broadcasting from New York. Calls himself The Wayfaring Stranger."

Later Daddy had reached Burl Ives up north, and offered to help him gain recognition in any way he could. And now Burl had come to the Coast, to rehearse with the cast of a morale show, "This Is the Army." He was our friend, and he was singing in our living room at that very moment. After a bit Daddy took out his own guitar and sang, while Burl sipped another brandy and nodded his head in kindly, generous approval. Then Burl sang once more.

The blue sky up above me, the green grass all around;
I've been looking for something that I have never found,

After I'd gone to bed, protesting, and was falling asleep, I thought for long, muddied minutes about Burl's coming into our lives, and about Daddy's going away.

"Timmy, come in here for a minute." Early morning, and I was getting ready for school. I turned away from the mirror, hair still tousled, went into the hall and on to their bedroom. It faced to the east and was filled with light. Yellow gold. Daddy was sitting on the bed he shared with Mother, naked, and gazing with proud delight at the puckered valleys on his left leg. "Just look at that. No more bandages for me. It's been five months since the operation and the damned thing hasn't opened once. And look at that scar tissue." Silver-white, and satin smooth within the grooves. I focused my eyes, carefully, rigidly, upon the scars, avoiding the center of power between his thighs, and then he spoke again and I looked at his face. There was pride there, fierce pride, but also something wistful in the eyes.

"As you know, I'm going away next month."

This was a formal speech, and called for a formal answer. "Yes, sir."

"First to Washington, to talk to people at Army Air Forces HQ. I may not be able to hike to the war but, by God, I can fly to it! And then to Philadelphia, to talk with the editors of the *Saturday Evening Post*—I'm going to England to write about the war for them—and then to New York to get my uniforms, and to talk with Syd Sanders, and with your godfather, Tim Coward. And then I'm going to get a ride overseas."

He paused. I didn't want him to go. I knew, of course, that he couldn't be hurt, but—for him to go away? I'd miss him so. We all would miss him.

"Now, I don't know how long I'm going to be gone. Maybe four months, maybe a year. I just can't say. But"—and his face was solemn, was gay, as he spoke—"I do know this. We're in a war. We're in it for just one reason. To protect democracy; to protect freedom. To save the things we love, in our country, in England, and all over the world.

"We each have a job to do, no matter how young or old. My job is to tell people what it's like over there. You have different duty." When I heard that last word my body straightened, just as it did at school when we recited the Pledge of Allegiance. "While I'm gone you have to be the man of the family. You have to take care of your mother, and of your sister too. You have to help them just as much as you can. You're a fine boy and I know I can count on you."

"Yes, Daddy." And then he relaxed, and kissed me on the cheek, and hugged me tight.

"Now get out of here and comb your hair, or you'll be late for school."

As I left the room I wondered when I'd have pubic hair, like Daddy.

"If only your father were here!"

A muggy June night in Florida, with tree frogs at their song in trees beyond the window screens. Defiant Layne-o sat, rigid, on the living room couch, her face taut and angry, staring straight ahead. I was pacing about, my hands clasped behind my back. (Sometimes Daddy clasped his hands that way, as though to constrain them from lashing out, when he was upset.) Mother stood in the middle of the room. There were tears on her cheeks, and her voice was trembling, desperate.

"If only your father... He'd know what to do. Layne-o, darling! I can't even trust you any more."

My sister turned to me and glared. "Little brat! Tattle-tale. It's all your fault!"

In a way it was. Fifteen-year-old Layne was in love with the most wonderful boy in the world. A boy of whom our parents disapproved. She had been forbidden to see him more than a few times a week, and she had done so anyway. She had been forbidden to speak to him on the phone more than once or twice or thrice a day, but she had also done that, and I had heard. And I had Told. I may have done that in part to fulfill my role of The Man In The Family; I had certainly also acted out of pure brattishness. (Layne and I had drifted into the usual big sister–little brother enmity, just as our father and *his* sister had years before. We had detested each other for over a year, for at least six hours out of every twenty four; we would continue to cherish that mutual loathing for several years to come.) So I had Told, and now Mother Did Not Know What To Do.

She bargained with Layne, she dickered, and she cried. And Layne-o cried too. I was upset by all the unhappiness my tattling honesty had inspired, and my own tears threatened. "If only your father were here!" But he wasn't. He was far away, and I was lost and lonely. I walked out onto the screen porch, and paced some more. I knew that I must be the man of the house—Daddy had told me so—but I didn't know how. I felt completely inadequate.

Be a man? Right then I hardly knew how to be a boy. And so I struck my hands together, just as Daddy sometimes did, as I stared into the dark.

12

Up Above Everywhere

At times, that summer, Mack felt almost like a child. A child invited on sufferance to a party where only the grown-ups were allowed to play. He felt at times like an actor playing a role—a mere pretender. As though he was just dressed up in borrowed khaki remnants from the past—from the days of The Company or the Scouts. At those times he'd look at the uniform he wore and shrug in deprecation. It was well-made, well fitted, and yet it didn't seem real to him. There were no insignia of rank upon his shoulders; just the black brassard around his left arm, with that damned white *C* for "Correspondent."

There were no wings upon his breast.

And yet, he'd done his best. It was late in August of '43 and he'd been in England for five months. England and Scotland. In London he'd experienced the tag end of the Blitz—he'd heard the sirens warn and mourn at night, the defiant ack-ack bark of antiaircraft guns nearby, the brutal crunch of bombs exploding, he'd seen searchlights grope across the sky—and he'd written about it for the *Post*. He'd witnessed the determined, understated gallantry of the British public, and reported that. He'd flown a mission with the Coastal Command, but they'd found no subs. He'd flown over Germany with the RAF, seen tracers stitch the dark, but that night they'd encountered few fighters and little flak. By chance he'd gone down to a base called Chelveston, in Northamptonshire, where the 305th Bomb Group of the Army Eighth Air Force was stationed with its four squadrons of B-17s. He'd liked, been awed by, the commanding officer, a colonel named Curtis LeMay, whom the kids called "Iron Ass" behind his back. He'd liked the kids as well—most of them were in truth kids, young enough to be his sons—and he'd laughed with them, drunk with them, sung with them a little. It was easy, in a way. So many of them knew his name from stories in the magazines, or from the movies or his books. He had done everything with them but fly. He had written the necessary articles, good articles, and he'd written a poem which he thought wonderful, but inside he felt small sense of pride. He was just a visitor to this war, a goddamned tourist! He didn't feel that he'd been blooded.

It was the Eighth Air Force that was at fault. The RAF had welcomed him, but not the Americans, not the Eighth. They'd wanted him to be just a gangplank correspondent. To wait back at the base while the flight crews— young men he'd come to know, to admire, even to love—went off on a mission, and then to go up to those who got back and ask, "Hey, what was it like? Were the fighters bad? How was the flak over the target?" And get a weary, scornful, dismissive glance in consequence.

Mack wanted none of that. His common sense agreed with pride: you could not tell others of the romance—he thought of it as romance—and the fear, sheer terror, boredom, the stubborn discipline, imposed by combat unless you'd experienced them yourself. Ever since he'd written that poem, about a pert, engaging young kid named Bailey who had tumbled out of the sky instead of coming home ("Up there on oxygen, / Up above everywhere...")—hell, ever since he'd written Long Remember—he'd suffered a stubborn, nagging, secret doubt. "Did I get it right?" And ever since he'd told his silly, adolescent lies about trench fighting in France he'd wondered how he would behave if faced with ugly fact.

He looked out the window of the train carriage he was riding in, at the neat and tidy miracle of the Bedfordshire countryside. The small precision of fields and hedges delighted him—a storybook illustration, one-quarter of the world away from the endless reach of Iowa fields which he'd known long ago. There were hayricks, dun-colored, piled high in the distance. He thought of that stack of straw —"For ghosts glide in the hayrick"—on which he'd slept one night. Straws had pricked him then, they pricked him now. He shook his head. ͵

Then he thought of a car falling, and of unremembered flames, and his body eased a bit and he smiled. A smile appropriately, deliberately grim. There was a savory piece of private knowledge which he owned, which he seldom shared with others. When that car had driven off the cliff back in Lehigh, Iowa, just over twenty years before, and gone hurtling down to crush and tear the branches which received it (once he showed me the very site, but never did he tell me this), the driver and three other occupants had gone spinning out to crash through leaves below. Mack and one other, a girl named Dorothea Western, had remained inside until they hit and Mack went tumbling free. His smashed leg was a fierce dark numbness to him—the hurting would come later—and glistening, jagged shafts of bone had pierced his flesh, his trousers; but he smelt a stench of gas and saw a wicked fire grow.

"Dorothea!"

"*O-o-oh.*" He crawled into the car; he dragged her out.

He didn't remember that, neither rescue nor the flames, until they told him later.

So, by God, he'd be all right, once he got in combat, up at altitude. He wouldn't wet his pants, more than others.

Air combat has romance, but it makes me wet my pants ...

He'd heard young men of the 305th sing that song, fierce and frightened, in the Officers' Club at Chelveston; he hadn't felt he had the right to join them. But now things might be different. At Eighth Air Force Headquarters in High Wycombe he had pleaded and he had pestered, to no avail, until he'd met Fred Anderson. Fred was lean and tall and tough, and he was different from most of the brass. The HQ types. For one thing, he wore the Distinguished Flying Cross, a peacetime DFC, and the old Army Air Corps had not given those away lightly. There had been very few awarded, and those had been hard-earned. For another, Mack and Fred liked each other. They were roughly the same age, and shared that jarring sense of mutual recognition which can come to men of vastly different backgrounds. (Mack sometimes thought that, if he'd gone to college and joined the ROTC and then become a Blue Cadet at Randolph Field, back in the twenties, he might have ended up like Fred. He was wrong about that, he knew he was, but it pleased him to think so.) And Fred was a one-star general, he had clout, and he understood Mack's yearning and the warrant for it.

"Look, Mack, I understand what you're after. You want to tell folks back in the States what it's *really* like up there. What our guys are going through."

"Damn right, General."

"But, Mack, things are rough right now. We're losing men and machines like crazy. You've been around here long enough to know the score. We're averaging losses of over four percent per mission. Four percent of the aircraft on each mission. In theory that means that not one crew will finish its tour of twenty-five. What kind of damn fool would want to go against odds like that?"

"Me." That devil's grin of his. "I need to do it to tell the story right. And, I'm lucky."

"Yeah. But the crews would resent your presence. They don't want an extra body going out, over target, or coming home. They'd think you'd just be in the way. And I'd think so, too. I'm sorry, but that's Air Force policy."

"General, the '17s have two cheek guns, fifty-calibers, for the bombardier and the navigator, and sometimes—even when there are fighters—the bombardier has to fiddle with his bombsight, and the navigator has to navigate. And I know you people have set up a school over here, training cooks, bakers, drivers, file clerks, as gunners. Because you're not getting enough replacements for the guys you lose. Now, if I went through Gunnery School, I could get a story out of it, and—if I qualified—I might come in handy."

Fred Anderson laughed. "It's against the rules of war for a noncombatant—"

"If I did get shot down, I'd have my correspondent's ID. Who the hell would know what I'd been doing?"

Mack had qualified. He'd hated machinery all his life, and field-stripping a .50-caliber machine gun he detested, but it was *necessary*. When it came to practice firing on the range, he thought of the rabbits he had shot so long ago. *"There is one, Mack. Shoot him!"* Or of wolves. Or Focke-Wulfs.

He came in second in his class.

"Congratulations, Mack. Pity you're a civilian, or you'd be wearing wings."

"I don't care, sir." A lie. "Just as long as I get to fly. Fred, when..."

"How about the 305th? You've been around them. You know people there..."

Mack nodded slowly, his face dour. Yeah, he knew a lot of folks there. And he had known others.

> *Somebody's chute was a little red rose—*
> *Somebody's chute and his life were a crumple,*
> *Little black crumple all the way down—*
> *Twenty-two thousand feet deep into Nantes.*
> *Six of you wistful and six of you sailing,*
> *Sailing and swinging,*

All the way down, four full miles to the ground.
Bailey. Who burned?

This is the way that I think of you always:
Cocky and walking untrammeled and quick.
This is the way I shall see you forever:
Tough face and monkey-mouth wrinkled and pert.
Leather arms swaying, you walk at the base,
Dingy gold bars on the loops of your jacket;
Childish forever you swagger and sing.
Always your cot with its rumpled gray blanket,
Always your pin-ups with lingerie leer,
Always your silken-limbed blondes on the wall,
Always your tongue running loose, and some fellow
Hauling you off of the bed on your fanny,
All the way down to the floor with a bump.

All the way down
To that checkerboard Nantes.
(Tell me, O Bailey, who burned?)
All the way down to the barbed-wire fences—
You, who said, "Heil!" for a comical greeting—
Down to the Achtung! *and* Blitzspiel *you gabbled.*
Six of you drifting, three dead in the ship,
Or battered so badly they couldn't bail out,
And another, lone flower, a-burning.

Had he got it right? "Yeah, I know people there. Knew others."

Fred Anderson shrugged. If you are a good man it is not easy to send others risking, while you remain at home. "Curt LeMay's no longer there. We've bumped him up. He's got himself a combat wing now. But the 305th's still under his command. I've spoken to him, and he likes the idea of you going along for the ride. He's passed the word to treat you right—to let you fly as official correspondent, and unofficial gunner. I've had orders cut, and they'll be expecting you."

Back to the English countryside. In Northamptonshire now. Still trim and tidy. Mack reached into his pocket and pulled out a cablegram he'd received the day before from the editor of the *Post*. He unfolded it and spread it on his knee.

1943 AUG 27

MACKINLAY KANTOR WAR CORRESPONDENT
SATURDAY EVENING POST AMBIHO LDN =

HAVE DECIDED BREAK RULE LONG STANDING AND
GIVE BAILEY POEM TWO PAGES UP FRONT WITH
FULL COLOR PAINTING STOP ASSUME NO OBJECTION
OUR MENTIONING EDITORS NOTE THAT POEM BASED
ON ACTUAL INCIDENT STOP COULD YOU SUPPLY
BAILEY'S FULL NAME AND HOME TOWN FOR EDI-
TORS NOTE =

BEN HIBBS.

Mack was pleased with that cable. Hell, anyone would be. Any writer.
That cable gave him joy. But he'd made use of Bailey, however honorably,
and Bailey was not a writer at all, he was just a kid from a small town in
Kentucky. He'd sought immortality not in print but in the flesh, and now
he was gone—perhaps—beyond all joy or pride.

My father had to justify himself to Bailey. The train wheezed and sighed
into the station in Wellingborough. On the platform a sergeant approached
him and saluted. "Mr. Kantor?"

"Yes."

"They sent me over to give you a ride to Chelveston."

Two nights later, during the early hours of August 31, Mack lay restless on
the bed in the room assigned to him. Someone else had bunked there until
the day before, but that someone else was gone into limbo, and now his
sack was empty and Mack was glad he hadn't known him. And, perversely,
regretted that he hadn't. That he couldn't put a face, a personality, to the
specter which lay beside him in the dark.

His left thigh hurt a bit, he'd been working that leg like crazy for the
last few months, but he was used to that and shoved the thought of pain
away. All physical pain, and he mused a while as he sweated toward the
morning.

"Why then did we come, why are we here? Such a damn-fool question
and such a necessary one. Why did the man who lies beside me, whose
breathing I can almost hear, whose flesh I almost smell, who isn't there at
all—go into nothing? Disappear. Dissolve. Or shrivel, crumple, as paper

crumples when it's burned. As, maybe, Bailey burned. What possible gain would justify such waste? And what was wasted? I don't even know.

"I'll have to give him a name. Put clothes upon his nakedness. I'll call him Quinn. Tom Quinn. And Tom Quinn came from an anywhere town, maybe a little like Webster City. All towns in America are a little like Webster City. He chased butterflies when he was small. Ran with jar and lid after fireflies through the long, late dusk of summer. And he was happy, desperate, he bested, was worsted, during all his young life. Was chaste, was lecherous, a saint, a shit, was human—until yesterday. Filled with spice or blandness, but surely filled with life. Life which he wagered—which he surrendered—at our behest. Hell, the kid probably didn't even know why. Nor can I name the reasons. But there is an obscenity, a blasphemous cloud, spreading over Europe, a savage avarice in Asia, and I know they must be stopped. And there is a vigor and a virtue which has nurtured me, and all I love. They call it the American Dream—but it is not dream, it is reality. The man who lies beside me, he risked himself for me and mine; I'd hug him if I could. I'd hold him close in fond embrace. I'd buy him drinks in thanks. I'd..."

Mack slept at last.

Air combat has romance...

It was different in so many ways from what he had expected, and yet in other fashion so like his imaginings. Almost familiar. (He'd laid siege to Vicksburg once, and ten years ago he'd charged with Pickett's men at Gettysburg.) The differences were in detail: the tinny, crackling sound of voices on the microphone, the squeak of the diaphragm in his mask, and the harsh, rubbery taste of oxygen when they were at altitude (he'd observed these phenomena when he was with the RAF, but now he *knew* them), the eerie serenity of flight up there above the clouds, particularly in the Plexiglas nose of a B-17. It seemed that he was riding on a magic carpet—he thought of a phrase from a hymn which Eva used to sing: "Safe and secure from all alarm"—until the Nazi fighters started coming in, or he saw black bursts of flak. No training film had prepared him for the fighters' speed, the "rate of closure," and it was funny about flak: it seemed so innocent. A bombardier had once told him that the first time he'd ever seen flak had been through the eyepiece of his bombsight, and it was so dense he had bitched about the "cloud cover" over the target. And when they were off oxygen, starting their ascent or coming home, it was surprising how quickly, sharply, odors spread, ten thousand feet above the earth. That was why everybody groaned and made bad jokes, if they'd been served baked beans before a mission.

The similarities: well, he'd lived through the adrenalin rush of fear and challenge for years at the typewriter, and often in his dreams at night. It filled him with a holy joy, pure exultation, to know that, if he was weak enough to suffer fear, he was also strong enough to master it. And he was there voluntarily, he thought, out of a sense of duty. Most of the others couldn't understand his eagerness to share the risks which they dreaded and abhorred. They teased him and admired him. They shook their heads and said he was crazy.

But they didn't know.

Young Mack and a pretty blonde: *"We'd just reached the first line of German trenches, outside of Mons."* He could laugh about that now, and he did. Privately, publicly—for all to know and be amused—he laughed.

What he didn't like, what no excess of sentiment could prettify, were the losses. The Army Air Force had a nicer, vaguer, word: attrition. You sat at the bar in the Officers' Club one night, or in the pub in nearby Rushden, talking with some guy—learning about his folks, his girl, maybe his wife and kids, or dreams of kids—and two days later he came back dead, or without an arm, without a face, or he didn't come back at all. Death undid so many that fall. On the fourteenth of October the 305th went to Schweinfurt for the second time. They put up eighteen aircraft and three aborted due to mechanical failure (maintenance was ragged, overstrained, in those bad days). Fifteen B-17s went on to Germany, to bomb the ball-bearing factory which was the target. Two came home.

Mack was unholy glad that he hadn't received authorization to go on that particular mission; glad, and somehow ashamed, unhappy. What right had he to breathe, to eat, to drink, to sing, to touch, to pound his flesh into another's—the grease and slide of love, of lust, of affirmation—when they could not? Idiot question, he told himself, as he drank or sang, or thrashed his way toward dawn. Idiot question, as old as the measure of time and foolishness. Humanity. *"They hid and watched the wagons burn."* Went hunting Indians in the corn.

He left that question behind when he went on missions.

The first had been the easiest. Five hours only—a milk run to Amiens. (Six years before he had walked that battlefield with Irene.) Early dawn, and blades of grass a-flutter, as engines roared to life upon the hardstand.

The crew were reluctant and aloof, only grudgingly accepting. They didn't want a civilian along. He might panic, or just get in the way. And Mack knew he looked a fool: the supply sergeant had issued him a seat-pack parachute, the kind only pilots wore, which would be awkward and uncomfortable when he was riding in the nose. But the pilot, a guy named Rogers, was pleasant enough, and so were the others. Except for the tail gunner. He was a cocky young kid from Brooklyn named Marvin Sirus, with the build of a middleweight boxer, and he only half hid his amusement at the sight Mack presented. But Mack acted well. (Marv says now, "What else can I say? He was Mack. A little loud and brash. He told us about the time he'd put in with the RAF. About Gunnery School. He was Mack. I see him laughing now.") When they'd reached altitude, and jockeyed into formation, they drove on to France. Over the Channel they tested their guns. The P-47s and Spitfires assigned to give them cover turned back when they ran low on fuel, and the '17s went on alone. A drone of engines in the sky. When they were nearing the Initial Point, and the bombardier was busy with exotic knobs upon his bombsight, some German fighters came to tease them and annoy. To shoot them down. Mack took the right cheek gun, and he remembered the lessons he had learned. He didn't get a fighter that time, but he did get respect, and after that things were easier. Even though the missions were not.

It was on his third trip, I think to Wilhelmshaven, that he got—or didn't get—his Messerschmitt. (*"Then the swoop, and the fighter deflecting on in— / O swift like a fish, he is trout coming in, / Drawn taut by the line of his own tracer-bullets . . ."* And I, Mack thought, with his trigger depressed and his own tracers speeding—I wrote that before I *knew*. Before I'd ever flown as long or high as Bailey. I did get it right.) At debriefing, after checking with the crew, and with other crews as well, they gave him a "Probable Kill." He was proud of that. Almost as proud as of his words.

Rogers had gone down by then, and so had many more. That night Mack felt privileged to sing with others.

> *. . .but it makes me wet my pants,*
> *It's for the eager, not for me . . .*
> *I wanted wings till I got the goddamn things,*
> *Now I don't want them any more.*

But Mack still did.

It was on the fourth mission that he dropped those bombs. I think it may have been George Harkavey who was the bombardier that time—slim and tallish, older than most of the others, with the scarred pits of acne on his face, but handsome nonetheless, and possessed of wry charm and enormous vitality. I like to think that it was Hark, because he was so important in Mack's life in years to come. And in Irene's life as well. We came to love him. All of us. And so the Nazi fighters dropped away, after the '17s had passed the Initial Point of their bomb run and the flak began in earnest. Hark looked up from the bombsight and said, "Look, Mack, you've been plaguing me for days, and now's your chance to play boy bombardier. Find out how it feels. This is the salvo release lever. We're dropping on the leader. When you see his bombs go, just press it down." Mack waited, crouching, twenty-eight thousand feet up.

A lot of flak.

Little steel lever.

Mack waited; he saw a ship go down. Then he saw bombs falling, and he pressed. The aircraft bucked, relieved of death, and turned sharply to the left. Through Plexiglas he saw red flowers blooming far below, and knew that some were his. And some of the flowers blossomed further, into flame. Oh God, what if they had missed the railroad yard they'd aimed for—were killing innocent civilians, maybe children or young shop girls, instead?

He thought of the last time he'd been to London, and seen the aftermath of a German raid. Near no railroad yard or factory at all. Remembered bombed-out flats; the pathetic fragments of small, of noble, lives. He remembered a shop girl he had seen, lying on the pavement, as if she were asleep. Her blue skirt had been hiked up to her thighs, displaying the ugly, rationed cotton stockings which she wore. She'd had pretty legs. A pretty face. He looked behind him, and saw red fires burn. And then he shrugged, and looked at Hark, and turned his eyes away.

The last mission was not too nice at all, they lost a lot of people, and Mack was glad when, debriefed, cleaned up, and in fresh uniform, he got to the Club. Sitting at the bar alone he ordered a drink, humming a song he knew. A song about death, and the words echoed in his mind.

> We stand 'neath the looming rafters,
> The walls all around are bare,
> As they echo our peals of laughter,
> It seems that the Dead are there.
> So stand to your glasses steady,
> This world is a world of lies.
> Here's to those who are dead already,
> And here's to the next man who dies.

Mack stood and, in bitter emulation, he raised his glass carefully, so as not to spill, and toasted. And then he sat again, and toasted to his luck. No Vicksburg for him yet. He had lasted through his little dance with death. He was going back to the States: he had bills to pay, stories to write, a family to care for.

But he'd come back again. He felt he owed too much, to too many.

"Mack." It was the pilot of the crew he'd flown with that day. He sat down, and others clustered round. "Look. We spoke with the Group CO, Colonel Wilson. He checked with General Anderson, and with Iron Ass himself. They cleared this. They agreed. You've done five missions. If you were in the Service you'd be due for an Air Medal. They can't give you that. Shit, we aren't supposed to give you these, either." He held something clenched within his hand. "But you should have them. You earned them at Gunnery School. You earned them flying with us. With the guys here." He gestured with his shoulder. "And with the guys who aren't. Here. Wear them." Air Crew Member's wings. Mack saw their silver shimmer through his tears, as they pinned them on.

He had his wings, and Fred and Curt approved. He had his wings, and he was going back to the country he loved, alive and kicking. Kicking even with the left leg. Going back to Irene and the kids.

I see him there, so lean and taut and proud. He had his wings. For that one minute, on that glorious night, he thought that he had everything.

But, when they got him back to his quarters, staggering all the way—singing, "Bless them all, bless them all, bless them all, / As back to the barracks they crawl..."—when they got him settled on his bed, not only the room, but faces real and imagined, went spinning still around him. ("Otis is with you, and with you is Scott...") And he smelt the stench of Bailey, "Tom Quinn," and all the others. He smelt their sick-sweet stench, and smelt their virtue, and both those scents would linger with him always.

Still, one thought shone through all his wooziness: He had his wings.

13

That Will Be Glory, *Glory for Me*

I felt inglorious indeed. Just as my father had been gaining his wings, his spurs, I'd been losing mine. The previous spring I had ridden high. I had, not strutted, but strode—strode with ten-year-old confidence through my young life. I had bested the bully in the schoolyard, and that little girl had displayed to me her nipple. Spring, summer, and now into the fall, and so much had changed.

I could still remember, do still remember sharply, a day in California (all of us who are fortunate have had green-grass days which will never end). There were white clouds and a kindly sun and a strong breeze blowing, and the sky was blue. Not blear with filth because, although I was in Los Angeles, which smog would later soil, it was only 1943 and the world was still young. Or so it seemed to me. Young and clean, and filled with a golden promise which outshone the sun. Through streets, along avenues, also clean, I rode on my bicycle to a favorite spot of mine. A haunt, a refuge, where all the city seemed far away. Parked my bike and made my way through trees, old they seemed to me, and came out upon a hillside swept clean by the wind. Swept clean out of place and time. I felt private there, and gloriously alone. There must have been buildings far away, but I do not remember them. Only grass and the clouds, and the wind blowing past my ears. And a sense of peace; of power. I was free there, and felt that I owned the world.

I didn't feel that way again for years.

If the sense of freedom and of power I felt on that wondrous day re-

sulted from my being away from, free of, my father's dominion—a thought
which had never occurred to me until I came to write this sentence—I nonetheless depended upon him totally. He did not just dominate my world: he
had succeeded in making himself the center of it. And then he had gone
away. He had deserted me. The emptiness, the uncertainty, the *silence* which
he had left behind were all enormous. I think my mother sensed my feelings but, since she shared them—she had built her world on him at least
as much as I—she didn't know how to help me. She barely knew how to
help herself.

After Florida—*"If only your father were here!"*—I'd been shipped off to
a summer camp, where I managed to make myself thoroughly miserable.
Despite all distractions of a war to be reported, to be fought, Daddy wrote
to me regularly. Fondly. I looked forward to his letters but, after I'd received them, the strange, mechanical V-mail—the microfilm enlargements
demanded by logistics—made him seem more distant still.

That fall Mother, with help from Tim Coward, found an apartment in
New York. The house in Sarasota remained "home" to us, but it became a
vacation home for years. Otherwise it was rented infrequently, or left empty,
or occupied by friends to make sure that all was well. The apartment was
on the fifteenth floor (the fourteenth, actually, but the people of Manhattan
are superstitious). The building was at Ninety-sixth Street and Fifth Avenue; the windows looked out over Central Park and the view was magnificent. And the rent, in that long ago, rent-controlled time, was very modest.
In constant dollars, the money my parents paid for rent would serve only
for a one-room apartment today. But we had three bedrooms with two baths,
and a long, wide hallway lined with Kurz and Allison prints of the Civil
War. (I have one of them still—the *Fall of Petersburg*—and Yankee soldiers pour over the revetments even now. As I write I can see them charging, see them fall.) There were also a living room and dining room, both
large, a pantry and a kitchen, and two tiny maid's rooms with another, also
tiny, bath. That apartment seemed huge to me then; in retrospect it seems
large still.

I think I behaved all right at home, I know I was at ease with family
friends, but at school I fell apart—into uncertain little pieces—just as I
had at camp. I was noisy, foolishly assertive, in class. I gave a sad, un-
popular little girl a hotfoot, so that others might notice me; yet I retreated
from schoolyard challenge. Perhaps because it was only a game, not real,
I welcomed challenge when playing soccer: I rushed into combat ardently,
until both my knees were kicked or strained too hard, too often, and ruined
for years. (Later I would trudge over mountain paths in Latin America, or

run short distances while photographing riots there or demonstrations on Fifth Avenue, but one of my knees still can trick me now—my left knee, though I think that is due to happenstance, not sad empathy.) Soccer aside, and English and History aside, I'd lost all confidence.

I did make a few friends, but they were largely like me: bright, perhaps, but diffident when facing the world, and emotionally uncertain. At ten or eleven one is not prone to self-analysis. I didn't even know I hurt; I only knew that I was frightened. I had shriveled in Daddy's absence. Like a candle guttering in the dark. Like a parachute burning, crumpling as it fell, with my self suspended.

Daddy was home. His voice filled the rooms. Thanksgiving Day 1943, and I felt that I had much to be thankful for. It was cold outside, cold and bright. But inside the apartment it was warm. Part of that warmth came from the hissing radiators, and part from his proud, loud, and beaming presence.

He was home, and though I had grown in his absence he seemed taller than ever. He had told us—with a mixture of eagerness and delight, of pain and revulsion—a little about his experience in England.

About the wonder of flight at high altitude. "...so peaceful there, and beautiful. And one day we went to Amiens, Irene! Just think of it—twenty-eight thousand feet up over that battlefield, where you and I walked six years ago. To see the trenches."

"Oh, *Mack*." Irene didn't think of trenches; she thought of graves instead.

He had told us about "his" Messerschmitt, and by then it had become, in his own mind, "his" for certain. We were properly awed by that. And he had told us about the sadness of losing young men he had known. "We had two little dogs over there—Scotties. Sort of mascots. Their names were Whisky and Whiskers. One guy would look after them, usually, and they'd sleep under that guy's bed. Whisky and Whiskers moved four times while I was there, as their masters kept going down."

And he'd told us about Bailey. We had all read the poem, of course, when it was published in the *Post*, but he'd read it to us again. We all cried when he did so, and Daddy cried too. "You know, Layne-o, he was only nineteen and, when I told him that I had a daughter who was just four years younger, he asked if I had your picture. So I took out my little folder—the one I always carry with me—and he whistled and said, 'Oh, boy. She's a knockout! She looks so nice. I'd sure like to meet her when I get back to the States.'" And Daddy had whistled in emulation of Bailey's wolf-call, and Layne-o had cried some more.

Thanksgiving morning, and we could already smell the turkey. Layne and I were setting the table. Daddy came from an inspection tour of the kitchen and said, "Good God, Irene! You've got enough in there to feed an army. We'll be eating leftovers for days."

"Well, darling, I wanted this to be a very special day for all of us." And, smugly, "I've been saving ration stamps for months. And you always love leftovers."

He strolled over to the windows, craned his neck, and looked down on Fifth Avenue. People were walking, in cold, stiff parade, along the walk beside the Park. "There sure are a lot of uniforms down there. I'll bet there are a lot of lonely kids with nowhere to go—kids a long way from home, maybe from Iowa, who can't afford a good Thanksgiving dinner; who'll be lucky if they can get in at the USO. And who may be in a pretty rough place, this time next year. Or maybe no place at all. How about Timmy and I go out and pick some of them up to share with us?"

"Mack, we can't *really* serve an army." Mother shook her head indignantly, but there was a softness in her eyes, and her Irish mouth was only halfway firm.

"How about *two?*" He was smiling; he knew he'd won.

She went to him and kissed him. Then, turning: "Layne-o, set two more places."

"Timmy! Come on and get your coat." Layne's delighted smile, and Mother's look of bemused adoration, trailed us out the door. Brown grass and barren trees in the Park. Sharp, thin sunlight. A strong wind driving clouds across the sky, catching at our coats and teasing, chilling, up our sleeves. We took a cab down Fifth, until Daddy spotted two young privates whom he took a fancy to.

That Thanksgiving is one of the happiest I remember. One of the soldiers really was from Iowa, and Mack thought the other looked a bit like Bailey.

Mack went down by train to see Ben Hibbs, in his office in the vast mausoleum which was the *Saturday Evening Post*'s headquarters in Philadelphia. They talked of assignments and stories, past and future, and they gloried in the success of the poem about Bailey, which had triggered an enormous flow of mail. And then Ben Hibbs, a slight man and kind, and a giant in the world of magazines, stayed the conversation with a flick of his hand. He grinned a little. A tiny grin. "Mack, I've got a question."

"Yes, Ben."

"Why is it that your expense account is so much smaller than that of any other correspondent we have?"

Mack was a little embarrassed. In his mind he held the notion that it was somehow wicked to note down expenses for drinks, for food and housing and transportation, when he was fighting a war he would have attended anyway. "Hell, Ben, sometimes I forget to write things down, I guess. When I'm busy—and, by God, I've been busy—I'm not too good at keeping records."

"Well, I've never said this to a correspondent before, and I probably never will again—but you've been screwing yourself. Here. I had them make out a check for an extra thousand dollars."

Mack was pleased by that. He glowed for days. He could use the money but, more important, it meant that he was not thought to be a cheat, like his father. Like his father who was now in Sing Sing prison. Imprisoned for fraud. Mack had cheated nobody, except possibly himself.

How we kids had laughed when he told us about that imprisonment. How he had laughed. And how, inside, he had suffered hurt (*he ran on again, thinking about fathers*), and he had cried.

But nobody, not Ben Hibbs, nor Bailey, nor any other, would ever call him cheat or liar.

Sometimes, after lunch or dinner, Daddy would put down his napkin, push back his chair, and sigh in exaggeration of real pleasure. He'd glance at us and then grin at Mother. "Vinnie, that was a *damned* good meal." We children would giggle, and Mother would respond to the compliment with a strained half-smile. Recently we had seen *Life with Father* on Broadway, and Daddy had identified completely with the part of Clarence Day, Sr., the Father of the title. Father's loud assertiveness, his apparently serene conviction that he knew everything he needed to know and that he was always right, his domination in the household and his crusty tenderness, even his self-importance: all these delighted Daddy immensely. He played the role of Father whenever he thought to do so, and that was often. Which would have been fine with Mother, except that he had also decided that Mother—who did indeed look a bit like the actress who had played the part when we saw the show—was the incarnation of Father's wife, Vinnie. Vinnie was careless about keeping financial records and uncomfortable with numbers, and so was Mother. Vinnie was vague and sometimes impractical, but charming and beautiful and very long-suffering; Daddy felt that Mother shared all those qualities too. And, Daddy said, Mother had been often known to go out of Saks or Bonwit's and march briskly off in the wrong direction, and he was certain that Vinnie would have done the same.

For years, Daddy was Father and Mother was Vinnie in family jest. Daddy had made that jest in all fondness (unaware of condescension, feeding his ego as he mocked it), but Mother didn't always enjoy it.

Nor did she enjoy it when, at lunch one day, coming out of some strange reverie, I announced that I could imagine Mother dying, but that I couldn't picture Daddy ever doing so at all. That made Daddy laugh. He roared with pride and pleasure. But Mother was upset and her eyes leaked tears until, contrite, ashamed, and finally aware of what I'd blurted out, I found some way to make a stumbling amends.

"Hail, Columbia, happy land! / Hail, ye heroes, heav'n-born band..." Mack sang and sipped as he sat in his drawing room on the *Twentieth Century Limited*, bound for Chicago. Chicago, and then Des Moines and Webster City. Heading home. Almost two years before he'd been sitting in a day coach in Pennsylvania Station, sweating out the fate of *Gentle Annie*, and desperately searching out an idea for a novelette. ...*maybe something about a kid from a town like Webster City, who was drafted. No. Volunteered, that was it. The kid would volunteer.* Despite all the Hollywood excitement of that day and night, the idea had clung to him, or he to it. Later, in the spring, in between screenwriting chores, he had written *Happy Land*, a short novel or long novelette about an Iowa boy who had enlisted in the Navy and been killed in combat, and about his family's hurt, and eventual acceptance of their loss. It was not a justification of the young man's death— Mack was not such a fool as that; rather, it was a celebration of the land for which the boy had risked and died. America, as Mack saw or dreamed it.

The *Saturday Evening Post* had featured the story in late November of '42, Coward-McCann had published it the following January, 20th Century– Fox had bought the movie rights, and the Office of War Information had issued translations in over ten foreign languages—from Italian to Indonesian—as propaganda for the American Way of Life.

Mack was especially pleased with that last, pleased and proud, though it brought no extra money. His words were being read by people all over the world—helping to fight the enemies he loathed, helping to protect the land, the dream, he loved.

"Hail, Columbia, happy land..." And, by God, it was a happy land. And beautiful. It was dark outside the train windows; only occasional lights of scattered farmhouses flickered by, and the beckoning warmth of small villages, and, more rarely, the harsher glow of larger towns. But Mack felt gifted with an inner vision born of understanding. During the past month or two he had been visiting the homes of the dead. The dead or missing. He'd been inside half a dozen such homes, ranging from farmhouse to urban apartment, from easy quarters to mean. He had not gone visiting out of any sick curiosity, nor any foolish wish to amend death or loss. He had gone out of curiosity both journalistic and sentimental: a need to understand better the roots of men he'd known briefly, known and loved, and now could know no more. He'd also gone because he felt he owed a debt to those he had outlived. ("This is how he behaved, and I did like him so. He had a funny way of saying...")

He had dreamed to ease, or deaden, death.

He had brought happy recollection, even laughter, to homes which suffered emptiness. And had been rewarded in return. The virtues, gentle or hearty, which he had encountered among the folks he met—even the occasional taint of smallness or of evil, for he knew well that Americans were human, and susceptible of vice—all combined to confirm him in the image he had painted through the years. Years of hurt and striving; years of loss and glorious fulfillment. And that image he had confected, he had spun, from threads of legend and of truth. That image was, to him, America. Webster City, etched large upon his mind.

America was worth living for—or dying for, as Rusty had in *Happy Land*. As Bailey had, and others. America, his America, would last in all simplicity; because of love, in spite of loss. And now Mack was on his way to see the premiere of the movie in Des Moines. It was good of the producers—it might be good publicity, but it was also *good*—to schedule the premiere there. Good of them to attend the dinner in Webster City the following evening.

By God, he was showing the folks at home.

And here he was, going to see a movie of his made by 20th Century–Fox, and riding the *Twentieth Century Limited*. Twentieth century. A damned good century in which to be alive. He stared at lamplight flickering through the dark, and detected warmth and kindness in the homes from which it came.

"Hail, Columbia..." It was a happy land.

*   *   *

During that summer, the summer of '44, our house in Florida, on Siesta Key, became a combination Bachelor Officers' Quarters, open bar, and beach resort for veterans of the 305th. George Harkavey and a few others who had finished their twenty-five missions had been reassigned to the Army air base at Sebring, less than a hundred miles away, to instruct yet other young men in the niceties of flying combat. On weekends the men from Chelveston would fill the house with the sound of their laughter, decorate the beach with the sight of their women. An eagerness of tan skin and admiring eyes. ("Oh who would not sleep with the brave?") Mack and Irene presided—kindly, grateful hosts—while we kids looked on in awe and wonder. And there was a part of Mack, a part detached from song and booze and bawdry, which looked on too. Also wondering.

These boys—no, make that men, young men—had been to a wicked place. They all bore scars from the fires which had scorched them, though only some were visible to the civilian eye. He wondered what would happen to these, who had left so many behind, now that they were home. Surrounded by folks who could not understand. Hell, even Irene sometimes looked at them funny. And at him.

In August Mack hitched a ride with George Harkavey's crew—a training mission out to Lockbourne Field in Ohio. It was fun being in a '17 again, but he had another reason for the flight. Some senior officers from the Eighth Air Force were also home, assigned to the Third Air Force—the training command—and they had recruited Mack to give orientation lectures for crews bound overseas. (*"Did I get it right?"* He had, and the Air Force knew it.)

When they landed at Lockbourne a message awaited. Hollywood had been trying to reach him. Donald Friede.

"Mack?"

"Yes, Donald."

"Sam Goldwyn wants you to write a screen treatment for him."

"No! God damn it, Donald, I've got to get back to the war."

"Now calm down, kid. Calm down. He wants a story about veterans. About guys coming home. He wants you to do it, thinks only you can do it right, but if you don't get out here right away he'll give it to someone else."

Mack gave his lectures, and then, armed with his AGO—his Army identity card—he hitched rides in aircraft headed west. Hitched rides, rode trains and buses. Three days later he and Donald had reached agreement with Samuel Goldwyn.

There were parties, there were "babes," and Mack worked his head

off. Tried and tried, but nothing came out right. Nothing rang true. School
was starting, and Irene had taken us back to New York. Mack thought he
might work better there, with his family around, and so he came east. Commercial transport was governed by "priority"; he hitchhiked once again,
using his AGO.

Wherever and whenever he could, during those months and years, he
recited the poem about Bailey to anyone who would listen. Who would listen and would *know*. To radio audiences in their tens of thousands; to an
audience of one, in some tired aircraft aching through the night. And people always loved it. It was on that trip that the notion came to him. The
story of these men come home was a noble one. It demanded special han-
dling. Why not tell the whole story in verse, just as he had done with Bailey?
It was on that trip, on September 17, that he wrote the first lines of the
book.

> *Fred Derry, twenty-one, and killer of a hundred men,*
> *Walked on the width of Welburn Field. The cargo ship*
> *Had set him down in noontime haze of early spring.*
> *He smelled the onion farms:*
> *He heard the trucks in Highway 52,*
> *He saw the signboards, and the ugliness*
> *That was a beauty he had dreamed.*
>
> *Fred Derry, green of eye, with lids pale-washed in pink*
> *(The way the eyes of bombardiers and gunners grow)...*

He looked over the original scribbled words, and made a few changes.
Then he nodded in self-approval. *That* was the way to do it. That was the
way to honor them: men, and women too, from hovels and from mansions,
and from modest, comfortable homes of the middle class, which, now that
the depression was over, were spreading across the land and which would,
in peacetime to come, spread farther still. Like clover spreading in an empty
pasture, waiting to nurture those who, in time, would come to graze and
thrive.

So he had Fred Derry, ex–soda jerk, ex-bombardier—with the Eighth
Air Force, of course—coming back to a future he had bought with blood
and risk. Coming back all unprepared to a hovel he no longer belonged in,
did not deserve. Mack needed an older voice, as well, to provide experience, a smidgen of wisdom. Let him come from the mansion, or perhaps a
fancy apartment. Returning to an easy life, to comfort, after squalor, after

horror. Make him a *banker*, by God, but also a human being. A man whom war had gentled, softened, even as it toughened him. Mack thought of a train, rattling across the state of Iowa, and tears of gratitude, and an envelope from "your friends at the bank." His banker would be like that, the son of bankers who had been like that. Who based their loans on trust, who were willing to invest in human striving because they were willing to believe in—give credit to—honor. (Ah, Adam McKinlay! It was Elton King, wasn't it, who had said, "I'd be willing to advance Adam McKinlay any sum of money, just on the strength of his word.") And the banker, *his* banker, would get into trouble with his bosses—typical of the petty, cautious minds, the scrawny souls, of folks who seemed to run banks nowadays. He'd make a loan to some returning vet, a loan based on faith and gratitude, with only human virtue, human striving, as collateral—and there would be a row. The guy would quit his job, and turn to cultivating things, living things—to cultivating life instead of money. And there'd have to be a kid from an ordinary home, very dull and middle class, and the kid would have been wounded. Badly wounded. And he'd have a girl, some young babe with guts, who'd help him back to life. To what folks who hadn't been to war called life. Called normality.

So he had his people, and he'd build his story, and he'd tell it all in verse.

He built, he told the story, all through the fall. First in New York—I remember the rumble of his voice as he dictated behind closed doors—and then, with May Greenwell in the apartment to keep an eye on Layne and me, in Baja California with Irene, Dick and Tye Whiteman (friends from Iowa days, from childhood), and a secretary stolen from Sam Goldwyn. And, it seemed to Irene, with half the Mexican navy to fill the nights with tequila and with song. But, even so, Mack got the story down. He got it done.

> *They looked, they saw an angry past*
> *Commingled with the future in a storm.*
> *Oh, they would feel the lightning part their hair,*
> *And hear the thunder deafen them once more.*
> *A war? Perhaps. Or maybe....*
>
> *But savage too the weather of a peace—*
> *When glare exposes class and race*
> *With bludgeon lifted for a blow—*
> *When staring flash reveals a blackened face*
> *As monster to the babies in their beds,*

And to the blacks reveals a monster pale.
When Star of David is a curse, a jeer,
A lodestone and a sacrament in one.
When grasping claw goes round a neck
And strangles song before the singer sings—
When jealousy is hail to sting your eyes,
And love is hurricane to blow the lilacs down.

. . .

A keen voice yelled, "Attention!" in the sky—
For, mounting out of prairie rim
And sunset glare,
The wild-west clouds were galloping again.

He needed a title. He thought of love, of risk and longing. He remembered Sunday evenings long ago, with the late sun still burnishing the polished floor at home, and Grandpa McKinlay calling down the stairs. "Effie, play the Glory Song." He saw his mother's hands upon piano keys, their tone, their tune, came resounding out of memory, and he remembered words as well: "When all my labors and trials are o'er / And I am safe on that beautiful shore.../ Oh that will be / Glory for me!"

That was it! *Glory for Me.*

Sam Goldwyn said, "Mack! It's a wonderful story. A terrible title. Wouldn't sell any tickets. But a wonderful story. But what do I do with it? I ask for, I pay for, a screen treatment, and what do I get? Poetry! I get poetry. You owe me. At least do me the favor of writing the screenplay. A real screenplay."

Irene returned to the East and Mack remained in Hollywood, working on a shooting script. It was good, he thought, damned good. And—by the time he had it two-thirds done—Frances Goldwyn, Samuel's adviser and confidante as well as wife, swore it was the best screenplay she'd ever read. But it was February 1945, and in Europe the clock of war was running down. It wasn't right that he should be safe at home, working on some damn fool script—however fine it was—and lunching at Chasen's or the Brown Derby, his ass ensconced on the softest leather. Not when, overseas, young men still rode the skies with *their* asses firmly placed on the harsh discomfort of their flak jackets, to protect their balls from flak.

It wasn't right at all. He had to go back.

Sam Goldwyn screamed. "You can't do this to me!"

"The hell I can't, Mr. Goldwyn." Mack felt filled with military and patriotic virtue and, anyway, Sam Goldwyn was impossible to work for. Always interfering; always wanting a rewrite. Everyone in the business agreed on that. "I did what you hired me for, and I'm not under contract. You've got your story about the vets. Get somebody else, maybe Bobby Sherwood, to do the screenplay. I've *got* to go back, before it's too late."

"Mack, don't be childish. You've done your part. Let the young men fight the war. Stay here. Write good things and make money. I'll tell you—I've been planning to talk to you about this anyway—I will make you a deal. I like what you've been doing, I like the other things you've done. A contract, Mack. I offer you a contract. A seven-year contract. Two thousand a week for seven years! And you want to go play soldier?"

Mack smiled. His body suddenly felt hot and tense; he felt the same surge of adrenalin he'd experienced when fighters had come boring in, or when they'd passed the Initial Point on their way to the target. Two thousand a week to be Goldwyn's slave?

Almost thirteen thousand a week in 1987 dollars.

He smiled, and then he laughed. He was behind on the phone bill back home, and he owed a little rent, but he had a war to go to, and books to write. "Sorry, Mr. Goldwyn." Goldwyn was still sputtering when Mack left the office.

Out in the parking lot laughter came anew. He remembered an evening back in New York, before the war, in the house on Eighty-seventh Street. Steve Benét and Sherwood Anderson had been there, and some others. They had been playing "What If?" and one particular "What If?" had stirred scorn and anger. "What if you were writing the Great American Novel, or Play, or Poem, and you were behind in the rent, and one of the kids needed an operation, and your wife was pregnant and didn't want an abortion, and another kid needed to go to a special school—and Hollywood summoned you? Offered a nice fat contract?" Steve and the others had maintained that they'd opt for art, and had been shocked, outraged, when Mack had said that of course Irene and the kids—domestic obligation—came first. They'd called him a Philistine, a sell-out. He wondered what they'd call him now.

Would they understand, would they approve, or would they call him a damn fool? A war lover?

He shook his head and, laughing still, he went to the Brown Derby. For drinks, for lunch, for a final taste of Hollywood luxury. And while he was lunching—amid all the fawning and the glitter—he sent his mind wandering. Before he went back to war he needed to write a short story or two, to take care of the phone bill, and the rent.

February still, or early March. Daddy was pacing up and down the living room in our apartment on Fifth Avenue—game leg, fife, and all, playing the "Garry Owen."

Layne-o thrilled as she listened, but also she thought of Bailey, of Rogers, and of others he had mentioned. "Daddy, do you really have to go?"

"Of course I do! There are kids getting killed, while I stay here safe and comfortable, and that isn't right." He stood there, tall and fierce and gay. "And maybe I'll get lucky over there." He played a few more bars of music, then put down the fife and mused a moment. "You know, Layne-o, I kind of hope I don't come back."

"Daddy!"

"Well, hell, I'd make a lousy old man."

The future, seeming cold and comfortless, came and rang the buzzer beside our door. April twelfth, and Layne and I were early home from school, or else still on Easter vacation. A nasty boy lived a few floors below us. He was perhaps two years younger than Layne, two years older than I. His people were conservative politically; also he liked to brag about the cleverness his older brother had displayed in getting assigned to the civilian Air Transport Service and thus avoiding the perils of flying combat. The future, embodied in such nastiness, such triviality, came to press the buzzer by our door.

The future smiled a foolish smile. "I thought you'd like to know that your precious President is dead. I just heard it on the radio."

We were devastated. Cast adrift; at sea. Our moorings all destroyed. Every cliché of loss applied. I had been less than five weeks old when The President, Franklin Roosevelt, was first elected. He had been President all my life, and I could not conceive of another in his place.

Layne-o cried, and Mother cried, and I went pacing. I remembered Daddy telling me of our driving south, in early November 1936: we had come upon torchlight parades in small towns, and people singing in the night, because The President had won again. And now the future had come to rub my face into its dirt, and I could not fathom it.

There was mourning too at Chelveston that day. When I was five weeks old many there had been six years old, or eight, or twelve. And Mack, well, he'd been older, perhaps had loved him more. He remembered a glorious Sunday afternoon when he and Irene had been invited to Hyde Park.

Later he would write a song, with music by Harry Rosenthal, which

Josh White used to sing. ("I'm dreaming of a man we knew, / He loved us all, we loved him too...") But that afternoon at Chelveston there was no song, only sorrow.

Usually, when the flag was raised or lowered, folks would hide away. Go scurrying for temporary haven, in order to avoid the tired ritual of attention and salute. But not this day. This sad day, at this odd hour, as word of loss spread wide the flagpole became a magnet. People, in ones and twos and groups, were drawn from duty and from quarters all across the base. Bodies rigid, right arms angled stiff for edge of hand to touch the visor or the brow, they stood still and grim and lost as the flag was lowered and then raised again. And lowered to half-mast.

Mack thought that the world he knew, the solid, homely land he loved, was slipping away from him. Drifting into the past.

The air war was different in that spring of '45. When the '17s revved and taxied in the early mornings they no longer droned of death. They chanted loud of victory instead. The German fighter defenses were a shambles, compared to the bad, mean days in '43. The flak was still there, but in only half its former nastiness—diminishing, and fading fast. (No longer did bombardiers complain of "cloud cover" over the target, unless the "clouds" were clouds indeed.) Mack had flown two more missions with the 305th, but really just for old times' sake. There was nothing new to learn.

He went to France, and flew a few missions with the B-26s of the Ninth Air Force. Still the V-2s were striking hard at London—the dead still splattered on the streets—and he went back and hunted stories there. (He was a correspondent for *Esquire* now. The *Post* was getting weary of the war.) There was a combat pilot at Chelveston who had finished up his tour of duty—thirty-five missions, now that things were easier—but who still managed to hang around, painting pictures. Pictures of air combat. His name was Francis H. Beaugureau, and they called him Beaugy, and he was good. He'd been a painter in civilian life; he was a painter now. But to most of the brass he was just another pilot. They thought he should go home, as an instructor.

Mack liked Beaugy, and was impressed, moved, by what he was doing. The '17s and fighters, the watercolor contrails and painted bursts of flak, came alive as he drew on skill and memory.

Fred Anderson had his second star by now, and was working for General Carl "Tooey" Spaatz, with the new U.S. Strategic Air Force, Europe, headquartered in France. Mack went to Fred, and Fred took Mack and

Beaugy to see Tooey Spaatz. Captain Francis H. Beaugureau showed his paintings to General Spaatz, and became an official Combat Artist that very night.

Tooey had work for Mack as well. The Air Force (still the *Army* Air Force, but with very much a mind of its own, and looking toward the future) was sending in a team following on the heels, hurrying in the tank tracks of the ground forces then racing into Germany, to survey the damage, to factories and rail and road junctions, which strategic bombing had achieved. Would Mack go with them to help write their report?

It was a week later that they reached Buchenwald, the day after the camp had been liberated, and found damage not caused by bombs.

Mack had been fascinated by tales of Andersonville Prison, and of the Union soldiers who had festered there, ever since he was a boy. Ever since he'd worked on *Arouse and Beware,* a novel about escaped prisoners of war, he had teased himself with the thought that a Civil War novel—*the* Civil War novel—could be written, centered on the horror that was Andersonville. Horror he had only read of.

Now he encountered horror with his own eyes, slipped as he walked in it, smelt it with his nose.

April 24, 1945

Dear Irene—

I hope you can read this. The ribbon is very faint, and some of the letters are misplaced on this queer German typewriter (made in Leipzig, not very far from here). If anyone ever tells you again that the atrocity stories are a lot of hysterical propaganda, just tell them politely to shut their big traps. I am sitting here in some damn German family's upstairs sitting room, with horrible oil portraits of Grossmutter and Grossvater staring stupidly from the wall: there is the smell of a good dinner being gekuchen, but I can hardly smell it— the smell of death is too persistent in my nostrils... the smell of the prison camp some five miles or so away—the sour-sweetish odor of rotten bodies, of pallid dead skin, of burnt bones and flesh—the perfume of burning, typhus-ridden rags and shoes, the latrines oozing with their rich concentrated filth, the old and new pools of vomit covering the ground. There are nineteen thousand prisoners still in the camp—nowhere else for them to go until a transportation path is opened through the battle-lines, for many of them are Russians, Czechs, Poles and Jugo-slavs. They are being moderately-well fed for the first time in months and in years, but their poor wizened stomachs can't take it—they keep vomiting up the stuff they eat. And the people who come to the camp—a lot of them vomit, too.

We stood and stared at the piles of dead—scores of them, heaps, trucks laden with the newly-dead who could not survive the shock of liberty and salvation. We poked about among great stacks of half-consumed human bones, and saw bodies still half-burnt in the none-too-efficient cremation furnaces (the good Germans ran short of coke recently: ja, ja, they have shortages over here too). They looked like broken, shriveled black wienies that someone had forgotten and left on the grill too long.

But worst of all, to me, was the children's quarters—both in the *hospital* (smile when you say that, pard) and in the regular children's quarters. The dear Teutons—think how they have enriched our language: they gave us the word *kindergarten*. A true child's garden, was this. "This section for children from 5 to 15." Boys, all of them—just boys in this camp— I kept imagining Timmy there. It was not too delightful, as you might say, but I imagined it. The marks of the children's last meal could be seen, if you poked around among wooden tables and filthy old comforters long enough. And good enough for them, I daresay: potato peelings, all dried and curly now—*gut* vegetable for *der kinder, ja?*—and square biscuits which were part of the dog food for the Dobermans and Shepherds of the SS guards. The kids had tried to cook those thick, brown-bone-meal crackers. And in the middle of the mess was an egg-shell. Whence came that egg? From the Easter bunny, without a doubt.

I saw a lot of pulverized cities today—smashed, ruined, pounded to extinction. I wish to God that all of Germany was laid in such ruins.

I can't write more now. Good night, baby and children. Bless you all. See you soon, I hope.

Mack

Sealing that letter he thought of the Germans. Goddamn Germans! But he knew that inhumanity was not limited in such fashion. America had produced its own horrors during the Civil War. Not such intended, concentrated evil, on such a grand scale; far smaller, not nearly as horrendous, but still—emaciated bodies, and vomit on the ground. People eating vomit. Eating shit. He thought of Johnson's Island and Camp Douglas in the North, of Belle Isle and Andersonville in the South.

He thought of Andersonville.

We had to throw trash into the garbage can in the kitchen, for the waste-baskets were dedicated to other use. Ever since we'd heard the news, over a week before, that some strange secret weapon—an "Atomic Bomb," whatever that was—had been dropped on Hiroshima, and that Japan would likely soon surrender, we had been shredding newspapers even as we read them. Making confetti. Homemade confetti which we then stored, in eager hope of celebration, in those wastebaskets.

We had no notion of the consequence of the power loosed over Hiroshima and Nagasaki. It would be months, be years, before we understood that August 6, 1945, had brought change more mighty than the death of any President could. That the world had lurched into a future more frightening than our imagination might conceive. (Like so many of his generation, Mack never did fully understand that watershed.) We only knew that many had died, and many, many more had been saved. And we had special interest in such salvation, because our father-husband had been scheduled to go with Beaugy to record the war in the Pacific, for the Air Force.

Now they need not go. The news had come. It was final. It was peace.

I think it was early afternoon when the word finally came. Still I see my mother (this time I can see her face), slim and trim and so very pretty, sunlight glinting in her red-gold hair; she is aflame with, almost consumed by, joy. She believes, she *knows*, that she will not lose Mack now. Not ever. She is sitting by an open window, on the radiator cover, seizing hand-fuls of confetti to thrust upon the wind. Layne and I are busy also, and the fine shreds of paper drift from our fingers. Dad—for so he has now become; my thirteenth birthday is coming near—is standing in the room, smiling benevolently, broadly, grandly. At first he is only tolerant of our paper-madness, but soon he puts aside his drink and joins us. We look out the windows to see our paper flowing on the wind, and are amazed, delighted. All down Fifth Avenue, and across the Park on Central Park West, there are flurries, squalls, exultations of paper. Horns are blowing in the streets, and we are laughing, crying.

Dad has put Beethoven's Ninth Symphony on the Magnavox. (Germany is known for more than evil.)

That night we went to Yorktown, for further celebration at Eberhardt's Cafe Grinzing on Eighty-sixth Street. I had been gifted with a Boy Scout bugle which I had never learned to use, but I blew it loudly from the taxi's window as we went on our way. And still car horns were honking. At the Grinzing Gypsy violins were at work, alternating with the *oompah, oompah* of the band. (Germany is known for more than evil.) We ate, and we sang. "Bless Them All." "You'll Never Mind." "Roll Me Over in the Clover." Veterans brought their relief, their pride, and their girls to the table, and joined our song. Dad got drunk, but he was still in command of his words, and none sang louder, none seemed happier, than he.

Later, an angry sorrow came to etch his face, and that I thought I understood. He was grieving for people he had known, and those he hadn't known; he was grieving for the entire world's great loss.

But now I think that he was also mourning a private loss, which even today I cannot name.

Other losses, other bruisings, were in store for him, in the winter coming on. *Glory for Me* was published (dedicated to George I. Harkavey) and—while there was some praise for a true and tender, an important story—most critics savaged it. (Orville Prescott, in the *Times*, was especially negative, and Mack swore he'd punch him in the nose if ever he encountered him.) Mr. Kantor, they said, should stick to prose. Tim Coward snarled in his nasal voice, "If, instead of poetry, you'd written the same story in good, masculine prose, we'd have had a best-seller!"

Also, Mack didn't like the title Samuel Goldwyn had picked for the movie version any more than Goldwyn had liked *his* title. After a door-to-door survey—"Which of the following picture titles would you most like to see?"—the film was called *The Best Years of Our Lives*.

Mack thought that was silly. *Worst Years* would have been more like it.

The movie itself he thought was wonderful. Robert Sherwood *had* done the final screenplay, and Mack thought that, though they'd cut out most of his fulminations about banking, the story was true to his in both character and event. Willy Wyler had done a fine job of directing—he'd been overseas, he knew a bit about the war—and Freddie March and Myrna Loy and Dana Andrews were wonderful. But, damn it, Sam Goldwyn had a long memory, and he hadn't liked Mack's desertion. His rejection of that contract. When the screen credits rolled they said that the film was based on *a* book by MacKinlay Kantor. There was no mention, in any of the publicity, of *Glory for Me*.

That didn't help sales of the book, and Goldwyn hadn't intended it to. Still, he had other books to write, and he was alive, and so were others whom he loved. On December 29, he and Irene gave a party for their New York friends—the Cowards, the Sanderses, and a bunch of others—and, most especially, for men from the 305th. There were quite a few in or near the city, and Mack had made a point of tracking them down. Perhaps a dozen were there, with their women. Each touching the other, to remind themselves that they were still alive.

There was food, and drink in plenty, and a photographer to commemorate the celebration, and a piano player from Asti's—one of Mack's favorite restaurants. Strong voices rose loud in song. The voices of survivors. Layne-o was there of course, with some young kid, and she was becoming a woman now. She looked so very pretty. And Irene was as beautiful, and looked almost as young, as she had been the day they first met. *"Are you looking for the Graeme Players?"* And Timmy was circulating, bug-eyed in the presence of the uniforms, and the confident masculinity they dressed and honored. The confidence owned by those come back from death.

"Come back from death." The piano player was taking a break; Mack finished his drink and picked up his guitar.

A chorus of voices. "Oh, Mack! Please sing."

"No, we'll all sing." Strumming the guitar, and waiting for silence.

This is my story, this is my song . . .

(Eva used to sing that hymn, but not this way.)

> *I've been in this Air Force too fucking long . . .*
> *I wanted wings till I got the goddamn things . . .*
> *You'll never mi-i-ind, you'll never mi-i-ind . . .*

And other songs after those. Other songs and other drinks. Bailey, and "Tom Quinn", and all their fellow shades stared from the edges of the room. The pianist was back at work. Mack shook his head, and lost himself in a trance. Reciting in his head a little passage from *Glory for Me*. Ah, some Glory that had brought him. Fuck Goldwyn. But. . .

> *When you come out of War to quiet streets*
> *You lug your War along with you.*
> *You walk a snail-path. On your back you carry it—*
> *A scaly load that makes your shoulders raw;*
> *And not a hand can ever lift the shell*

That cuts your hide. You only wear it off yourself—
Look up one day, and vaguely see it gone.

You do not see yourself in malformation.
The men and girls who have no shells
Of War upon their backs—You count them well deformed.
You recognize the other snails by eyes or ribbons;
You speak your perfect language to their ears,
And they to yours. You look with solemn eye
On those without a shell. You do not scorn,
You do not hate, you do not love them for it.
You only say, "They have no shell."

With other snails you crawl the quiet street
And wonder why you're there,
And think of folks who aren't.
You polish up your shell for pride
Until you tire of it.
And one day it is gone if you are wise.

With the clarity of alcoholic tunnel vision he looked around the room. Tim Coward? He'd never worn a shell. Too young for the last war; too old for this. Poor Timmy. Always telling him not to risk his ass. Mack laughed. Now, tough, gentle Sid Lovitt—with seventy-five missions, more than any other navigator in the Eighth Air Force, he was still wearing his shell, and it was shining bright. George Harkavey—Hark—laughing over there with some pretty babe? He was losing his. He was, by God, molting! And young Marv Sirus, not long back from prison camp, and minus his left arm? That was pretty rough, especially for a kid who'd boxed in the Golden Gloves. But Marv would handle that just fine, and Mack would help him if he could. He wondered if Marvin had ever worn a shell at all. Small sign of it now.

Mack Kantor, who had written such wise words for others, reached up behind his shoulder blades to touch his own shell. It was still there, and he found a certain glory in the thought.

14

A Game of Cards

I have a stack of notes on my work table. Notes I've made to myself, at odd moments of the day or late at night.

I have notes stacked upon the table. Notes stamped upon my mind. I pick up a stack—a deck—of notes and I shuffle. And I deal.

I was only fourteen, and not tall for my age at all. I paused in the lee of our building and lit an illicit cigarette, to make myself feel older, and then... *Kantor steps out into the wind as he throws his match away. He holds the cigarette in his mouth at a jaunty angle, but his lips are set in a firm, grim line, and there is a hint of sadness in his eyes. Close-up shot. He is considering the harshness of existence in a difficult, dangerous world. But then he shrugs and smiles a wry smile, the cigarette held more jauntily than ever. Wide shot. Kantor turns, he has made his decision and, as the camera dollies backward, he strides with increasing determination toward the corner, with the wild wind tossing his hair and catching at his coat as he goes.* Kantor caught a bus, and went to the movies.

It sometimes seems to me that, in those years, I existed only in scenario. That I preferred to view the world, and myself, only from the outside, rather than from inside my head, where I belonged. And when I did penetrate those threatening caverns in my mind, I rarely knew that I was there.

*   *   *

Dad had a gun. Of course in Florida we had guns. Lots of them. There was a 30-30 rifle, Dr. Von Krog's Winchester repeater, and my own little single-shot .22, which I'd been given on my eighth birthday. Also there were revolvers: Dad's .44 Special, Mother's dainty .22-.32 (for the bedside table drawer, when Dad wasn't there), and my special pride and delight—a .22 Colt Woodsman Automatic, which Dad had presented on my twelfth birthday. ("Here, Timmy, you can handle this now.") And another automatic, a P-38, which Dad had "liberated" in Germany. But that was on the wild west coast of Florida. In our New York apartment there'd been no gun at all. But now there was.

A .38 Police Special, for Dad was riding with the cops. Doing research.

He was writing a book about the life of policemen in the city—a novel called *Signal Thirty-Two*. (I'd hear that harsh cry come over the radio years later, when *I* was riding with the cops. It meant "Assist Patrolman!" It meant "All Cars." It meant "Now.") He was the first writer, other than a working journalist, ever to be allowed to ride and work with the police on a daily basis, and he was proud of that. Just as he was proud of the friends he'd made "downtown," among the senior officers, and of friends he'd made among the working policemen with whom he rode, and limped up tenement stairs, and responded to the radio's crackling commands. He was also proud of the special identification and the gun permit he'd been issued, and of the gun he wore. He wore it all the time. "Cops do, and so should I," he said. Mother cut and hemmed little slits in his shirts so that, when he was wearing a jacket, the strap of the shoulder holster wouldn't show.

My father had a gun.

He rode with men of the Twenty-Third Precinct—regularly sometimes; intermittently, when he was at work on other projects—for almost two years. Long after he had any need to; long after he'd finished *Signal Thirty-Two*. Because he prized the risks he shared with his friends, and cherished their respect. Two of those friendships would last his lifetime.

At some point during those months I wrote a story for my English class at school. A very long story, it seemed to me—almost two pages typewritten. Double-spaced. It was called "The Gun." It was about a boy my own age whose father had given him a gun as a present. A Colt Woodsman. The boy was very proud of the gun his father gave him. He lived on an island much like Siesta Key, and one day he took his gun and went in a small outboard boat to an automatic lighthouse not far away. He climbed the ladder on the steel tower and, from its platform, he watched for stingrays swimming through the clear, shallow water below. He shot several, but then, while aiming at another, he tripped over a steel bar and shot himself instead. He fell into the water and drowned. "And the gun which he had loved, and which had killed him, lay at his side." I was very proud of that story.

My teacher gave me an A-minus, and a very odd look. It wasn't until years later, when I knew more about "guns," and about phallic imagery as well, that I realized what I'd written.

But at the time I wrote that story, I'd been determined to realize as little as I could.

Some nights George Harkavey stayed over at our apartment, and I was pleased that he did. He often stayed when Dad was away, and I always welcomed his presence. He'd had a long war. He had initially enlisted in the old U.S. Cavalry, back in early '41, before he went on to ride wild horses in the sky. Perhaps he still carried scale upon his back; certainly his soul was filled with irony. He approached life with a wry and wary eagerness, but that eagerness was real and expressed in a jauntiness which charmed. He had too many of the casual human graces to be happy as the loan officer he was, or the senior banker he became. I do not think that he wished to take the world seriously, but he took me—with all my adolescent humors—seriously indeed, and I valued that.

Often he'd stay up late, talking with Mother, after I'd gone to bed. (Layne-o was away at college.) In the morning I'd wake up and find him asleep on the other bed in my room. He would wake, and so would Mother in her room, and the three of us would breakfast. And would laugh.

But there were a few times when I awoke in the dark hours, long past midnight, not to the sound of music and conversation in the living room but to silence, and I'd turn to see Hark's bed and it was empty. I'd lie there sleepily, wondering—could Mother and Hark *possibly* be...? Impossible! Ridiculous. I'd dismiss the rest of that thought before I found words to give it shape, and drift again—retreat—into sleep.

I did not *realize*. I did not wish to.

But when, several years later, Dad decided that it was time to add to my education with tales of his own philandering, I was not truly surprised at his answer to the question I strained my gut to ask. The question I asked in a whisper.

"You've known all these women. Had all these love affairs." It seemed monstrous to me that Mother should have persisted in lonely fidelity through all those years. "Did Mother ever...?"

"Oh, sure. Hark and she had a big deal for years." He looked grim for a moment—forlorn—and then he laughed, and savored his drink. "We almost got divorced. You see, at the same time that she was having that deal with Hark, I was all tangled up with—in love with—Glenda, out on the coast. God knows, *she* wanted to marry *me*. And there was Hester. You know Hester, she was my secretary down here in Florida. She's a nice woman." I did know her, and indeed she was. "And, up in New York, there was Kelley." A family intimate for years. "And your mother was absolutely mad for Hark. And he loved her. But there were you kids to think about and, the real problem was—your mother and I *love* each other."

He mentioned the names of two other men, family friends, with whom Mother had also had affairs. One of them was laughable, dismissable—the kind of idle or desperate mistake that most of us make at some point in our years. The other was a nice man, though I found it hard to believe that women would find him attractive. I thought—still think, and I'm sure Dad thought—that his major attraction for Mother was the fact that he was husband to a woman with whom Dad was, at the same time, having an affair. Sauce for the gander, and for the goose. But loving Hark—that was different. Mother had exhibited good taste in loving him. That I was certain of. After all Dad's infidelities, Mother had had her moment in the extramarital sun. A moment which had threatened him. I thought that only proper.

But also I was impressed by the fact that Dad had remained Hark's friend, close friend, despite all jealousy. And remained so, long after that affair was over. Until Hark's heart betrayed him.

But all Dad's screwing, and her few affairs? I spent most of a lifetime "making it up" to her for Dad's wandering. Enmeshed in (and often rewarded by) serial monogamy or its extralegal equivalent.

If Mother had asserted herself sexually—and romantically, with Hark— she had also happily surrendered to another passion, a passion that necessity had smothered for years. A passion which would challenge, frustrate, and reward her into the last day of her life. She went back to canvas and to paper, back to brushes she loved, to colors she could use so well. Back to painting.

In Chicago, years before, she had made deliberate sacrifice. As she had told Dad when they first met, she wanted to paint. Before their meeting, she had applied for a job as an illustrator with an advertising agency. They had said that they liked her work, but there had been no opening, no opening at all. And so she had worked in humbler jobs, dreaming all the while of Opportunity. Dreaming to use her hands, her eyes, her mind; to use her special gift.

The day after Dad received the offer from the *Cedar Rapids Republican*, the offer which would enable him to write full-time—which would open doors into the future—and they had held high celebration, and quit their jobs, and made travel plans, Opportunity had announced itself to Mother, to Irene, in a letter. That advertising agency had found room on its staff. They had indeed admired Miss Layne's work, and hoped that she could join them. The job would pay twenty-five or thirty dollars a week.

Irene had crowed, all to herself: her talent was wanted. And Irene had wept, for Mack was a genius and she was not, they were both certain of that, and he must write and write and write. She could not deny him now his chance. ("Whither thou goest..." She remembered those words from Sunday School, where her father had been the Superintendent, and from her mother's Bible as well. Those words were from the Book of Ruth, and her sister's name was also Ruth, and Irene would miss her. "Whither thou goest, I will go...") She had laughed, almost gaily, when she told Mack about the letter.

"Of course, I'm going to tell them that I can't take the job now. I won't be here. In Chicago."

His voice had been dull when he spoke. "But that's what you want to do. And we'd be making fifty-five or sixty dollars between us. And I could still write part-time."

"But you need to write full-time!" And they had kissed, and hugged one another. Later in the night, he woke to find her crying.

But that was long ago, and Irene, Mother, was proud of, glad of, sacrifice, because it had not been sacrifice at all. It had been investment, and that investment had brought rich dividends.

During the war, with Dad away, Mother had gone back to art school. To the Art Students League in New York, and to various private instructors in Sarasota. And she found that she was good. Very good.

If she had had more confidence in herself, been more willing, more determined to trust and cling to her own wise first intent, she might have been a painter of considerable consequence. But just as Dad was too stubborn, too determined to ignore criticism from any source, so Mother was too willing to listen to any comment—to listen, and to bend. Too often she would work until she had a painting right, and then—listening to uninformed opinion, or to her own dubious second thoughts—she would work until she had it wrong. But she was no Sunday painter. She had talent. She could paint.

Dad was honestly delighted. He thought it was wonderful that she was exercising what he privately, only privately, considered to be her modest gift, and so he praised each painting she made. He had an unconscious knack of dismissing with great praise. "Irene! That's magnificent!" And she would pause, eyes straining at the canvas; the brush held, uncertain, in her hand.

Despite all the emotional pulls which stressed its fabric, our family life during those years was fond and intense. Sometimes peculiar.

When he was courting Layne, my future brother-in-law, Bill Shroder, once observed that going to visit the Kantors was like going to a performance of *You Can't Take It with You*. Donald Friede used the same analogy. "There is no need," he said, looking both owlish and bemused, "for George Kaufman to *write* wacky plays about wacky families. He should just come and live with the Kantors for a while."

There was a lot of laughter in our home. A lot of laughter, a lot of disagreement and argument—about politics, about people, about life, about which restaurant to go to or which movie to see—and there was a lot of jockeying for center stage.

And all of it was loud.

His sister Virginia once told me that Dad had come into the world with a squall, and that he'd been yelling ever since. Layne and I had early come to know that, if we wished to be heard, we had to raise our own voices; we did, and often we do so even now. For Mother it was more difficult. She had learned to project her voice from the stage when acting in amateur theater, but her natural voice was soft and gentle. Sometimes, when the rest of us were ranting, she'd feel frustrated, ignored, drowned out—and then she'd assert her feeling or opinion in a scream. It was a tiny scream, but it commanded attention.

She swore that someday she'd write her memoirs—correcting all matters of family history which Dad had distorted—and that when she did, she'd call the book *I Learned to Shout*.

In June 1946 Dad was working on a script for Paramount. Like so many scripts, it would eventually die of Hollywooditis before it ever came to life on the screen, but Dad couldn't know that, and he was in high spirits. The contract Donald had negotiated called for Dad to write the screenplay in ten weeks, and to be payed two thousand dollars for each of those weeks. He was finishing the damn thing within three. Twenty thousand, he announced loudly and happily, for three weeks' work, was *damned* good pay. Now he could get to work on his next book.

One June afternoon when he had finished dictating and Phyllis Gossling, his secretary for many years, was busy at the typewriter, she paused and looked around the living room. The day was bright; full of sun, and shimmer from the beach. Mother was hard at work on a portrait of her sister, our beloved Aunt Ruth, on the screen porch which opened off the room. Aunt Ruth was sitting for the portrait, wearing an evening gown. Layne-o, just back from the beach with her swimming suit still wet, was practicing some strange new dance step all over the place. I was throwing darts—very sharp darts—at the dart board with great intensity. Our friend Marvin Sirus, who had come to visit us at Dad's urging—and who would stay in Sarasota to work, to marry, to raise a family—was stretched out in the middle of the floor, cleaning revolvers with the hand the Germans had left him. Beverly, our current collie, was asleep upon the couch. And Dad had just found an entire litter of kittens asleep on the bottom tray of an old tea cart we had, and was pushing the loaded cart around the room, to see how far he could push it before the kittens woke and jumped.

Phyllis looked and looked, and shook her head. "My word," she said, in her brisk, Australian voice, "what a household we are!"

Nor did we confine eccentricity to our home. We carried it with us. And we went, it seemed, almost everywhere.

Back to Webster City a few times, where Dad was treated with all the respect he'd yearned for. But not his son. Some of the local boys had heard, at home and in school, far too much about the famous-home-town-lad-made-good, and they were inclined to take it out on me. Once a few of them tried to bully me, and I let them. I still had to grow my legs. When I told my father about it, his reaction lacked all his usual bluster. He spoke gently. Firmly. It was often so: when he saw the necessity, he was often wise. He did not laugh or scorn, or make me feel more ashamed than I already was. He gave me a pep talk, and helped me to feel angry instead. Then I went out hunting my attackers. I didn't find them, but the effort made me feel better. It was a tiptoe toward confidence.

One summer we drove out to Bryce Canyon, passing Plum Creek, in Nebraska, on the way. The ghosts of the massacred hallooed as we passed, and Dad's narration of the history of the land we were crossing rose above the sound of the engine as we drove. We went on to Grand Lake, Colorado, up in the Rocky Mountains, and spent a few weeks at a dude ranch. (I worked there, as a cabin boy, the following summer.) We explored an old mining camp, and found bits of glass from bottles broken and discarded over seventy years before. We wondered at the beauty of the mountain forest, and at the naked majesty above the tree line as we drove to Estes Park. We worshipped the endless blue-white reach of the sky above the plains, and the muscle of the land which stretched out below the clouds: open, empty, vast and clean. And colored by Dad's words.

Driving east from the Rockies, we found another use for words. We went on a punning spree, and all our puns had to concern themselves with the supernatural or—we loosened the rules—with mundane death. And so: There was a little ghost-boy who went to the drugstore and got sick, because he drank too many vaulted milks. Then he went home, and his mother gave him a psychic. Later the same ghost-family visited New York, and marveled at the Vampire State Building, and went to Boney Island. And later still the ghost-boy grew up and joined the Air Force. He went to England and flew Flying Coffins (a sadly real nickname for B-24 bombers), and he flew to Germany and bombed a pall-bearing factory. And so forth, all across the continent. Long minutes of silence, sometimes stretching toward an hour, and then, "Aha!" and one of us would offer yet another silly pun. Silly, perhaps, but we enjoyed ourselves, and thought we were very clever.

I think it was in the summer of '47 that we spent a month at a resort in Vermont, on the shore of Lake Champlain. Rustic cabins tucked into the woods, and a central dining room where, on Sundays, they served cupcakes with icing of many colors, many flavors. There were black raspberries in the fields around, and the lake was still and clear. There were rocky, piney islands nearby which, Layne and I swore, seemed never to have known a human step until they felt the press of ours. And the lake was clean. (If there were papermills then, vomiting their chemical filth into the lake, they were far away.)

Dad was at work on some manuscript or other—he'd lugged his old portable typewriter along—and he was half-delighted, half-annoyed, to be so immersed in family. Mother had brought her own gear, and was painting, and was annoyed herself because "Mack was being difficult." Layne was suffering some adolescent trauma, something having to do with boys and curfew, and was fighting constantly with Dad. (Her main problem with Dad at the time was that she fought him constantly, whenever he wished to limit her autonomy. Mine was that I didn't.) Except when Layne-o wanted—with romantic intent—to go on moonlight canoe trips, without my company, I felt relatively relaxed. I felt that I was visiting in Eden.

That was when we met Peter Kellaway. Peter was a very tough, gentle man. He was a neurophysiologist with a very impressive past and a more impressive future. His father was the fine character actor Cecil Kellaway, and that fact may have accounted for Peter's very understated, unactorish, presence. He was capable of taking—had taken—brave, decisive action in this world but, when we first met him, he was inclined to stand back and observe. And, as he became a friend of ours, during those few weeks, he did stand back, he did observe. One night he said, half-seriously, "You know I like you all. But I think most of you are crazy. I think that Tim is the only sane member of the family." I preened myself on that remark. But even then I wasn't sure that he was right, and now I'm sure he wasn't.

Now slam the years together once again, and pack them full—just as life is filled—with contradiction and with irony.

Dad had encountered few black people during his early years. "The color line had never been drawn with distinct sharpness in Webster City, purely for the reason that there was almost no one to place on the sinister side of it." But, when he was nine or ten, a group of black laborers was brought to town to pave the streets.

> ...the men toiled around the cooking cauldrons of tar in the town's streets or stamped about with wooden clogs strapped to their feet, pushing long-handled brooms and scrapers over the steaming surface of the asphalt. They sang as they worked—deep-throated, sweaty chants....I don't know the songs they sang. I wish I did; I can hear them singing vaguely, far away in a dream now.

> I dreamed violently about them while they were there....They were strange; they were new and greasy and wild and ragged. They did not speak as the townspeople spoke nor wear the same garb; they did not eat the same food; poor things, they had not a garden to their names. Living long before the unionized generations, they were probably paid a miserable wage by the men who had fetched them there.

> "If you don't be a good little girl, I'm going to have a great big black nigger come and get you!" That was the wise admonition spoken by certain Webster City women more than once, before and after that time. Negroes, black-snake whips, bloodhounds, lynchings, floggings, night riders, cannibals, voodoo, rape...these horrors shaped

and foamed in a ghastly montage. Just who was the villain and who was the victim I did not know...pursuer and pursued were confused. In floundering imagination I heard the baying of mastiffs and the tinkle of banjos, the thick rumble of negroid laughter and the pound of pigmy drums. Victors or vanquished, masters or slaves, missionaries or converts, they were all figments of a disorderly juba-dance....

Long during the night I dreamed about Negroes—a whole gang of them, with wooden clogs on their feet. They were singing and working and digging—digging a hole to put me in. Unreasoning, asking never for comfort and reassurance from those who might have given it to me, not willing to abide by the evidence of my own experience, I was like a vast white portion of America today—wound in the soggy ropes of fear and prejudice, unable to loose myself, perhaps not even caring to.

Those words were written in 1946 or '47, and they are not the words of a man possessed by prejudice. Or, if they are, they are surely the words of a man struggling to loose himself from it.

And yet...

In the late winter or spring of '46 Layne-o had a party. The private school we both attended at the time was integrated, in a fashion: there were a number of black children from upper- and middle-class families, and even a few on scholarships, who might be poor but were very bright. There was a black kid in her class whom Layne invited to her party, and the Irish doorman (who had forgotten, or never known about, want ads of fifty years before: "No Irish Need Apply") had insisted that the boy use the freight elevator. Layne was outraged, and complained to Dad.

"Fred was perfectly right. That's the custom. If you have to invite a black brat to our apartment, let him come up the *back* way!" And Mother sided with him.

Layne-o was flabbergasted, and so was I when she told me about it. We had not been raised steeped in prejudice. No black bogymen had haunted our childish dreams. And our parents had never made any comment about Negro children at our school. (*Negro* was the proper word to use then. *Black* was a nasty epithet, until black pride wrested the word from whites, and invested it with dignity.)

"Goddamn nigger kid," Dad had said, and shook his head.

And yet...

In 1939 Dad wrote the first short story ever to appear in the *Saturday Evening Post* in which a black was the central, and very sympathetic, character. His name was Dewey McCue, and he was a colored kid (*colored* was accepted then, and used by both blacks and whites)—the only colored kid in yet another Webster City, and he wanted to join the Scouts. "But," his parents told him, "the Boy Scouts are for white folks, little boy. Don't you step out of place." And so Dewey nurtured his dream in private—became a pretend Boy Scout—and studied a battered Scout manual which his father had retrieved from trash he hauled, and learned the lore of signaling and bird watching—and first aid. *And* the scoutmaster's daughter had an accident, and Dewey saved her life. Using skills he'd learned in the manual. *And* the scoutmaster, after thanking him, said, "But, Dewey, why didn't you tell me that you wanted to be a Scout? Of course you're welcome." *And* the real Boy Scouts praised him, and they welcomed him.

It was a sentimental tale—beautifully written and touching. Dad had climbed into Dewey's skull when he wrote it.

The publication of the story kicked up quite a storm. Letters poured in, filled with praise or nastiness. But, to Dad, the most important letter came from a young black man in California, a young man who dreamed of writing for the popular magazines. Writing about blacks. "Now I have hope. Until this ice-breaking story of yours, I do not think there has been such a story used—"

The Scouts were also pleased. To his great pride, they asked him to serve on the National Council of the Boy Scouts of America.

And yet...

Working with the New York cops in the later forties, when he was writing *Signal Thirty-Two*, he not only adopted the prejudice they owned, he bathed in it. He smelt as much of prejudice as he did of the cigars he loved to smoke. Or of Frances Fox hair tonic.

Nigger. Jig. Black bastard or *bitch. Goddamn PRs* (for Puerto Ricans). *Spik.* I heard all those terms—he *used* all those terms—to the point of sickness.

And yet...

In the forties and the fifties Sarasota, Florida, reeked of prejudice even more than many other Southern towns. This was due, even more than to the innate, inane bigotry of the native-born whites, to the blithe indifference, the icy dismissal and disdain, of settlers from the North. Folks from places like Michigan and Ohio. The streets of Newtown, the black neighborhood, were largely unpaved, the sewers uncovered, and the books the black kids read in their segregated schools, the uniforms their football team wore, were all weary rejects the white schools had chosen to discard. Sarasota is a coastal county, and there were miles and miles of the whitest beaches in the world, but no black foot might tread upon them. Much of that sand was privately owned, and the public beaches were reserved for whites.

In 1956 there came a great controversy: people campaigned for, and the county commission actually considered, proposals for a "Negro beach." Those proposals caused much reaction in the community at large, much of it negative, much of it nasty. The county commission dithered, and Mack Kantor got upset. In September he wrote a Letter to the Editor of the local paper, the *Sarasota Herald-Tribune*. (One of many which he wrote through the years. He often thought the world needed his chiding. In this case he was right.)

Sir:

Last night I had a perfectly dreadful nightmare, and it might help now if I told you about it. Seemed like I was walking along out here on Siesta Key, and suddenly I came face to face with Richard Barber, a boy who used to be my yardman. Richard was the son of Henry and Rosa Barber, who live out in Newtown. It was odd to meet him, because he has been dead more than twelve years.

He wanted to know how things were in Sarasota county these days.

"That little old Gulf of Mexico," he said. "Sure like to see it again. I hear they got them a colored folks' beach."

"Well," I said, "that'll cost you. First you'd have to buy gas and drive up past Palmetto. Then you'd pay a dollar-seventy-five at the toll gate. Then—"

"Ain't they got them no colored folks' beach round Sarasota yet? They was talking about it fore I left—"

"It was suggested," I told Richard, "that they have such a beach out on Longboat, but the Longboat people didn't want it there. Later it was suggested that they make the colored folks' beach at Midnight Pass, but a great many objections were voiced by Siesta Key residents."

Richard asked humbly, "Such as?"

"Well, some people said that it would bring about a definite increase in burglary and crime on Siesta Key. And—"

"You mean they got them a crime wave in Sarasota now?"

"Just a little one," I admitted. "The other night the assistant manager of the Florida Theater got beaten up by a gang of teenagers. And a kid pulled a knife on a ticket-taker at the Ritz. And—"

"Colored boys done that?" asked Richard in horror.

"No," I said, "they were white boys. But—"

"I 'spose," said Richard gravely, "it would cost a lot of money to fix up that there colored folks' beach. You just don't find money laying around."

I agreed. "Certainly not. And a great deal of money must be earmarked for other purposes. For instance, a local storekeeper has just pledged ten thousand dollars to help purchase a site for a proposed university to be located in or near Sarasota. And—"

"Maybe he think university folks come and buy lots of things in he store," opined Richard sagely.

"Nonsense! It was a generous civic gesture."

"Maybe colored boys go to that university, too?"

"Don't be silly, Richard. It's to be for white people only. And then a local architect has just submitted a wonderful plan for a waterfront development in the bay. Picnic shelters, water-skiing, something they call an 'aquarena'—I'm not exactly sure what an 'aquarena' is. But it might cost four hundred thousand dollars. And—"

"That's a lot of money," said Richard. "You think a colored folks' beach maybe cost that much?"

"Richard," I said, "you're getting entirely too uppity for a nigger! Will you please get back to that United States Military Cemetery in Northern France where you belong?"

> Sincerely,
> MacKinlay Kantor

I still can hear the pride which thrilled his voice when he told me of that letter on the phone, pride because he knew that I'd be pleased with him. He had also, in an interview in the paper, threatened to write an article for a national magazine entitled "Sarasota Cheats Its Black Children," and there was further pride in the note he wrote when he sent me a copy of the letter. "The Ku Klux Klan threatened to stage a demonstration on the road in front of our house last Sunday, and I announced that that was fine. I said they'd find me sitting on a chair on the lawn, with my 30-30 on my lap. A few cars did come by, with idiot faces glaring from the windows, but they took off fast when I picked up the rifle."

And yet...

He referred to Martin Luther King, Jr., as "Martin Luther Coon."

And yet...

In later years, when he came back from acting as a consultant on psychological warfare with the Air Force, or otherwise playing flyboy, he'd make a point of mentioning this or that "outstanding Negro" general or colonel he had met. It was as though Air Force blue or silver-tan could ennoble skin of any hue, and rob black pigmentation of all its threat.

And yet...

"Long during the night I dreamed about Negroes—a whole gang of them, with wooden clogs on their feet. They were singing and working and digging— digging a hole to put me in." Such dreams recurred throughout his life. In April of '58 he wrote a long letter to Dr. Giorgio Lolli, a distinguished psychiatrist and an authority on alcoholism, with whom he consulted for a number of years. (Dad was fond of quoting Dr. Lolli as saying, "Mack, you're not an alcoholic. You just like to drink.") The letter contained a drink-by-drink recounting of his current alcohol consumption, and also a long discussion of his dreams. ("The point I wish to make is that dreams of complication and clarity almost never occurred to me during the times when I was on the wagon. I am prone to regard these as evidences of a creative force and ambition now stirring...") He described one dream in great detail. It centered on physical threat from an unknown black man, met in a strange place.

I think that, as a child, he had absorbed ancient European folk memories, folk values, reaching far back before even the first encounter with Africa. "Black as night. Black as sin. Black as the Devil. He's not as black as he is painted."

And yet...

Five years after Dad died I met and dated a bright, accomplished, and attractive young woman—who happened to be black. I first told Mother of this romance when I invited her to a party I was giving, and described the lady who—among other friends—would be there. Mother had conniptions. Her son with a black woman! What would people say? How could I do this to her? All the hoary bugaboos went raging through her mind. She said that not only would she not come to the party, she would disown me as well. But Mother was, however skewed her feelings, a generous and warm-hearted person. After a few days she undisowned me, she did come to the party, and she was pleasant to everyone there. Including my friend.

But had Dad been alive, he would have behaved differently. He would have, at first, ranted and raved about the "black wench" I was dating. Then he would have agreed to meet her, been charmed by her, and exercised all his own charm in return. Because he liked her, in spite of all foolish prejudice, and because he loved me, in his mind he would have dressed her up in Air Force blue.

He was often more capable of wisdom than he wished to be.

In 1935 he wrote a little short-short story entitled "Spoils of War," about ragged, scarecrow men who met, in passing, at the end of the Civil War. Men who had been imprisoned in camps both in the North and the South. A nice little story, which created quite a fuss. The Daughters of Union Veterans complained, and so did the United Daughters of the Confederacy. There had been no Camp Douglas in the North; no Andersonville in the South. In reply to some angry woman in Virginia he wrote (he always did reply to fan mail both admiring and foolish), "I have found that prejudice sits in a closed room, without door or window."

"So Pat said to Mike..."

"So Abie said to Ike..."

Dad loved funny stories, "clean" and "dirty", and often the stories he told were ethnic. He told them beautifully, and he could go from Irish to Jewish to Scottish to Cockney to Iowa to Southern dialect with hardly a break. There was little malice in those tales; only when he told stories about blacks was there any sting of venom. He particularly delighted in telling "pansy" stories, and he had every gesture, every shrug of shoulder, every lilt of voice of the extremely effeminate down pat. He loved trading such stories with our homosexual friends, just as he enjoyed swapping Jewish stories with Jews.

And excelling most of them in mimicry.

Considering the forces which worked on him when he was young—both personal circumstances and the texture of the world in which he lived—he might have been expected to "grow up" to be both a self-hating anti-Semite and a man who scorned and detested, because he felt threatened by, homosexuals. But his happy acquaintance with his grandfather, Joseph Kantor, saved him from being the first, and—despite his mother's overwhelming presence in childhood; despite of, because of, all his "babes" in later years—a basic, happy awareness of his own sexual identity saved him from the other.

Our family was unchurched; our parents had long since abandoned formal religious observance. Dad knew the Bible better than most preachers did or do but, for him, it was great literature, a repository of wisdom and apt myth, and so I came to regard it too. Still we sang the hymns of his childhood, and of Mother's, but when Dad took out his guitar, or when Burl Ives came to play and sing, we were likely to mix songs of faith with songs of fornication. "Beautiful Isle of Somewhere," "The Battle Hymn of the Republic," "Barbara Allen," and "Minnie the Mermaid" all seemed to us relevant to the human condition.

Many of our parents' friends were Jewish and, because of the schools we attended in New York, most of Layne's friends, and most of mine were. Jewish ethnically, if not in faith. We took pride in that portion of our heritage, just as we gloried in our Irish, English, and Scottish ancestry.

As for homosexuality: Dad thought such predilection mysterious and sad. Such folks were *missing* so much. So much fun. But he did not think them wicked. During my teen years I spent quite a bit of time with two especially fond friends of ours—a "couple" named Jake and Harry. Knowing this, other friends, foolish and ignorant, questioned Dad. "But how can you let Timmy spend time with them alone? They might..." And their protestations trailed off at thought of the unmentionable.

"Oh, bullshit! Jake and Harry are about as eager to attack Tim as I am to rape some twelve-year-old little girl."

Jake, in particular, was an exceptionally fine man. And talented. And I loved him. Years later, he and Harry came to my wedding.

Expand the years once more. Fill in their chinks and crannies. Dad stood above us, and he leered. "I think it's time you met your dear grandpa."

I had only met our grandfather once, when I was three or four. Dad's recent financial success was evident from publicity in the papers, he and Mother were away on a trip, and Grandpa had come to prowl, had come to spy. Layne-o and I had been left in the care of the maid, and she was overawed when John Kantor knocked and announced himself, importantly, at the door. He had come to see his dear grandchildren, and she let him in. He made much of us but, after a little while, she found him looking through Daddy's mail, and browsing through the contents of his desk. She remembered cautions she'd received, and told him he must leave.

I didn't remember that occasion at all, and my sister barely did. All we knew of Grandpa was gleaned from our parents' tales about him. We knew that he'd been sent to Sing Sing prison for a very complicated swindle.

(Dad always said that his father had spent four years there. Westbrook Pegler later mentioned in his column that John Kantor had served twenty months for that particular felony. I don't know who was right: Pegler was noted for his inaccuracy, but Dad loved to exaggerate.) We knew that Dad had publicly disowned his father and declared that he would not be responsible for any of his father's obligations—after years of pathetic entreaty through the mail or on the phone. ("Your father talked me out of my life savings... Your father owes me for this grocery bill.")

We knew that Grandpa was a charming, brilliant, mystic being.

When Dad made that statement, we agreed. We said, "Yes!"

"All right. Now, you mustn't let your grandfather know that I put you up to this, because I don't want the old bastard trying to get friendly with *me*." He paused and ruminated, and then he beamed in delight with his own invention. "Layne-o, you call him—he's at the Saint George Hotel in Brooklyn, with his current wife. Tell him that I'd skin you alive if I knew about this, but your mother and I are out of town, and you're dying to meet him."

So it was done, and Grandpa invited us to dinner.

Reaching into my head for vague memories retained for almost forty years, I can summon up a brightly lit restaurant dining room. The table linen is snowy white, and light sparkles off silver and large glasses. The wife is a handsome woman, and pleasant. And subservient. The waiters are obsequious. Layne-o's chin is almost down to her chest, and so is mine. Our grandfather is tall and stately, a little stout, and his handsome face is jowly—as our father's face would become in time; as my own face threatens to become. At first his speech is slow and rambling, and I wonder if prison has rendered him senescent, even senile. (It does not occur to me to think that he may be as nervous about this meeting as are we.) He asks me what I am studying in school, and I mention ancient history.

The strong, broad face lights up, and his rich voice quickens. "Oh? Have you studied the Assyrians?"

"Yes!" History is my favorite subject. "We're studying them right now."

"Really? What can you tell me about Tiglath-pileser I?"

"Well, he..." Tiglath-pileser, Sennacherib, Assurbanipal, the fighting with the Chaldeans and the Elamites—he is familiar with them all. We have found an interest shared, and most of the rest of our conversation is devoted to it. He seems to know more about the Assyrians than does my teacher, Mr. Kovacs, or even the men who wrote my textbook. His charm and knowledge make the room glow, even brighter than before, and his face comes alive. But his eyes (I think they were brown) are cold, and dead as stones.

Perhaps he had called my school, introduced himself as my loving grandfather, asked them what I was studying, and then done some research in order to impress me. Perhaps he had once been fascinated by those ancient folk, read widely in the field, and had an enormously retentive memory. Perhaps both.

We thanked him and his wife, awkwardly but politely, for our dinner. Dad opened the apartment door as we got out of the elevator. "Well, what did you think of him?"

We never saw him again, but I remember his eyes. Dark they were, and still as any stone.

I was elsewhere when the bell rang. Dad stumped down the hall to answer it, emoting, growling "Goddamn little bastards," and his eyes flashed fire. False fire. He opened the door to snarl a welcome to Bob Selig and Don Barth. "Come on in, and I hope you lose your asses!"

They laughed. "Hi, Uncle Mack."

"You know where the booze is, and Timmy is someplace or other." I came to greet them. There would be six or seven of us that night, assembled for our weekly poker game. Penny-ante, befitting teenagers' allowances. Though not mine. Dad was still making up to himself for his own early deprivation, and so indulging me. He gave me the ridiculous sum of twenty dollars each and every week. I spent some of that on movies, and gifts to the family on birthdays or at Christmas time, and much of it on books. And the collection of ancient Greek coins, which were relatively cheap then, and laden with beauty and with history; I had a happy passion for them.

It took me years to truly understand that money cost work.

We greeted others as they came. We made our drinks. (Dad had the notion that, if kids were going to explore the joys and perils of alcohol, it was better for them to do so at home. Rather than illegally, in some bleak bar.) Last of all to come was Mike Loewenthal.

Mike was a brilliant boy, and eccentric. He was the son of Austrian Jews who had emigrated barely in time, in 1938. (Germany is known for more than evil.) I think he came, those Friday nights, for socializing—not for gaming. He played poker badly, and rashly, as though he thought the game beneath his intellect and interest. Also, he was awkward in the use of his body. He was uncoordinated; he tripped, he stumbled. Once he tripped on an area rug in the hall; he slid into the dining room, where we played our game, sitting on the thing. Waving and laughing. After that, in self-mimicry, he made the same entrance every time. And then he'd laugh, and be clever, and often lose.

A few years later he was at Oxford, on a very prestigious scholarship. He had too many pints at a local pub one evening, and then stumbled back toward his quarters. He tripped on the way, and fell into a ditch. He fell face down, passed out, and drowned in three inches of water.

But I remember Mike laughing. I was fond of him, and fond of the others. And even fonder of Dad, of "Uncle Mack," who came home with Mother just as we were playing a final, foolish round of Red Dog. He came back just in time to congratulate the winner, and to sneer at the night's biggest loser.

"Uncle Mack" was a title the other kids had accorded him spontaneously, and he delighted in it. If Ernest Hemingway could be Papa, why could Dad not be Uncle Mack? He referred to himself as that for a number of years, but, to his sorrow, no one else ever used the phrase.

Mack sat on the toilet seat, and he strained. Always he had been afflicted by constipation; always he would be, almost until the last. (I remember that, when I had occasional trouble when very young, he would say, "*I* know what *you* need!" And then he'd advance toward me, fiendish grin in place, fond but threatening, flourishing an enormous, pasty white suppository. He, himself, seemed to derive an almost sensual pleasure from the damn things. Being generally of looser inclination, I have no interest in them.)

He sat, and he strained, and he cursed.

"Goddamn world!" Good people had died to save an old world which he loved, but they had bought a new world instead, and he didn't much like it. Take Burma Shave, for instance. He didn't use it himself, but he imagined it was as good as most shaving creams. Before the war, during the war, immediately after, they'd only advertised on road signs. A half mile of tiny, oblong signs on country roads displaying, one after the other, a silly verse, a clever slogan. And so you strained to watch, strained to read. Hell, those signs had helped his kids *learn* to read. But now they advertised on radio. Even television! Idiot box with idiot faces, scornful of all taste, all knowledge, all history. By God, he'd never have a TV set in his house, his apartment.

The men he'd known had fought, he had fought, for a storybook world—a happy, comfortable vision, like the world he'd sometimes dreamed of in the pages of the *Saturday Evening Post*. A world imagined by the pioneers, by the kids who fought at Vicksburg or Petersburg or Belleau Wood. By Bailey, who died. But take this goddamn Levittown, out on Long Island. What did such an artificial creation have to do with a *real* town. Like Webster City. Where were the local shops, the neighbors whom you knew—had known forever—where were the maples or the elms, the butterflies flickering, a sense of certainty, a sense of the past? Sad, nervous little men, in sad, nervous little suits, commuting to the city on the train, and coming back to restless, uncertain kids and sad, nervous little wives. That wasn't right. That wasn't Webster City.

That was wrong.

And take the fucking Commies! Oh, once he himself had said mad things, during the agony of the Depression years, but now he was sane. He chuckled as he strained. He thought of a room full of startled faces. Faces which had been sad, and then were shocked.

He thought of Will Crawford. Of "Uncle Bill." Thought of an ancient, wispy, shaggy-haired, almost elfin creature whom he had known and loved for years. Will had been a great illustrator of the olden days, of Indian lore, of the West. Right up there with Remington and Charley Russell. Will had celebrated America as fondly and fiercely as Steve Benét had done, or Mack himself. He could glide through the woodland like a fawn; he could draw like a kindly fiend. And he had been a Communist. An idealist, visioning all mankind living happily in one vast wilderness commune. Until the Winter War in Finland—the treacherous Soviet invasion. Then he had quit the Party, and his sister had said, "Will, I think you're lost." And Will had told that old story about the Indian found wandering in the lonely woods, and folks had asked him if he was lost, and the Indian had replied, "Indian not lost. Tepee lost."

Back in '44, at the memorial service for Will Crawford—for Uncle Bill—after the remarks by Jimmy Cagney and the others, Mack had told that story, and some of the people there had gasped. But, damn it, the Commies were lost, and creating havoc wherever they ranged. And the unions weren't much better, and the developers of all these lousy new suburbs, and the colored agitators—they all wanted to *change* things. And the advertising people, and this goddamn new TV.

They were muddying the world he'd known, altering it, making it strange. Bastards! And the Russians—killing their own people, and taking over Europe. God! How he'd love to ride in the first bomber over Moscow.

He swore, as he finished his labor and cleaned himself. He had a sudden, swift remembrance of the outhouse which was Vicksburg. Recalled the scent of aging wood, and other, very human, smells. Flies would gather there, in summer. That ancient world he'd known had not been sanitary, but it had been sane. Now everything was clean, and chemical or plastic, and mad.

He pulled up his trousers and stalked out of the bathroom, shouting, "God damn it! I don't belong in this world. I'm a nineteenth-century man!"

I labored on a bluff near Pierre, South Dakota, digging up Indians. Archaeologists with trowels and brushes, and kids like me armed with shovels, were racing bulldozers constructing a dam on the Missouri River. The Oahe Dam. A village site some eight hundred years old would be covered over, and we were trying to retrieve and catalogue all that could be saved. My throat was parched, and I paused to drink from our jug of water. The Dakota sun was blasting from the open sky—it was over one hundred degrees in the nonexistent shade—but I was barely sweating, for the long wind blowing off the Plains was fiercely dry. Another drink, and then I smoked a cigarette and found great pleasure in the act. It was a Chesterfield. I remember that because it was the last cigarette which ever pleasured me—though I smoke cigarettes to this day, and to my shame. I stood there amid the others, listening to their wind-torn voices, enjoying flavor in my mouth and fire in my lungs, and I experienced déjà vu. I *knew* that I had stood in that same place, and watched those same forms, before.

I was stunned, and it took me several minutes to sort through memory and find the source of that illusion. There were deep gullies on either side of the bluff which converted it into a sort of promontory shoving into the river, and there was something suggestive about the positioning of those around me. The wind seemed to make their voices small. And then I remembered—thirteen years before: *...one late afternoon we walked through damp woods, two rows of us children, hand in hand, down to a rocky promontory which thrust into the lake....The light was sharp, the colors clean and clear, and the voices of children and adults echoed softly in the air.*

It was the summer of '50, when the Korean War started, and there were veterans of the ground war in Europe among us—young archaeologists made excellent reconnaissance troops and combat engineers—and they talked long into the nights, mixing harsh memories with new fears. I listened, but their talk of combat seemed to have little to do with me.

They were grown men, they were adults, and I felt strongly, weakly, that I could not claim to be a man.

Night wind, but no stars at all. Just thick mist all around. I lay beside a hedge, on the road from Wells to Bath, wrapped in my raincoat and with a musette bag, borrowed from my father, under my head for a pillow. I was eighteen, and I felt sorry for myself and for the world.

I had graduated from high school the previous spring, just before I'd gone to work on the dig near Pierre. (Dad had gotten me that job, through friends at the Smithsonian.) I had graduated spang in the middle of my class—A's in English and, I think, in Spanish; barely C's in Math and Science: results of effort or its lack—and I was sick of school. I'd been accepted by the one college I had applied to, Brown, but I hadn't wanted to go. I wanted a breather, and Dad indulged me once again. He gave me six months in Europe instead.

In London I had dinner with one of his wartime "babes" (though I didn't know that then). She was an accomplished writer who had been young with Auden and Spender. In Paris I gave a prostitute some francs and my virginity. I spent six weeks wandering in Spain, and nailed down a solid, basic knowledge of Spanish which would be a blessing in the future. In Madrid there were snowflakes on Christmas Eve, when I went caroling through the streets with some Spanish kids I'd met; in Sevilla the oranges were bitter, but the people lusty and engaging. With thousands of others I ate twelve grapes at midnight, one for each stroke of the clock—and time hovering over me—to welcome the New Year. In Cannes I worked for food and drinks at the New Yorker Bar, and touted its virtues and passed out leaflets to sailors of the American 5th Fleet when they came ashore on liberty, all along that coast. In Antibes I was arrested for the first time in my life, for soliciting, but I pretended that I had no French at all, rather than the little phrase-book, barroom bit I did possess, and they let me go and simply kicked me out of town. Someplace along the coast there were bright rocks under clear water, and a pillbox left over from the war, and I sat and leaned against the pillbox and wrote bad poetry. All about lost love and loneliness, and the ending of the world. (Stalin was still in his restless, wicked glory; the Bomb was new, and as threatening as it should be still. Wise men feared the world might not last ten years, much less almost forty.) I went down to greet the spring in Sicily. Almond blossoms flecked dun hills and, in Agrigento, with a friend I'd met in Rome, I toasted old gods with raw red wine on the steps of a crumbling temple. We ate bread and cheese. In Florence I saw Michelangelo's *Dawn* and *Dusk*, *Night* and *Day*, a Medici come to sit in judgment, the Slave within the stone, and I reeled. I stayed in that chapel for hours. Back in Paris I met another prostitute (in those harsh postwar years many girls had little alternative) and had the kind of experience that foolish youths might dream of then.

I met her at the bar in Morgan's of Oregon, on the Rue Pigalle, which was owned by a Ninth Air Force pilot who'd stayed over after the war. She was pleasant to talk to, and very lovely, with fine features, black hair, swarthy skin, and slender body. Only a few years older than I. I asked her name, and she told me, "Françoise." But I had been in the south of Spain. I recognized the set of her dark eyes, the tint of tawny flesh. In my bad French I said, "No, I mean your real name."

She stiffened a little and drew away (prejudice is pandemic, and not confined to Germans). "What do you mean?"

"I mean that you're a Gypsy. You are very nice, and very pretty, and I would like to know your true name." I added, "My name is Tim."

She looked at me a moment, and then she softened. "And mine is Jiska." Her knee came back to press mine once more. "Tell me, Tim"—and she switched to English—"where do you come from in the States?"

"Florida."

"Florida! Where in Florida?"

"A little town called Sarasota."

"Sarasota!" And now her knee was pressing hard. "The guy who got my cherry, he come from Sarasota!"

We had a lovely night, most unprofessional, and achieved all kinds of happy feats. Jiska was making love with her first lover, and I was making love with Europe, and with history.

And history again in England, when I walked through a sweet-scented pine plantation to the ruin of Wardour Castle, and later when I was overwhelmed by the still magnificence of Stonehenge. I was stirred by the past, yet crushed by it. And I was oppressed by thought of the future. The world's future, and my own.

The world faced then the probability, what seems still the probability, of maniac destruction. It was, and is, no question of wiping out a wagon train or a squadron. *They hid, and watched the wagons burn....Two came home.* Men, and cities, have faced forever the threat of destruction. "And we razed the city, and slew all who lived there, and before its ruined walls made a pyramid of skulls." I had enough historic lore to know that such had happened in the past, but always there had been the possibility of survival of a culture, the certainty of survival of the species.

All that had changed before I was thirteen, and when I was eighteen I knew it had.

I was frightened, and I pinned to my fright all personal fears and doubts. I had written poems through all those six months, and thought them good. They were not, but I thought them so. I had written two or three pages of the start of an imagined novel. (And perhaps those pages, long discarded, *were* good. Something about the decline of the West. Of the world.) But always in front of me loomed the commanding shape of my father. I thought that he was a brilliant writer, and how could I possibly compete?

And women, girls—despite all unlikely serendipity in Paris, they daunted me. Perhaps I might not be charming enough. As charming as he. Surely I was not as handsome. I knew that I was more than adequate in bed, but what did I have to offer to lure girls or women there? And where was that wonderful girl who would open her soul for me, and seek to open mine? And what was I to do in this world? I knew that life demanded competence, and felt I had small share of that.

I took a country bus to Glastonbury. I climbed its Tor, saw the shimmer of the Bristol Channel, and disturbed young lovers loving. What had I to do with them, or they with me? I took another bus to Wells, stirred the ghosts in the cathedral close, and then went tramping through the evening, and into my own adolescent night.

It is dreadfully unpleasant to be bright, and uncertain, and eighteen.

North of Wells, at ten o'clock, I came to a pub, its bright lights bleared by the mist. I heard music and laughter, and I wanted to go in but I didn't have the guts. I felt too much the outsider—alien to, and undeserving of, all human warmth. Hugging misery close around me, like the cloak my father once had worn, I turned and walked away. Later I grew tired, and stretched out on grass beside the road. Until a slight noise roused me, and I saw a white shape threaten through the dark and mist. Ghost or cow, I wasn't quite certain, but I got up and traveled on.

All the world seemed misty to me in those years, and uncertain. I dared not look upon it clearly, to bring it into sharp focus, for others then might look at me clearly too, and find me lacking.

In late June of '51 Dad took us down to Cuba. Mother, Layne-o, her husband—Bill Shroder, a bright, engaging young man—and me. It was their twenty-fifth wedding anniversary. *He had given the minister three dollars, and Mack had to ask Irene for trolley fare, after he'd taken her home.* Now he took us all to Havana, flying first class. We stayed at the Sevilla-Biltmore, we drank daiquiris at La Floradita, and the third day we took a car out to Finca Vigía to spend an afternoon with Ernest Hemingway.

Dad admired Hemingway more than any other writer of the time. Part of that admiration was due to Hemingway's prose, and part to his pose—to his demonstrated courage, and his deliberately cultivated aura of masculinity. But they were only acquaintances, not friends. Since the death of Steve Benét, in '43, Dad had avoided—and, in the future, always would avoid—friendship with major writers of the time. He knew many of them, he'd met them, but he tended to shun them, for it was important to him to be the center of any group of which he was a part. He *needed* to be the center. He did not seek for rivals in his social life.

Yet "Papa" was different. He'd been no gangplank correspondent, and Dad knew that Hemingway could write. He thought *A Farewell to Arms* the great novel which it is. We arrived about noon, and Papa was an amiable host. He poured mighty drinks for us all as soon as we arrived, and more drinks still before lunch. He had a yacht cannon by the pool, and delighted in charging it and firing it off. He seemed tight, even drunk, and I was smugly certain that, as I whispered to my sister, "Hemingway is through." He'd make no more fine books.

At that very time he was rising at five in the morning and, after stretching his aching back, would stand at his lectern and, in the longhand he loved to use, would write another few pages of *The Old Man and the Sea*. So much for my youthful smugness, clouded by mist.

There was one other event of that visit which shouts now through the years. Layne and Bill Shroder always remembered the sight of Dad and Ernest Hemingway sitting on a couch together, talking about their work. Hemingway seemed familiar with all of Dad's books, and Dad with few of Hemingway's.

"I'm a nineteenth-century man, God damn it! After Dickens and Tolstoy, they don't matter." Or mattered too much.

In the fall I went back to school, at the University of Chicago. I got good marks, because I could write clever papers, but I wasn't working hard and I thought that I was learning little. I wrote bad poems about Jiska and Agrigento. There was a girl who was only sixteen and thus too young, or so I primly felt. Pathetic "dry humping" was the limit I allowed. I don't think she appreciated that. On weekends, drinking too much at the University Tavern, I argued with friends about the necessity of the Korean War. I thought, and said loudly, belligerently, that it had to be fought. Eventually the obvious finally occurred to me—blasted its way through my adolescent mist. While I sat, safe and noisy and protected by my academic deferment, young men from farms and filling stations, who had no notion at all of the reasons for the war, were getting killed. Which was not right. I walked off the campus, in the middle of the quarterly exams, and enlisted.

In the Air Force, of course. Mother was upset, and furious with Dad. She maintained that he had influenced me, though he had never said a word. He was very proud of me. He was delighted. He had just finished six missions over Korea as a correspondent, in B-29s. Perhaps I might ride a '29 there too. Up to the Yalu River, as he had done.

I spent four years, two months, and three days in the service, and I counted every year, every month, every day, still enveloped in a sort of haze. I did well in basic training but, when Sergeant Allen, our drill in-structor, nominated me for a special award as the man in our flight who had made the most effort or most distinguished himself or some such, I stalked off to the training squadron headquarters, and asked to see the com-manding officer. I couldn't believe that I had earned that nomination on my own, and Dad knew a lot of senior officers—from both wars, and from his work as a consultant with "the assimilated rank of Lieutenant General" (a phrase he loved to use; in The Company, as a child, he had only been Captain of Scouts). I demanded to know if the nomination was the result of my father's influence, and was puzzled when assured that it was not.

As puzzled as the major who'd answered my question.

After basic I went home on leave. *"Mack, go on!"* . . . *"I will, if Timmy will stop his braying and let us sing."*

And then I trained as an observer in Cadets. As a navigator. My left knee still gave me trouble but the young men I was training with were mostly decent people and, if the knee gave out while we were marching, they'd pick me up by the elbows and shove me back in line. They hid me with their bodies, and none of our officers ever knew. I'd not been interested in math in school, I'd done poorly in geometry, but now I wanted to master the trigonometry which navigators must learn, and so I did. I gained no Cadet rank, and I'm sure I was regarded as an eccentric—the only one who lugged along a duffel bag stuffed with paperback books whenever we changed barracks—but, when the course was over, I was named a Distin-guished Graduate.

Dad gave me a Ford.

I was still in combat crew training when the truce was signed, which was fortunate both for me and for my crew. It usually took a navigator some three months after getting his wings to become really competent. It took me far longer. I was so uncertain, so afraid of making some simple mathematical error, that I'd add up columns of figures over and over until I did foul up. Even after we went to Okinawa. I was perhaps the only navigator ever to tell his aircraft commander that they were sixty miles west of the Philippine Islands when, in fact, they were sixty miles to the east. In combat such an error could have been unpleasant. Fatal.

Eventually I gained the confidence to feel, with reason, that I deserved the wings I wore, and I won another battle also. All through my teens, ever since Dad had first gone stumping off to war, I had suffered the fear of physical violence. Not just the awareness of the possibility of hurt or danger which any sane person feels. Nor any fear of death. I was afraid of *losing*. Losing a fist fight. I was afraid, not of bruising to cheek or jaw, to arms or chest, but of the look of triumph I might see in the face of him who bested me. Scorn, and triumph in the eyes. Contempt—I'd been terrified of that.

And so I had encountered contempt. Quite rightly so.

But that had changed. There was some anti-Semitic nonsense in the barracks once, and I responded properly, and successfully. There was a row which degenerated into a fight with another young officer, larger than I was, and stronger—a former football tackle—and I survived for five long, battered minutes, until others came to break it up. I felt surer of myself than I had in years.

And yet...

When I got back from Okinawa I had three weeks' leave, and I spent them in New York. I bought a typewriter or I rented one, and I holed up in a hotel room on Madison Avenue. I, by God, was going to be a writer. In those three weeks I wrote—or overwrote, according to some friends—a short story about a young American in Spain. I never did submit it to any magazine and, eventually, I trashed it. In retrospect, I think that it may have been pretty good, but the writing of it had been agony. I had all those words inside of me, but they came out lame and halting. I saw my father's strong face, confident and commanding, between me and the typewriter. Between me and each word I forced onto the paper. He was staring out from every letter, every key. Frustration and fear brought me almost to tears.

And that mist, all around.

* * *

Mack was crying.

Four months earlier, and I was still on Okinawa. Late at night, and Mack was pretty well liquored up. He had gone to visit friends. He had knocked on the door, carrying his guitar, and then lurched in when the door was opened. The friends were dear to him. So many of his friends were dear. Sally Glendinning was a reporter for the *Sarasota Herald-Tribune*; Dick had been a magazine editor in New York, and was also a writer of accomplishment, but he had not been as successful as Mack, was not as famous, and so he posed no threat. Mack had said, "I've come to sing."

He had sung, they had sung, for over an hour. Songs of the Civil War. "Many are the hearts that are weary tonight, / Wishing for the war to cease..." "We shall meet, but we shall miss him, / There will be one vacant chair..." And then drinking songs; and Mack had kept drinking too. His words had become more slurred.

At last he'd put down the guitar, and shaken his head, and cried out, "I am so *goddamned* scared! I'd rather be over Regensburg or Schweinfurt, facing a whole flock of Focke-Wulfs, or waiting for the flak. I have a chance, damn it," and the tears had started coming, "I have a chance to write *the* novel of the Civil War. The greatest one that's ever been written. But it's got to be a big book, a huge book. I've got to do what no one's ever done. I've got to show the soul of this country, the way it was then—North and South, rich and poor, white and black. I've got to live for months and months with filth and misery. Degradation. I know how to do the damn thing. Hell, I wrote about Belle Island in *Arouse and Beware*, that's eighteen years ago, and I've researched Andersonville Prison for years, and I smelled the stink of Buchenwald. I slipped in vomit there. I know the things that men can do to men. And I know about courage, I know about love. My God, I'm almost fifty years old. I've been training for this book all my life. But I don't know if I have the guts, the stamina. I see all those ghosts in blue and gray, and they frighten me. They keep challenging me."

The Glendinnings offered soothing words, but Mack went on plaining, with the tears still seeping from his eyes. "And this is my chance. This story. *Andersonville*. It can be an American *War and Peace*. It can be the big book. The big one. It can get the Pulitzer. Even the Nobel prize. But I'm going up against Tolstoy, and I don't know if I have the talent. The wisdom. And all those folks—farmer, tinker, banker, plantation owner; virgin, whore, hero, bully; blue and gray—they keep coming at me in the night. They want me to do it *right*. Jesus Christ, I'm scared. I've got everything riding on this book."

They poured him into his car—he was a fairly good driver when drunk—and he went home. He didn't want Irene to see the state he was in. He dried his tears, donned a cloak of alcoholic jauntiness, before he went inside.

During the next year and a half Mack slipped back and forth between the present and the past a thousand, a hundred thousand, times. He haunted the physical site of Andersonville Prison, and its history haunted his mind. He and Irene went to Europe for one long stay in '54. They liked Spain best. Torremolinos. They'd drive off into the countryside and find, perhaps, a hillside covered with olive trees, or a herd of grazing sheep. Irene would set up her folding stool, her easel, her canvas, her paints, and set to work. Mack had another stool he'd rigged to support his typewriter in their car.

Back home he dictated to his secretary. The words kept coming. Three hundred and forty thousand of them. Our Civil War, as best as he could tell it: he had brought those who fought that war, those who suffered it, back to life. The book was published in October of '55, and it sold, and sold, and sold. The *New York Times Book Review*—on its front page again—called it "the greatest of our Civil War novels." It was a Book of the Month Club selection, and Columbia Pictures bought the movie rights for a quarter of a million dollars.

Mack was ecstatic, and so was Irene, though she thought, he thought, everyone thought, that he was drinking too much. "How the hell do you expect me to come down from that labor, this excitement, overnight?" They were back in Paris, sitting in the bar of the Prince de Galle and having drinks before dinner, when a man came up to them. Gardner "Mike" Cowles. Mike Cowles was the publisher of *Look* magazine then, but back in 1930, when Mack was writing a column for the *Des Moines Tribune*, Mike had worked there also. Worked for his father, who owned the *Tribune*, and Mack and he had been friendly. Twenty-six years later, just a few days before, they had run into one another in Paris and had dinner together, and now Mike Cowles stood at their table, looking down and smiling. But the smile was somehow solemn. He said, "Congratulations, Mack."

Mack kept his face still and straight, although—the timing was right, and he'd been waiting for this—he thought he knew what Mike was going to say. He gripped Irene's hand tight. *"I'm going to be a great writer someday. I know I can be."* "Oh?"

"I just came from our local office. I saw it on the wire. It's official. *Andersonville* won the Pulitzer Prize." He shook Mack's hand, kissed Irene on the cheek, and joined them at their table. Mack ordered a bottle of champagne. Mike raised his glass, and said, "It's a long way from Des Moines."

Irene was laughing and crying all at once. She looked at Mack. "It's even longer from the Graeme Players."

Late that night, when he was muzzy with drink, tears came to Mack also. This time, they were tears of joy. Of pride. He thought of the pride his mother would have felt, and wept for her as well. Until a nasty thought half-sobered him. "And now I've got to do it all again."

A few days later they had further reason for champagne. Layne, aside from being a cosseting wife and busy mother, had—at the urging of her husband, and with Dad's encouragement—been at work upon a novel of her own. She had finished it, and submitted it to Dad's publisher. Toward the end of April she wired them: "Novel accepted. Hurray! John Kantor died yesterday. Love."

"Well," Dad said, "hurray, indeed, for Layne-o! And, at last, we're rid of him."

For most of my life I laughed at the thought of pompous, wicked John Kantor. But, writing this book, I came to take on my father's contempt for him, and my father's rage. Now, suddenly, writing these words, I feel pity for him. He was vital and vibrant and brilliant, and yet, like other moral cripples, he left such a puny legacy. His father would spit at the mention of his name. The voice of his eldest daughter, a very gentle woman, still quivers in anger when she speaks of him. And, when they heard of his death, his only son and his daughter-in-law celebrated with an especially elaborate dinner, and they ordered two bottles of champagne.

"...at last we're rid of him."

Not quite. When he went into the hospital for his final stay John Kantor persuaded the admissions office that his son, "MacKinlay Kantor, the famous novelist," would pay his bill.

They were quite upset when Dad refused to honor this. *"Do you love your Daddy, sweetheart?"*

My cameras sat on a shelf, staring at me with their big, hard eyes. It was almost noon but still I lay in bed, unwilling to move.

After my leave in the spring of '54, and my bruising at the typewriter, I had gone up to Maine. I'd been assigned to a tanker squadron, KB-29s, stationed at Dow Air Force Base, in Bangor. I shared an old white house with three other young officers. We flew training missions, and partied in between, and in the winter the summer kitchen became piled high with empty bottles. It was in Bangor that I met Nan—first, fierce love—and presumed, played at, maturity. But the future frightened me. I wanted to be a writer. I felt that I *was* a writer, by destiny and desire, and yet I dared not write, and I knew of no suppository for the mind.

After Maine there came Texas and Alaska, and then I was out. I was done with the Air Force and, a few months later and at her demand, I was done with Nan. That devastated me. I had felt that, by accepting me as her lover, she had given me my manhood—I would have made blustering denial then, but I hadn't yet learned that manhood grows only from within—and, in rejecting me, it seemed that she had taken it away. Done with the Air Force, done with Nan, I felt that I was almost done with myself. (My father striding, firm, on the edges of my mind.)

In the fall of '56 I went back to school, on the GI Bill, at Columbia. The Greeks had always fascinated me, and the Byzantines. I decided that I would become a scholar of Byzantine history. The past seemed safe to me, it seemed secure. I took a course in Ancient Greek, and I learned enough to know that it was a lovely language (even more beautiful, more subtle than our own rich English tongue). But, after a few months, it dawned on me that the Greeks and the Byzantines were dead, and that, however frightened I might be by the world, this present world which I inhabited, I wished to comment on it. To grapple with it.

I did not wish to live among the dead.

Nan came to New York for a brief visit, and I took her to lunch. The sight of her, sound of her, smell of her, stirred my guts. I started to write a novel, filled with self-pity, about young love, but I only got about ten pages into it before I froze. My father, damn him, bless him, getting in the way. Writing hurt—not as the exercise of any art or craft hurts as it makes its demands, but physically. It hurt to type, to beat out words. I told myself that I was in love, not with the act of writing itself, but only with the idea of being a writer. And yet I wanted to close with this world, and caress it.

It was then that I thought of a camera. I'd been given a Box Brownie when I was six, and photographed a few street scenes—I remember a shot of an old woman scrounging in garbage cans. I'd taken a cheap camera to Europe, but in six months I'd only used two rolls of film. It seemed then that the camera got in the way, that, with all its mechanics, it distanced me from the scene before me, rather than linking me to it. But later, in the Air Force, I'd picked up a 35-millimeter Canon, and a projector, and spent a few happy months making slides of friends, of Nan and her kids, of the many-colored fall. A few of those pictures had not been bad, had captured a little life, but I'd lost interest (I was going to be a writer!), and had sold the camera to a friend.

It occurred to me now that I'd been flirting with cameras for years. And, since I'd been a little kid, I had pored over the pages of each new issue of *Life* magazine. Its arrival each week had been, not only for me and my parents but for millions of others, an *event*. It had been our TV. The best of the picture stories had moved, even haunted, me; become part of my mental baggage. I borrowed another camera and, the first time I looked into the viewfinder, I seemed to see the world more clearly, more acutely, more intimately, than even when I'd peered out of childhood windows of long ago. When, later, I saw what I had first seen through the camera made still and eloquent in black and white, I was hooked. I might not be able to write about the world, but I thought that I could picture it. Capture life on film; seize elements from the whirl of life around me and bring them into balance. Impose order on a disorderly world. I dropped out of school. To hell with it. I was going to be a photojournalist.

I learned to see—to see light and shadow, color and form; to anticipate both motion and emotion—and my progress was rapid. More rapid than I believed. I tried to learn to process film and to make good prints, and my progress was slow. I turned to a professional lab, as did many neophytes in those days—heady days, with photojournalism the center of our world. The client, magazine or other, if there was one, would pay for processing. Dad supported me, underwrote my existence, and I learned. I grew. But every time I picked up a camera, to try to add to my portfolio, every time I went to see a picture editor or art director, I put myself on the line. That frightened me. Sometimes it seemed safer to sleep, or to lie in bed, only half wakeful. As long as I lay there, and made no effort, I risked no failure.

But there was film in the refrigerator, and the cameras kept staring at me, until I stirred.

Five years later, down in Ecuador. Almost five o'clock in the morning and the night was still black—black as the sugary coffee I was drinking to bring myself awake.

I had learned my craft fairly well. I had made myself competent. I'd sold pictures to this magazine and that one, I'd had small assignments from *Life* and others, I was making (almost) a living. I had spent six months in Guatemala, working on a book which never was published because the publisher folded. And because the fifteen thousand words of painful prose were not very good, and the layout was uncertain.

The pictures, however—well, I had brought some pictures home. I had tried *Life* and *Look*, but their editors weren't interested in Guatemala then. Or in Latin America. Because they thought—quite rightly, quite irresponsibly—that their readers weren't. But there was a little magazine called *Pageant*. Its editors had excellent taste, though a very limited budget, and it served as a sort of proving ground or showcase for promising young photojournalists. They ran a ten-page picture story of mine on Guatemala, with my own text—brief, written to character count, and hard-achieved—and it was very good. I had wandered all over the face of that tortured land, from poor-ass mountain villages filled with unconscionable squalor to the Presidential Palace and the Club Guatemala, filled with unconscionable, tasteless luxury. I had managed to get myself arrested once. (The camera, particularly with a wide-angle lens, is a dangerous amulet, for it can lead you in so close. You come to think that, through the viewfinder, you are only witnessing a scene; a scene made just for you.) The National Police had been beating a protester in a political demonstration, and I had photographed them doing so. They had turned their billy clubs on me, and sent the camera I held to my eye flying to the end of its strap. They shoved me, along with the young man they'd been beating on, into a police car, and took us to the city prison. It was a forbidding place, but I was out within two hours. We had been on television when they hustled me away, and influential friends I'd made had seen, and made phone calls. The cops even forgot to confiscate my film.

I had come to love that land and its people. I had even come to dream in Spanish. Most of the dreams were sad.

Up in the highlands I had heard on the marimba a wild and whining lament. "El Rey Quiché"—"The Quiché King." Back in Guatemala City there was the Tourist Bar, to which no tourist ever went. I liked the bar, the bartender, and the band. One night I asked the blind accordionist, and the clarinetist—who played also for the Guatemala Symphony Orchestra, whenever it was in operation—if they knew that tune. They did. After that, every night I went into the place, they played that song for me. I knew their land better than they did, I knew their language, I was not some goddamned Gringo, and I reigned there for months as "The Quiché King."

And now I rode through the dark, bleak streets of Riobamba, in an old jeep driven by the head of the CARE operation in Ecuador. Outside the city we turned onto a rough, unpaved mountain road, and lurched along until we came to a tiny village. We parked and went into a one-room school-house, where there were candles burning. On a shelf between two of the candles were an alarm clock, a blackboard, and a little battery-powered radio, all provided by CARE. The room was filled with villagers, Quechua Indians ranging in age from six to sixty, who—before their daylong labor in the fields, which would bring them thirty or forty cents—were trying to *learn*. Learn to write their own language, learn to speak and write in Spanish, learn to add and subtract. Learn to better themselves in the harsh world they inhabited. An instructor, with perhaps a fourth-grade education, stood at the blackboard and wrote as words came over the radio. It was a daily broadcast put out by the local Catholic diocese. It was one-quarter religious indoctrination, but the rest was sound instruction, amazingly effective. And they were all so eager, so desperate, to learn. I saw the earnestness in the teacher's eyes, the earnestness in the determined faces of two little girls who huddled together at a table, grasping pencils awkwardly. And, by God, I got them.

In the early dawn, so soft for so harsh a land, we trudged a thousand feet higher over long-beaten mountain paths, my knees hardly bothering me at all, to an even smaller hamlet. Coming down again, the valley opened out before us, all different shades of green, and tall trees, like cypress, growing toward the sun. On the path below us, two men turned to stare at us—as though we were visitors out of time—and one of them wore a bright red poncho. A gnomelike figure passed us, and the sun cast his shadow on a bank of stone. I got them all: valley, alien stare, and gnome.

Later, in the jeep again, we climbed over the high shoulder of Mount Chimborazo. We passed a merchant in the mist, leading a burro, heavy-laden. On a high pasture we saw a flock of sheep, and their ten-year-old shepherd squatted down and stared at us when we paused. We spilled over the edge of the Andes, and stopped for gas in a market town. There was a bus, a converted truck, parked nearby, and through a window I saw a man with a desolate face, clutching, cherishing, a bouquet of flowers. I used the camera with the long lens to get them, seize them, fix them on film: merchant and mist, and shepherd boy rising out of the ground, and mourner with the flowers.

That evening we crossed flat lowlands, and a river, and came to Guayaquil. There were the homeless in the streets, sleeping on the sidewalks, but for us there was a good hotel. In the morning there were hovels to be explored.

*   *   *

My God, I thought, they look so old! If they're eight they seem to be eleven or twelve, if they're twenty they might be thirty, if they're forty, sixty— sixty-five? It's their faces, the limited expectation, the knowledge in their eyes.

The line of women and girls curved out of the shack in which I stood and continued down a dirt street which ran between open sewers in the city of Guayaquil. Each individual held a bowl, a bucket, or a pan, and stood passive, patient, perhaps chatting quietly with a neighbor in the line. Their eyes seemed to brighten as they reached the doorway and could see their goal. It was right in front of me. A large cauldron of reconstituted milk, courtesy of CARE and the city's League of Ministering Ladies.

Outside, the sunlight shattered on particles of dirt suspended in the heavy air, producing a curious dusty glare. Inside, a rooster hunted bits of food in a corner of the shack, and flies attracted by the cauldron hovered, buzzed, and menaced. A neighborhood volunteer, proud of the importance her position gave her, presided with a ladle in her hand, doling out the milk to each supplicant in turn—one, three, ten portions, according to the number of children in each family. The hovels in which they lived lay jammed together all around us, as far as the eye could see or the nose could smell.

The kids, why weren't they in school?

Foolish question, and I knew the answer. To go to school they needed books, and writing pads, and pencils, and at a church school they'd need uniforms; and so, even if they were only six, they did women's work, and tried sometimes to play. The men I didn't ask about; I remembered now. They were working for a dollar or less a day, or looking for work, or pray- ing for work, or lying at home in a hammock or on a homemade mattress, sweaty or consumptive, empty-eyed.

I had to watch my exposure. It was dark in there, and bright as hell outside. I didn't want to lose their faces, and yet the background was im- portant too. A $1/125$ at about f/2.8 should do. I worked away, trying differ- ent angles, different faces. I spotted her when she came in the door, her old young face so grave and lovely. She couldn't be more than nine. Spanish ancestry predominated, but there was Inca too, in eyes and skin and rich, dark hair. Bare feet, forever-mended dress, walking so erect and proud. Flower on a dunghill. Flowers didn't last long, not in that environment. I wondered how long this one would last.

Well, by fifteen, I thought, she'll be a whore—that's one way out of here, the only way she'll ever find. But get this woman next, with the lined old face and hanging breasts, how many has she nursed? And look who's in the doorway, with Indian-braided gray hair. And now my little girl is here, she's holding out her bowl, staring at the milk so hard, and here's the ladle pouring.

Click.

Ten months later I got a letter from a couple in Connecticut. They'd seen the picture in a magazine, they couldn't rest for thinking of the child, and could I help them find her? I wrote and told them it was almost impossible, she was one of so very many, but I enclosed the address of the CARE office in Guayaquil and wished them luck.

In time, another letter came. They'd found the child. Arrangements had been made to help the family and they'd provided for her education.

It made me feel a bit like God, until the rent came due.

Back in the late fifties the success of *Andersonville* had made my father feel a lot like God, and for a far longer time. He was courted by publishers and Hollywood producers. Proudly, happily he received the honorary degrees he felt were his due—and none pleased him more than the doctorate from Drake University. Drake—where his mother and father had met some sixty years before. (When he spoke at the convocation, he saw Effie's face in the audience, filled with joy, and John Kantor's face as well—iced by envy, warmed by reluctant pride.)

He had indulged me and my sister in various ways, and he had indulged his love of private charity. (Once he had written, "If there is any better thing to do with money than to buy a contribution toward human delight, I have yet to hear of it.") He had indulged himself and Mother by having the house in Florida remodeled and expanded, according to Mother's design. There was a vast new living room, the old living and dining rooms had become the relic-encrusted workroom described long pages past, and the old garage had been made into a large, air-conditioned studio, complete with north light, where Mother painted away—busily, happily, productively. And he had bought more land on either side of the house, to preserve the jungle all around.

That had required a lot of money. Payment for the movie rights was stretched out over ten years, and so he had borrowed against those payments and other future earnings from "Big A." (That was how he always referred to *Andersonville*. He was not conscious of any affectation in using the phrase. It was, to him, just a simple assertion of the book's importance.) Out in California, in the early forties, Donald Friede had been in a financial bind and Dad had lent him some money. That money had long since been repaid, and now Donald—who had been the happy, enthusiastic, long-suffering editor of "Big A"—was well-fixed, and he lent Dad a large sum of money in his turn. Eighty thousand dollars, which was paid back carefully, scrupulously, through the years. Dad would be *damned* before he'd be like John Kantor. Years later his longtime tax and contract lawyer, Maurice Greenbaum, wrote, "He was the most honest man I ever knew.... He went through life on his own terms, with great style and, above all, with integrity." He had; he spent. He borrowed, and he gave. And with "great style" indeed, a style mixed out of generosity and self-centeredness, modesty and self-importance, humor and anger, gentleness and fury, confidence and uncertainty, all confused. Confused by a confusing world which he no longer recognized as his.

"I'm a nineteenth-century man, Goddamn it!" And into that century he had again retreated for his next big book. *Spirit Lake*. Memories of tales about the Spirit Lake massacre back in 1857, and visions of the lean, lined faces of survivors of the relief expedition from Webster City, whom he had heard reciting legends when he was five or six or seven, had lingered with him always. But it wasn't just thought of snow and cold, of barbarity and sacrifice, which had so intrigued him. He had the notion that by putting tales of different lives together, both white and Indian, like putting beads upon a string to make a rosary, he could make a sacrament to celebrate our frontier experience. Make it come alive as no one had before.

This time, by God, he *would* earn the Nobel prize. *"When you're a man, you've got to do great things."* He had harsh dreams at night. Black bullies threatened, and outcast Indians came to torture him.

The research involved was enormous. He was a historian of the first rank. Even those critics who questioned his literary accomplishment never challenged his accuracy. If he described a country doctor's practice in 1835, or Jenny Lind's extravagant, hysterical reception in New York in 1850, he was correct in every detail. As early as the summer of '56, when I had just bid hurtful farewell to Nan, he had asked me to go to Poland, Maine, to research local records about "the year without a summer." Eighteen sixteen—"eighteen-hundred-and-froze-to-death." And in New York, during the next four years, when his own enormous research collection and his contacts at the Library of Congress wouldn't serve, I received occasional requests to find information about this or that obscure event or personality. Partly that came of his desire to help me through hungry stretches in my work—he paid me for my time—but also it was due to his determination to get not one happening, not one fact, not one word, wrong.

He was no linguist—I used to laugh at the bastard Spanish he'd picked up in Spain—but, during several trips to the Rosebud Reservation in South Dakota, he gained a basic knowledge of Siouan. Because it was important to him to be accurate.

He and Mother crossed the Atlantic several times during those years. He liked to work at sea, in the early mornings when the other passengers weren't up, and he loved to work in Europe, away from all press and pressure. He was truly a noted figure now and, in Sarasota, the lion of the town. On the way to catch their ship they'd fly into New York. First Class, of course, for Dad felt that he had earned it, and because his left leg sometimes gave him trouble when he flew cramped in Tourist. Then they'd ride into town—no taxicab, neither red, yellow, nor green, for them now; rather a black, shiny, rented limousine—to the Algonquin, and to an extravagant, almost obsequious, welcome.

Dad liked all that immensely. Mother enjoyed it too, indeed she gloried in it (they were a long way from Wi*l*son Avenue, and from Wi*ll*son Avenue too), but she did worry about finances. To ease that worry, she'd go out and buy another dress.

Sometimes, during their stay in the city, they'd go up to Scarsdale, to visit Layne and Bill Shroder and their children. Mother would be anxious and warm and eager, a youthful, sweet-scented, atypical image of a grandmother. Dad would usually drink too much, and always he would want to perform and preside—singing songs, reading to Layne and Bill the latest chapters of the manuscript he was working on, reading to the kids excerpts from children's books he had written, and seeming to ignore totally—display no interest in—their reports on their own doings. Later he would exaggerate and boast about their achievements to friends, and to strangers met abroad.

And always, back in New York, there would be a ritual, repeated numerous times. Dad and Mother, with these friends or others, and often with Layne and Bill and me, and sometimes with my current love, tagging on behind. Dad was, in his own estimation and because the world had told him so, a great man then. There would be drinks in their suite at the Algonquin, then cabs summoned, and then the grand procession to a table, with greetings from the manager or owner and a scurrying of waiters, and drinks and dinner and laughter, at this favorite restaurant or that. And, at the end of the evening, he would insist on taking the check for everyone, and tip quite grandly. *"What model ever did I have?"*

He moved through some of those days, during some of those years, in a bright alcoholic fog. Sober as a stern, demanding judge in the mornings; foolishly benign, foolishly angry, late at nights.

*   *   *

Spirit Lake was published in the fall of 1961, to mixed reviews. One critic hailed it as the Great American Novel; *Life* called it "a gigantic sweeping symphony"; *The New York Times* was generous—*Time* and *The New Republic* sneered. The prose was deliberately ornate, more so even than in *Andersonville*, and far distant from the crisp, clear words he'd spun in the thirties and early forties. He had thought that he had a mighty saga to relate, and must find words to suit.

Mack Kantor put all he knew into *Spirit Lake*—a lifetime of observing, reading, and remembering—and he made a mighty world. All of America's westering experience was cherished in its pages. Surely the past he loved had burned within him when he wrote, but some reviewers felt that he had smothered that past, that world, in words.

Summertime of 1962, and the work was slow. All the picture editors and art directors were off on vacation, at Fire Island, or Martha's Vineyard, or Cape Cod. It was about noon, and I was working on yet another idea for a picture story, to be submitted to *Life* or *Look,* when the phone rang and my father's voice came pulsing down the line. Vibrant and tough, and yet somehow uncertain.

"Tim!"

"Yes, Dad. How are you doing?"

"Not so good. Are you busy right now? Do you have any assignments?"

"Well, you know, the summer..." My hand shook, and almost my voice did, too. To report lack of success to him, who seemed still to me to be always successful, was abhorrent.

"Thank God. Look, I'm out here in Webster City, staying with Ax Crosley. I've been drinking my way across the country—the booze had started to build up before I left Sarasota—and I've been drinking here, and last night they had a party for me. At six o'clock this morning I woke up, and found that I was staring at the goddamn trees. I'd passed out on the lawn. And so," and there was more annoyance and weariness in his voice than shame, "I decided that it was time to climb back on the wagon."

"That's great, Dad."

"Yeah! The trouble is, I've got the shakes. Bad. I'm due in New York in a few days, to talk to Donald Friede and some other people, but I don't dare drive the car. And yet I hate to leave it here. I wondered..." Now his voice became diffident. He hated to ask for help from anyone, even, or especially, me. "I wondered if you could possibly fly out to Des Moines tomorrow, I can get the car that far, and drive me back east. I know it's a hell of a thing to ask..."

"Oh, Dad, for Christ's sake! Sure I will."

"...and of course I'll pay for the ticket."

The next morning I flew west.

It was perhaps the fourth time in ten years that he'd gone on the water wagon. Almost literally. He reacted badly to caffeine, it made him exceedingly nervous, he disliked most forms of soda drinks, and so he'd limit himself largely to water and spicy Virgin Marys. He'd eat more, he would make a batch of fudge, with a recipe learned from Effie; or Mother—beaming at the thought of his sobriety—would make brownies. Her brownies were wonderful. In the evenings, he'd make popcorn and, lying in bed and reading, spoon it out of a bowl of milk. Gradually the tension would seep out of him, but also, he complained, creative energy as well, and—after three months, six months, a year—he'd go back to social drinking. And boast proudly of how moderate he was. And then his drinking would slowly escalate, particularly when he was coming off a long stint of hard work, and the whole pattern, the whole agony, would have to be repeated.

When I got to Des Moines he was there to meet me at the airport—smiling, a little rueful. We shook hands in greeting, and I was suddenly acutely aware of the first time we had done so, rather than hug and kiss. I had been fourteen, and coming back from a summer job. I'd been working as a cabin boy on a dude ranch in Colorado. Dad had come to meet me at the airport and had stood apart from me, extended his hand instead of embracing me, when I got off the plane. I knew that it was a sort of rite of passage and felt flattered, and at the same time curiously bereft.

His hands were trembling when he gave me the keys to the car. He shrugged and said, "I damn near didn't get here, even though I only went at thirty miles an hour all the way."

We drove through the gold and green and loamy black of Iowa farmland, with tall clouds marshaled overhead and the sun kind to the earth below. We talked a little and he talked a lot, which was the usual pattern when we were together. To have learned all that he had learned about different people and different ways of life, he must have been at one time, in other circumstances, a good listener, an excellent audience for other people's tales. But not now. Not with me. He would ask eagerly about any minor professional triumph I might have had—but never the details; details bored him—and inquire if there was a new "babe" in my life, or if an old flame still flickered. He would ask me if I needed money. We could chat briefly about other members of the family, or friends we held in common. We might, particularly in the evenings, particularly after drinks, argue about politics: I was moderately liberal; he had grown increasingly, angrily, conservative. After such talk he'd end up calling me a "little Commie bastard" and I'd call him a "goddamned old fascist," and we'd move on to other things. Such dissension was allowed, but I was expected to laud everything he ever wrote, and he offered unthinking, facile praise for every photograph of mine he ever saw.

Mostly, on that trip and at other times, he talked. Brilliant, uncertain soul, lodged in a vigorous body. He would hold forth in constant monologue, sometimes spontaneous but often well rehearsed from other tellings. Stories about the country we were traveling through or about people he had known; stories, almost invariably, about the past.

"This little village up ahead. Back in '92 Dvořák, the Czech composer, spent the summer there. The town was filled with Czechs in those days. Immigrants. That's where he wrote the *New World Symphony*. You remember the largo, with all of America in it," and his voice crooned, "'Going home, going home...'" Crooned all through town. He said, "Take it easy, and I'll show you the house he lived in." An old frame house with, it seemed, no music left inside.

"Your mother saw a ghost, once. In an abandoned farmhouse not far from here, where we had to spend the night... And once I saw, or almost saw, a ghost. In a rooming house in England. And I wasn't drunk!... " He was an ardent supporter of the American Society of Psychical Research. The thought of ghosts made the world more pleasing to him. "And once your sister saw a ghost. Met with her for nights on end. You remember about the Pink Lady?" I lied and said I didn't. Partly that was politeness or deference, but also I enjoyed listening to his stories. I'd been listening to them all my life—an engaging, sometimes enchanting, ever dominant drone in my ear. In my mind.

"It was back in late December of '31, just before you were conceived. Just after Mother died." His facial muscles tightened, the way they always did when he mentioned Effie's death. The sun was sinking low behind us. Almost dusk. *"For ghosts glide in the hayrick..."* A good time for ghost stories. "After Mother became ill again, and came to live with us on Germania Drive, in Des Moines, she shared the other bedroom with Layne-o. Layne wasn't quite four yet, and she still liked her crib, but Mother would take her into her bed at nights, and tell her stories. About a little black cat, our cat, who had adventures. Went to the moon. Things like that. Layne-o loved those stories. Then Mother had another heart attack." He gestured toward his own breast. "She wasn't doing too well, and we moved Layne's crib into our bedroom. When Mother died, the day after Christmas, and they'd taken her body away—poor, sad piece of clay—we cleaned out that room. Your mother and I. Sorted clothes to give to charity, and things to keep. We washed the bedclothes, and I took out the mattress, to air it and beat it free of death. I guess nowadays they'd call it therapy. That night we told Layne-o that she was sleeping in her old bedroom again, and she went without protest." He laughed. "She'd been jumping on that aired mattress, once I'd put it back, all afternoon and evening, and I figured that her childish glee had chased away all ghosts. But, for days after that, she was so eager to go to bed! We asked her about it, and she said, 'Oh, I *love* to go to bed! Because, before I go to sleep, every night the Pink Lady comes to visit me. She sits beside me on the bed, and tells me such wonderful stories.' We asked, 'Who is she?' And she said, 'Just the Pink Lady.'"

He paused, for dramatic effect. "Mother had had a pink dress, one of the things we gave away. Those last months, she used to wear it a lot."

About eight o'clock we found a decent motel, complete with restaurant and bar. When we went into the dining room, found a table, and the waitress approached us, Dad ordered a Virgin Mary. I hesitated. It had been a long day, but I didn't want to introduce temptation—add to the discomfort I knew he was feeling. He laughed. "Go ahead. Have a couple of drinks. It won't bother me. You've earned them!" His hands were still trembling, but he stuck out his jaw, prognathous and challenging. Challenging life. "The booze is my problem, not yours." I had a double Manhattan, the first of two, and we ordered dinner.

Sipping the drink, I thought about his courage, and his strange nature. He would rage because there was no milk in the refrigerator, curse in anguish because he'd stubbed his toe, make a grand production over any minor annoyance. But his reaction to major disaster was different. Once, in Key West, he'd slammed the car door on his thumb. He'd opened the door again, looked at his thumb, and shrugged. "Well," he said, "I guess I've lost it." He stopped the bleeding with a handkerchief, we got him to a doctor, and he hadn't lost it after all. But he had thought so, and he'd shown grace. *Spirit Lake* had been the major effort, the greatest gamble, of his life, and the sales had been disappointing, many of the reviews tepid. He had clung to the few raves and other positive reviews for reassurance, muttered "goddamn bastard critics" about the others, and gone on grimly working. And now his hands were trembling and he wanted a drink very badly, but he sat across the table from me, and joked and laughed as I finished mine.

During the next two days we crossed the rest of the continent, with Dad talking, declaiming, all the way—recalling in fond detail the American past, and damning the American present.

By the time we got back to New York his shakes had almost disappeared.

He had an extraordinary gift for friendship. He and Bob Richardson, the son of the doctor who delivered Dad, were friends from the time they both could crawl, and remained fond friends until Dad died. Dick Whiteman, who was a few years younger, became Dad's friend in early youth, as soon as they decided that age was irrelevant, and they were intimates for the rest of Dad's life. Mother and Dick's wife Tye became close friends also. Often Dad would see the Whitemans in Los Angeles, where Dick had an advertising firm—with Mother, if she was there, or else with a "babe" in tow. Sometimes, when business demanded or vacation permitted, the Whitemans would come to New York, and we would hold happy, high reunion. (It was Dick's father who got young Mack Kantor that job on the *Cedar Rapids Republican*, and Dad never forgot it.)

Sometimes Dick and Bob, working out of childhood memory, would call Dad "Benjy." And from them, because he loved them, he accepted it.

All through his adult life he kept adding friends. A few he lost through politics or pretension, but most only through death. He and Tim Coward—of Coward-McCann, Dad's first publisher—had been close friends for years. There were long car trips to Washington or to the country, and golden days together: golden days and groggy nights. And all of them declamatory, for Timmy liked to talk and argue just as much as Dad. They got into professional rows a number of times, but the relationship lasted until the winter of '46–'47, when Dad finished a book which Tim didn't want to publish without extensive revision. Dad refused. There was still something in him of the little-boy tyrant of long ago. *Mack crying, Mack writhing in a tantrum, Mack screaming, "I want to go too!"* He'd be damned if he'd revise that book—which needed it—and took the book to Random House instead. In April Tim wrote to him a long diatribe.

> ...I'm sorry indeed you are gone from us. It marks the end of an epoch.... I think you have been on the wrong track for years & I blame myself for not facing it & risking a showdown. I probably owed it to you, but whether you would have paid any attention I doubt.... Peggy criticized, but not the right things &, of course,

Irene has never had the courage or perhaps the knowledge to stand up to you in things that really count.... You surrounded yourself with inferiors or people who so admired you personally they were incapable of a sound critical attitude toward you or your work.... All those who didn't like your work were bastards with some axe to grind.... You have resolutely refused to grow up so that a remarkable, fresh talent has been put to little use for the past 10 years. *Glory For Me* thoroughly thought out and with four times the time given to it that was and written in decent, straight-forward masculine prose might have been a great novel.... It's getting late & the discipline of a full length novel is going to be harder & harder to suffer. A few more years of Hollywood & its quick silver written under high pressure will be all you will be able to do.... I'd like you to make a smashing success with a full length, fully thought out, digested creation worth divorce from any thought of Hollywood that grave yard of serious literary talent. No one would shout Hosannas louder or be more pleased to point to the fact that C-McC first published you.... I have too much respect for the writer I once knew who *was* a writer and not an appendage of the movie industry. If this letter makes you grind your teeth & swear "I'll show that x-xxx?@ so & so" I'll be delighted...I still care about you...

Best

T

Uncle Tim (so I always called him) did care, and so did Dad care about him. After a long, cold silence they went on corresponding fondly through the years and, when *Andersonville* was published by World shortly before his death, there were few more pleased and proud than Thomas R. Coward.

Dad had an absolute need to blend business and personal relationships. He loathed, as did many others, Bennett Cerf, the publisher at Random House. It was because of his extreme fondness and admiration for Bob Haas, a senior editor there, that he stayed with them for a number of years. (Robert Haas was a charming, civilized man, an able editor, and, perhaps most important to Dad, he'd been awarded the Distinguished Service Cross when flying in France during the First World War.) Dad's lawyer, Maurice C. Greenbaum, became a close personal friend as well. They corresponded regularly, talked frequently in person or on the phone, and, out of gratitude and admiration for Maury's ability, Dad praised him loudly and brought him other clients. And out of affection, Dad paid Maury his ultimate compliment: he named his last dog, a Treeing Walker coon hound, after him.

And, if Maury (man) was and is a prince among lawyers, Maury (hound) was certainly a king among canines. I can hear him howling still, summoning neighbor dogs to his command.

Just as there was a Maury dog, there was also a MacKinlay cat. He belonged to Donald and Eleanor Kask Friede. Donald, who had been Dad's Hollywood agent, later became his longtime New York editor (and sometimes agent as well). The Friedes and the Kantors vacationed in Italy together, and in England. They traded visits—often working visits for Donald and for Dad—at each other's homes. They cherished and carefully observed the rites of friendship, which help to nurture it: the remembrance of birthdays and anniversaries of weddings and of other special happenings. The occasional gift; uncalled for, unexpected. Dad's correspondence with them was almost saccharine in its greetings. They were "Dear Ones"; Donald was variously addressed as "Donald, my baby," "Donald Duck Dear," and just plain "Dear Donald."

He had fond connection with his doctor, his dentist, and—for once, not wantonly—their wives. There were also so many others—the famous, and the unknown with private strengths, private virtues; the butcher, the baker, the candlestick maker, and couples met on this cruise or that. And folks he'd met when he was with the cops, or on active duty with the Air Force. He loved to draw people to him. He loved to share their lives.

And his own with them. Particularly with negative thoughts, he was sometimes more open and honest with special friends than he was—or could allow himself to be—with us. In the late winter of '63, perhaps six months after our trip back from Iowa, he went to the Mediterranean to research some project for the Air Force. A little while after he got home, on the eighth of May—at a time when he was telling me on the phone that he felt "grand"—he wrote a letter to an especially close friend, Colonel Micky Roth, a public information officer in the Pentagon.

> ... I started work on 16 April, which was three weeks ago yesterday. Everything I've done, coldly and cannily, is wooden, uninspiring, uninviting. I have put down a lot of cogent thoughts, and have not dressed them attractively from the standpoint of narration; nor even, I fear, from the standpoint of beguiling characterization. To say, however, that I have been trying hard is to put it mildly. I let nothing else get in front of me, and yet have constantly entertained the feeling that I was stricken speechless, that my tongue was actually torn out by the roots, that I was paralyzed, calloused—alternately a doughy shapeless uncreative lump, or else a rigid be-

ing encased in hard old-fashioned armor, with the visor of my helmet pulled tightly down, and excluding all suns and weathers.

During these past three weeks I managed to work myself very close to a state of utter mental, spiritual and physical collapse. For the first time since I was in my twenties, I didn't even wish to go on living. The tension grew to exemplify itself in the fashion of another monster dwelling inside my own body and soul—a creature made perhaps of wire-mesh or wire rings laced closely together, and extending from my finger-tips to my gullet, and up into the aching recesses of my skull, and down across my chest and into every organ and extremity.

Five days later Dad had an attack of congestive heart failure.

He survived, he almost flourished, eager and ranting once again. The doctor urged him to exercise and so, whenever he was back on Siesta Key, he would chop fallen trees for firewood, or work, in crisp air or humid, on clearing a path through the rich, thick jungle to the south of the house. He succeeded in that last task, but he never would, never could, clear a proper path through the jungle in his mind.

15

Her Eyes, Their Love, My Loss

I saw something in her eyes. I think I thought of it as wildfire.

There had been girls, even a few women, as I struggled to become a man; false love had spun past me through the years and, at least once, a hint of real love, too. I had roared in pleasure, gone crying through the night in pain, but now I was thirty and almost solvent, and I thought it time to settle down.

Time to get married. Love would buoy me, I thought; responsibility would make me grow.

Her name was Ruth Williams Bolté. Mutual friends had introduced us, "fixed us up," the night before, and now I felt fixed indeed. We were sitting at a table in a restaurant called El Faro, and talking. Courting. *El Faro* means "The Lighthouse," and the place had lit my way to romance, been my courting ground, for years. Ever since the fall of 1955, when I'd had leave and brought Nan with me to New York, and a friend had guided us there. (Later that night Nan and I had gone on to the Stork Club—first lieutenant on flight pay—and then returned to a borrowed apartment and made intense, young love.) Since I'd been out of the service every pretty female I'd met in the city, whom I had romanced and then made love with, I had taken there first. A propitiatory rite.

El Faro was on the western edge of Greenwich Village, with bad murals on its dingy walls, and a good bar, good wine, good laughter. There were Spanish records on the jukebox, and I played, over and over, one song in particular. A flamenco tune. "Sorrow, little sorrow, sorrow, / Sorrow of my heart..." The food, prepared in some steamy dungeon down below, was wonderful—paella, and shrimp in wine sauce, especially—and the service was friendly and fine. The owners and the waiters were all Gallegos, but their Castilian was as good as the food and the wine and, in the early years, they catered to me by suffering my Spanish. It was through such practice that I had kept my knowledge of that tongue alive, until I got down to Latin America for the first time. El Faro was my place. The people there had made it mine.

And now we sat there and talked, and I saw something in Ruth's eyes. Something I had never known before. Fey and beckoning. We sat there and we talked. She had a fine mind, and she was very lovely. We drank strong coffee; we sipped a liqueur. Later that night we went dancing in a place on Sheridan Square. As we danced I found myself snared within those eyes, and I told her so.

She laughed, and closed them tight. "I bet you don't even know what color they are."

"Of course I do. They're gray." She shook her head and opened them, and they were blue. But still we danced, and the world went spinning around me, vague and ill-defined. We married nine months later, and the world seemed to go on spinning for years. For we had not married each other—the living breathing, thinking, feeling person. We had married promises and dreams instead. Dreams of what the other seemed to promise, might become.

Now I must cheat, and be elliptical. My forebears are not here to protest their nakedness, and I have volunteered my own. But Ruth did not, and neither have our children. Enough to say our marriage, a sad thing of our own devising, was not a happy one. Enough to say that we can damn ourselves for marrying foolishly, and still bless the fate which gave us children such as ours.

Enough to dance and duck through the paragraphs which follow.

When we married, Jeffrey, Ruth's son from her previous marriage, was five. I had said to him, when we told him that we were getting married, that I was "marrying" him as well. That I would be his father. But I was new to fatherhood, and not particularly adept. And Jeffrey felt awkward in this new situation, and perhaps a bit resentful. (I note that I am using tentative words quite a lot here. I find it necessary.) In reaction, he picked at his food at dinner, scorning this vegetable or that piece of meat. I demanded that he finish his plate (I feared that the boy might weaken himself, might never grow at all), and we had a war of wills, and a series of unpleasant dinners, for many, many months. Even years. It wasn't until his sister, Lydia, came along, and I could watch her bloom from infancy, that I began to sense the rhythm of human growth. And realized that kids will eat what they need to eat, when they need to eat it.

It wasn't until I was over halfway through this book—reliving chants of "Eat, Timmy, eat, Timmy, eat!"—that I realized why I had been so compulsively rigid with Jeff. If he thrives today, it is not because of my dinner time admonitions, but in spite of them.

We made Lydia, and she was a gem. We made Melissa, and she was a jewel. I remember the negligible weight, the incredible warmth, of them as I carried them in my arms or, papooselike, on my back. And "Hush, honey! Hush, and lie still while I change you. I don't want any shit on the sheets." And walking them late at night, or pushing strollers, pushing swings, in the Park.

Jeffrey was a brilliant boy—he is a brilliant man—and I had been daunted by the thought of imagined "competition" with the man who had begot him. Could I father a child as bright as Jeffrey? I felt that I could deal with bright children, rewarded by the pleasure of nurturing them, but I was afraid that I might not have the substance or the strength to deal with one who was of ordinary intellect, or retarded. Fortunately I never had to address that fear. Each of the three turned out, in his or her own way, brighter than the others.

And Ruth was a marvelous, inventive, intuitive teacher. From the time they were toddling, and able to reach the walls to touch them, the children were surrounded with homemade charts listing the days of the week, the months of the year; listing and illustrating the names of colors, the progression of numbers. Celebrating thought and words.

Night wind again, heavy on my face, clawing at my hair. Night wind curls through this story, just as it curls through life. But this wind was not sweet off the prairie, nor damp with Somerset mist. It was hot and gritty; tainted. The wind which scoured Manhattan. It had combed the hair of the Tiger—"The Tiger In The Streets." Ruth and I had had yet another row, and I had gone up onto the roof of our apartment building, to get some distance and to look at the lights of the city. I leaned on the parapet as I listened to sirens sounding along the avenues sixteen stories below, taxis squealing when they came to traffic lights, a dog howling or a child crying in some sad apartment on West Ninety-fifth Street. I looked south beyond the brownstones there, toward the massive bulk of the Pan Am Building, Radio City, the tall lights of the Empire State. (There was a bronze plaque on the observation floor of that last building: "Whence rise you, lights? . . ." My father had written those words.) I looked east across the Park to apartment buildings far more comfortable than ours (I had lived in such one time), west to catch the color of Broadway, and north to remind myself of slums. Street light splattered on pavement down below. Yellow light spilled from individual windows, and I knew that there was a story behind each one. And I could have them all.

I could own the goddamn city.

I knew what was out there. I had chased after cops up tenement stairs, gone out onto other, more frightening, rooftops with them, pursuing burglars or rapists; I had outraced other cops across an empty lot, so that I could be ahead of them, catch them—kneel and shoot them with the wide-angle lens—as they pounded past me, responding to an "Assist Patrolman" call. A Signal Thirty-Two. ("You goddamn fool! We're the guys with the guns." Ah, amulet. But also, "'Kantor'? Is your old man MacKinlay Kantor? The one who wrote *Signal Thirty-Two*? I joined the cops because of that book." Everywhere my father seemed to precede me.

I had gone, of necessity and draped with cameras, into the city's sad ghettos and come back with photographic gold. I had shot drug users, and lovers young and old, in the city's parks. I had skewered the vapid folk who attended the April in Paris Ball—held, for some strange reason, in New York, in November, at the Waldorf. Laughing children in the streets, smug executives in their offices, the greedy madness on the floor of the Stock Exchange, Nobelists come to town, and Mayor John Lindsay—in conference, or riding high in a helicopter over the city lights. "Clean Gene" McCarthy, an earnest, frightened Hubert Humphrey, and a used car salesman named Richard Nixon. I had shot them all.

Dirty wind tugged at my hair and, far away, someone laughed. Someone screamed. City sounds. I had been told at lunch that day that I could own them all. Laugh and scream and eminence or notoriety could be mine to record, for all my working life. Since another happy lunch, in the spring of '66, I had not only worked regularly for *The New York Times Magazine* as a free lance, but I had also sat in for the *Times* Sunday Department photographer, whenever he was on vacation. At that time, that meant working for the *Magazine*, the "Arts and Leisure" section, the "News of the Week in Review," and the *Book Review*. Already I had been offered, and had refused, a job on the daily staff. Though the *Times* used photography well, the job seemed somehow beneath my imagined dignity —*"When you're a man, you've got to do great things"*—but now I'd been told that, when the current Sunday photographer retired, I could have his job. I tended to scorn that offer too. I felt that I should be working for *Life*. And yet the job would provide almost a decent living, and the city was out there, waiting to be seized.

I wished that I could seize it, seize anything, with words, but I knew that I couldn't. My father's shadow was in the way, hiding words.

The wind curled round me, and it was late. It was time to go back downstairs, and make peace with my wife. The kids would be asleep by now, and I hoped their dreams would be more pleasant than mine.

Back in 1964, a few months before my marriage, I had made another major error. I had opened my big mouth and, as a result, I had been blacklisted by *Life*. *Life* magazine was then, for photojournalists, at the center of our working world. If good pictures of yours had appeared in *Life*, people were impressed. If you were on the staff, or even merely a contract photographer, editors and art directors were overwhelmed. They offered you lunch; they offered you work. Assignments from *Life* could be exciting, demanding, rewarding. The stamp, the cachet, of *"Life* Photographer" could be rewarding also. But I had, in preceding months, received small assignments, and few.

One evening I gave a party. Many friends were there, and among them was Pete Turner. He was a close friend indeed. He was tall and charming and very talented, he had grown up in difficult circumstances, and he was driven to succeed—all just like my father. In my rare and reluctant attempts at self-understanding, I sometimes wondered if those similarities affected the strength of my admiration and fondness for him. Pete was one of my mentors in photography, and was already far more successful than I in the business of making images. He was not only very talented, he was also very canny—as he is today: one of the most able and admired of all professional photographers.

Nowadays color film is a relatively easy tool for the photojournalist to use, but then lenses and film quality made it more uncertain, and there were very few who had mastered it for use outside the studio. Oh, yes— perfect time of day and perfect light—it had been used for years. But they were rare who could go into some city canyon on an overcast day to cover a political rally, then into a fluorescent-lit office, and on to some event bathed in the glaring light required by TV, and come back with consistently acceptable color. It took a sophisticated knowledge of lens filters to do that, and Pete had introduced me to them. For months I had experimented with specially devised filters, mixing my own recipes of red, magenta, cyan, or blue. And I had learned.

At that party there were records on the phonograph, loud voices, and too much heat from the steam radiator. It was a Bring-Your-Own party, and there were pretty young women (Ruth was there—she was hostess) and sufficient bottles of booze. I got a little tight, and I got to talking with Pete about the new color pictures I had made. Some of them were very good, and I had an appointment with *Life*'s director of photography the next morning. I asked Pete if he had seen a recent spread in *Life* on a political primary in New Hampshire. All the indoor pictures had been shot under fluorescent light, and they had turned out green—a result of the light source acting on unfiltered film. He agreed with me that they'd been lousy. Inept. And I *knew* that I knew how to control color. Inspired by a mixture of alcohol and arrogance I exclaimed, "God damn it, I could make better pictures with no lens on my camera!"

I liked the sound of that phrase and I repeated it. Pete laughed, and he allowed that I was right. And then, born of frustration, there came to me a shimmering, foolish notion. "By God, I'm going to tell the guy just that when I see him tomorrow."

Pete Turner's face tightened, out of concern for me, and he said, "Now look, buddy, just show your pictures. I've seen them, and I know they're good. But if you say that, you'll offend the man. He'll get pissed. That's his magazine. You'll destroy yourself. You'll shoot yourself down!"

But I was struck by my own cleverness. I had long been convinced that my trouble with *Life* was that I was too soft-spoken, too diffident, too shy. Not brash, as a *Life* photographer should be. Smugly, I shook my head, and said, "No. I'm going to tell him that."

And the next morning, halfway sane and fully sober—and after the man had looked at my new slide portfolio, and made approving noises—I did. I added, "You've seen these new pictures. You know I'm good. *Use* me. Use me now!"

He looked at me for a long, cold moment. "Yeah. We did have some problems on that assignment," he said. "Good-bye, Tim." I felt like a schoolboy chided for some classroom mistake.

For months I labored, conceiving and submitting story ideas to *Life*.

They were all turned down. In September, with new material to show—aside from some assignments, I'd worked all summer on further control of color—I made an appointment with the new senior assistant director of photography. (The director happened to be on vacation.) My portfolio was greeted with raves—I was told that I was doing "just what *Life* needs," and that I would have a major assignment within months. I went home elated, with sugarplum visions filling my head. But, despite phone calls I made and letters of submission I wrote, I received no assignment at all. I got work elsewhere, but none from *Life*.

And *Life* was the center of my world.

A year later I went back again, with new and better pictures. Again the director was on vacation, again I saw a new senior assistant, again my work was praised. This time to the skies. I would have an assignment within weeks, I was told. By now I had become a little wary, and I suggested that I might be on a blacklist.

"Oh, nonsense. We don't do things that way here. We're interested in quality! What you're doing is good, and we need it, and you'll have a major story within weeks." The letters and the phone calls and the months went by. And always with the sickening, thrilling sensation that this might be the day.

In December an acquaintance, who was getting work from *Life* regularly, mentioned my name in the same office. "Why don't you use Tim Kantor?"

"Oh, Kantor? He's dead, here."

And so I was, for four more years. But alive and hurting all that time.

And thus, so wisely, during the years that followed, I took care of my family. And thus I continued to lean upon my father. I had thought that I might be as bold as I conceived him to be, but I leaned on him instead.

Still searching for my legs.

Finally—when it no longer mattered professionally, and by happenstance—I returned to *Life* in glory.

Dad and I had discussed for years the possibility of working together on some project or other—his words, my pictures; indeed we had once experimented with an idea, but it had not proved valid. Too vague. In the spring of '68 I was, as so often, and even with my work for the *Times*, hurting financially. Dad was aware of that and wanted to help, and we started trading ideas again. It was I who first had the notion of exploring rural America, and it was he who came up with the spine, the structure, for a book. I still

can hear his excited voice on the phone. *Hamilton County!* Webster City
was in Hamilton County, Iowa, and it was casual thought of that fact which
had led him to consult an atlas and its gazeteer. There are ten Hamilton
counties in this country—scattered as far north as New York's Adirondacks,
as far south as Florida's Suwannee River, and west to Texas, Kansas, and
Nebraska, with only two cities soiling their rural character, and offering
contrast.

Hamilton County. I loved the idea; I loved the title.

Dad made some phone calls, then flew up to New York. To the Algonquin. As always there was the ritual dinner out, though with even more
pontification and larger tips than formerly. The next day we had lunch with
the editors and publisher of Macmillan, and they bought the idea of the
book and offered a respectable advance. The book would be about one-
third words and two-thirds pictures, but we split the advance evenly. Books
of photographs rarely sold well then; they do not often sell well now. I could
not have gotten a substantial advance on my own. (No *Life* Photographer
was I.) It was the thought of my father's name on the cover, and the promise of his words, which brought enough money for me to do the book. Later
we had drinks, a lot of them, in a bar on Madison Avenue, and toasted
each other with pride and fondness.

I thought it would be fun working together, and I think that he did, too.

The leaves were beginning to turn in Hamilton County, New York,
when I started work on the book, and the corn was reaching high and
green in Hamilton County, Iowa, when I finished it. I had spent a total of
forty-nine days in shooting, on trips varying from three days to two or
three weeks. Then came the editing and printing of the photographs. Dad,
meanwhile, browsed through prints I sent him, and hunted inspiration.
To accompany the pictures he came up with a series of short stories, es-
says, and vignettes. I was moved and very impressed by a few of them,
and very disappointed by most. They did not represent Dad at his best. I
shrugged, and put it down to the old man left-handedly doing the kid a
favor. It was not until I came to pore over old manuscripts, while working
on this book, that I discovered that the best pieces were magazine rejects
from years before. Dad never told me that, and he'd worked his heart out
on the others. Now I know that—though he was still vital, even overwhelming, in person—he was losing creative force and imagination. He
was losing it, whatever "it" is.

I was proud as hell of what I'd done, and still am.

If our agent had asked, I would have told him that it was a waste of
time to submit manuscript and pictures to *Life* magazine for possible use

before the book was published in the fall of '70. Perhaps the manuscript, but surely not the pictures. I had been a nonperson, or at least a non-photographer, as far as *Life* was concerned, for six long years. I had wandered in a *Life*-created limbo, I had suffered professionally and financially, and I had no reason to think that that might ever change.

Fortunately, the agent never asked me. He went ahead and submitted the material to the magazine, to the wrong department, and the stuff bounced all over the place until it landed on the desk of Philip Kunhardt, the senior assistant managing editor. He loved the pictures.

He made of them the last significant picture story the old *Life* ever ran. It appeared as the lead spread in their issue for the Fourth of July. Eleven pages.

Text had been a problem. Phil asked me to pick out quotes which might accompany the pictures. Ruth and I sat up for two or three nights, laboring over the text, seeking out short quotes which were germane to the pictures selected, and to the layout. (Ruth had remarkable taste, for both the visual and the written image, and had helped me for years to edit my "takes" of photographs. I owe her much for that. It was one of the areas of being, of doing, which we shared, rather than fought over.) But Phil Kunhardt dismissed all our effort—we had tended to be overly respectful of Dad's effusions—and picked the quotes himself. And he picked well.

I think that it was in May that Dad came back to town, and we walked over to the Time-Life Building together, to see that layout and to meet the managing editor. I couldn't hear the Muzak in the elevator, as we rode up to the editorial floor. It was overridden by the flourish of trumpets, blaring all the way.

In the middle of July I received an envelope from *Life*. It contained a letter, addressed to me, from some motel in Louisiana. After I opened it I cried a bit, and then I crowed. I cannot quote the letter now exactly—it was later destroyed by wind, by weather, by happenstance—but it began, "Dear Tim Kantor, I wish to thank you for the pleasure your photographs, in the recent issue of *Life*, have given me..." It was signed by Henri Cartier-Bresson.

That was praise from a master, and I framed the letter and hung it on the wall. It was the one accolade I ever received as a photographer that truly mattered to me. I might not be the great photographer I aspired to be (had to be—I was still certain that my father was a great writer), but here was affirmation that I was indeed a very good one.

*   *   *

But *Life* was dying—they couldn't even keep their own photographers busy—and my connection with *The New York Times* was dying also. I had shot innumerable assignments for them. In one story, on one of the anti–Vietnam War demonstrations in Washington, they had published twenty-three or maybe twenty-six of my pictures—more than the *Magazine* had ever run before by a single photographer. And in the five years starting in 1966 they had run sixteen of my covers, and of those at least half were truly good. There had only been three by others to compare. Unlike the handsome *Magazine* today the paper and reproduction were of poor quality, and the layout was undistinguished. But still, there were times when I thought of the *Magazine* almost as mine, and there were times when I thought that the *Magazine* represented for me a nourishing, rewarding future. Gradually that future faded, as did that of my special friend and mentor on the staff. (Just as I dance around my marriage and my children, I must—out of fondness and respect—dance here also.) Eventually he was out, and I was out before him. He'd been accused of favoritism.

The accusation was unjust and foolish, but so are many corporate decisions.

After that spread in *Life*, and before I fully knew my fate at the *Times*, Dad and Mother took a working vacation up on Mount Washington, which straddles the New York–Massachusetts border, and they invited us to join them, in a cottage nearby. Dad was hurting for money then, though he minimized his worry and I could hardly credit it. (As long as I could remember he had, upon occasion, bitched about money in one breath, and said, "Don't worry," in the next. Always he had spent money, and always he had made it.) All summer long he labored on short stories shaped for another age—his age, the age of the *Post*. He labored fiercely; he didn't sell a one. Ruth and I fought almost constantly. Unpleasantly. One afternoon the children flew kites on an open hillside, and we all had a good time.

The *Chicago Tribune* had asked that Dad and I each write a short piece, a page or so explaining our experience in collaboration, to run concurrently with their review of the book. Dad did a nice little article in a few hours. It took me at least three days, parked each day in some forest lane with a typewriter on the seat beside me, to come up with three hundred words.

Still that pain when trying to write; still his face behind each key, behind each imagined word.

After the story had been published in *Life*, I tried to persuade Macmillan that it would help to sell the book if they made and mounted large reproductions of *Life*'s pages to send to bookstores for display in their windows. I was told that "research proved" such displays were not effective.

After the book itself came out, beautifully designed by Joan Stoliar, and the reviews came in—almost all very kind to the pictures, and some kind to the prose as well—I urged that Macmillan advertise in the Middle American cities, where *Hamilton County* might be expected to sell the best. I was told that "research proved" that such advertising was not effective.

The damned thing never earned out its advance. I doubt that it sold five thousand copies, and I imagine that the remainders have by now been shredded.

But it was a handsome book.

The next spring Ruth took the kids to Florida—to Sarasota—for a brief vacation, but they didn't come back.

Then came the summer, and there followed the winter of the Nixon recession. With thought of war and suppression of protest and economics in our minds, some of us combined two sad words and called it the "Nixon Repression." The big picture magazines, which had supported us, were going, or were gone. Some of the people I knew became teachers of photojournalism, but I did not wish to try to prepare a new generation for a world which seemed to me to be dying. *Look* magazine and the *Saturday Evening Post* were dead, *Life* was terminal, and the *Times* was to me only a fairly happy memory. Corporations were not eager in those months to spend large sums on glossy annual reports. To bring in money I drove a cab. I had none left over to send to the children and to Ruth, and so she leaned on my father—as I had taught her to, by example. That was my fault, not hers.

In the late winter of '72 controls on corporate spending eased up and I made quite a bit of money within a couple of months shooting annual reports. Rags to riches. The major companies paid very substantial sums to the photographers who illustrated their reports. The top names received $1,000 a day or more. I hadn't reached that level, yet even the $450 day-rate I'd established was still gratifying. But the work wasn't. I found it shaming instead. I had not become a photographer in order to make ugly, dehumanizing factories and machines seem pretty, nor to falsely celebrate "the happy people who work for us," nor to glorify crafty little Masters of Business Administration—little, whether slim or fat, short or tall—with their humanly insensitive, but oh-so-clever, cost-conscious, counterproductive ways. I had never enjoyed the act of selling my wares, my skills, even when showing my portfolio in the relatively comfortable, even welcoming, surroundings of the office of a magazine picture editor or art director. Perhaps that arose from lack of confidence in what I had to sell; certainly I didn't like it. And I detested doing the same thing while sitting across an impressive desk from some director of public or corporate relations—often an ex-newsman with a large alimony to pay, alcoholic and ashamed, just as I felt ashamed, who had sold not only his skills but himself. And I had neither the skill nor the desire to make pretty images in a studio.

I had become a photographer not only because I was afraid of using words, but also because I wished to comment truly on the world.

When I'd called the kids in Florida, as often I had done, I'd also talked at length with Ruth. We thought that perhaps we could "work things out." In April, with one major journalistic assignment, with hope and considerable fear, and with the help of some friends, I loaded a rented moving van with our possessions and headed south.

It was wonderful to see the kids again.

Six unhappy months later, about the time of my fortieth birthday, I retreated to my parents' home. The transformed home of my childhood. Reconciliation had not worked at all. Under excess of pressure, I had also botched the one assignment I had brought with me, and it had taken me months to get paid. My agent in New York had come up with little work. Nor could I find much locally. Small-town advertising firms were uninterested in quality, and unwilling to pay for it. The *St. Petersburg Times* was happy with its staff. I hadn't been so desperate, felt so inadequate, since my father had walked the floor with me at nights, while I howled in anguish; now he was carrying me once again. Ruth had found a job, and she was grimly, bravely laboring, but Dad was carrying the kids as well.

While I kept hunting photographic work for myself I also kept looking at his typewriter.

Words.

Words.

I had grown up bathed in them, and except through his loud and demanding presence, his masculine yet almost childishly assertive personality, my father had never, in any way, discouraged me from using words to explore the world, to make a living. Oh, often he had snarled, "Anyone who wants to be a writer is a goddamn fool!" But he was only speaking the truth—a truth which applies to all would-be writers, photographers, actors, dancers, or artists of any sort. They are all damned fools.

But some of them are lucky, and some are also wise.

If, out of the service, I had told Dad that I wanted to write, he would have given me as much support and encouragement as he did when, instead, I said that I wanted to make images. If he had daunted me, it was not by intent; it was I who allowed myself to be daunted. Perhaps there had been too much of my mother in me. Perhaps it was my first, painful contact with the world which made me so timid. Made me a coward—for it is cowardice to deny one's talent, to shrink from using it, or at least attempting to do so. It is not fashionable today among either psychotherapists or presidents to accept responsibility for one's actions, but that is wrong.

While writing letters and making phone calls seeking assignments, I kept looking at the typewriter.

I walked on the beach which, though vastly eroded by then, I had known since childhood. Maury dog was with me, and ghost crabs went scurrying at our approach. The sun was sliding deep into the west, and the salt breeze came hurrying off the Gulf. Pelicans beat homeward overhead. The wind shoved the present aside and made it easier to think. It came to me that I had a story to tell. A novel to write. The death of photojournalism as I had known it, intertwined with the death of a marriage. There was a novel there; I was convinced of that.

It would only take words.

Dad sat at his enormous desk, using his big typewriter or, often, dictating into a machine for later transcription. Sun or rain, land breeze or sea breeze or none at all, I sat at a long, wood table on the screen porch which opened from his workroom, and worked on an old Royal typewriter which once he had used, and now kept as a spare. On a phonograph in the living room the music of Telemann played, or Albinoni, Corelli, Biber, and others. Baroque "white music" to keep the world away, to bring it close. (I use the same table, the same old Royal, and play the same records as I write these words.) At last I found myself free—free out of desperation—to string words together, and there was a delight, triumphant, almost incestuous, in thus sharing in our separate labor.

My God, I loved that man. My God, I loved to write. In the early evening or late afternoon we read our work to one another and, with the power of our voices, convinced each other that the words were marvelous.

But if there was excitement, liberation, in my world, there was desperation also. The novel was halfway done, and I had not yet been able to sell it. (Nor would I. I ended up writing an autobiographical novel in which the protagonist—me—did not grow an ounce nor an inch from beginning to finish.) At about the same time that I had begun the book Ruth and I had started "dating"—indulging in the same sad, foolish rite which so many separated couples engage in, when both love their children and have fondness for one another, and neither wishes to admit to failure.

On weekends the girls would come to stay, and I would retreat from the guest bedroom which was otherwise mine. I'd sleep then on a couch in the workroom (the one that was not Maury's), unless Jeff had come as well—he was in his early teens, and sometimes we had difficulties—and then I'd sleep on a couch in the vast living room. All three of the children were always welcome in that house. They were loved by their grandmother and, if not more welcome, they were surely more tolerated in their childishness and youth by Dad than ever Layne-o and I had been.

There was a lot of laughter in the house still—Dad was never in his life a happy man, but he owned gaiety, a gaiety which could dismiss despair, and Mother joined him in it—but, for several years, I slept amid a foul, recurrent pattern of bad dreams. The career I had left behind, the money I wasn't earning, the book, or books, for which I could not find a publisher, the marriage which would be or had been lost, the love of children who must be abandoned. Night after night I tossed and clutched the sheet— spiraling down into an abyss of failure, facing or fleeing from a dilemma without any apparent happy answer.

Night after night.

Jeffrey was someplace else that Saturday, and so was Lydia—perhaps with the Brownies, or the Girl Scouts. Melissa and I had been off on some excursion or other, and now I had parked the car in front of the house where she lived. She was five and, because she was and is by nature a romantic, I felt perhaps even closer to her—at least I was able to identify with her— even more than with the others. I went round the car and opened the door for her, and she got out.

Melissa had been hearing an ugly, frightening word quite a lot by then, and now she asked about it. "Daddy, if you and Mommy get divorced, who will I live with?"

I was filled with self-contempt. I couldn't even support myself; I couldn't possibly handle the kids. "Well, honey, usually the children live with their mother. It's the custom."

"Oh."

No tears, but her lovely face grew still. It was the most hurting, hurtful monosyllable that I have heard in my life.

I said, "Come on, honey." I walked her to the door, and I kissed her and said good-bye. I left something of myself behind when I went back down the walk. Something of me; something of Meliss.

16

Living Room,
Bedroom

"Well? Should I do it, or not?" Dad's voice was addressed to us, but his eyes were directed, glowering, toward the lawn, the trees, the beach, the world outside the screen which covered the front terrace of the house that *Andersonville* had built. I don't think that he saw any of them. He was looking at the cold and misery of Valley Forge. Mother, Layne, and I had been summoned to a family council, to decide if he should undertake a big new book. And that was unprecedented. Always he had acted in his own mysterious ways, when it came to creative decisions, leaving us merely to marvel and applaud. But now we were summoned to council.

"My God," I thought, "he doesn't want to do it."

I couldn't understand why. Just the year before, in '72, he had published yet another book, a memoir of his early years with Mother. It was true that the reviews had been mixed (reviews often are) and the sales had been modest, but it was a fine and touching book. I said, "Damn it, Dad, you're still a wonderful writer! Look at *I Love You, Irene*." Mother and Layne-o added eager agreement, and Dad turned back to look at us, nodded his head as though he also agreed, and smiled at receiving our praise. But there was something wistful about his smile.

It wasn't until some ten years later that I discovered that all the best sections of *I Love You, Irene* had been taken from another memoir, a planned sequel to *But Look, the Morn*, called *In Russet Mantle Clad*. (He had also considered an alternate title: *The Maples Were My Gods*.) The manuscript had never been published, and I understand why. It suffers from Mack

Kantor's gift for total recall, and it trails off badly at the end. But it was written in the early fifties, when power over words still throve within him, and he had cannibalized it for the making of *I Love You, Irene*.

He had never told us that, I think from shame or embarrassment, and now his smile was wistful but we talked him into undertaking the enormous labor of a book called *Valley Forge*.

A good restaurant, with attentive service. Dad finished his first vodka martini as he ordered for us. "And I," he added with seraphic smile, "will have vichyssoise."

"Mack," Mother said, "please, darling..."

He smiled upon us fondly; he beamed upon the waiter. "Vichyssoise. And, I think, another round of drinks." While we waited for our food he told us that he'd just been writing about George Washington's problems with his teeth, and that he, by God, could sympathize. And he could. Several years before Dad had lost the last of his teeth, except for a couple of stubs which served as uncertain anchors for his dentures. Now he found eating not a pleasure, but a pain (he remembered sitting on a toilet seat, with head bent low, to ease such pain long ago), and he subsisted largely on a liquid diet. Slowly, inexorably, he was starving himself, and would listen to no caution, no entreaty. And yet, despite Mother's constant complaints and begging—"Please, let's eat at home. I'll fix..."—and even though she was a wonderful cook, he insisted on eating out. Which Mother felt, quite rightly, he couldn't afford.

Dad told a very funny story as he signed the check, and we went on to a piano bar. A sing-along place.

Dim light, smoke, and liquor, and loud voices, but the voices all fell still.

> *Jesus Christ, I hate the tourists,*
> *Jesus Christ, I hate the tourists,*
> *Jesus Christ, I hate the tourists,*
> *I wish they'd go away...*

Dad was singing his "Tourist Song"—a song cycle actually, set to various traditional tunes, which could go on for almost two hours and was one of the greatest hymns of hate ever written. When that segment was over the whole barroom, tourists among them, exploded in applause. All his life he'd looked far younger than his age, but now he looked far older, and he

was frail, but still his voice was true, and still he was a consummate per-
former. The tune for that set of verses, for instance, was borrowed from the
"Battle Hymn of the Republic," and when he sang his own words, his
"Tourist" words, he snarled.

> *In the glory of a cesspool,*
> *They were reeked and they were roiled . . .*

But when, in other circumstances, he sang the "Battle Hymn" itself,
his voice would soar, loud as a trumpet call.

> *The trumpet that shall never call retreat . . .*

Nor did his voice retreat as he sang, loud, proud, and defiant. Yet in
the last verse his voice would gentle itself and he would almost croon the
words.

> *With a glory in His bosom that transfigures you and me;*
> *As He died to make men holy, let us die to make men free . . .*

And virtuous people in that room would cry.

But now there were no tears; only laughter or, on the part of old-timers,
a reminiscent shrugging of the shoulders, a sad nodding of the head.

> *We used to have wildcats all over the roof,*
> *We used to have coons on the shore,*
> *But now we have bitches and bastards so thick,*
> *They come crowding in at the door.*
> *Oh, here's to the old Sarasota,*
> *The land of the lazy and glad,*
> *Where the sharks and the stingrays,*
> *Mosquitoes and mice,*
> *Were the worst enemies that we had.*

Sarasota, and the world, had been different once. Amid further applause
he came back to the table, smiling, proud, fond, and drunk. *"One of these
elderly Pucks."*

I drove us home.

Dad got up the next morning at seven, and had a tiny bowl of stewed
tomatoes for breakfast. He went to his desk and got to work, recreating the

snow and hunger at Valley Forge, and the pain General Washington suffered from his rotting teeth.

In the late afternoon he took Maury for a walk upon the beach. Beach where the water was no longer clear, and the sky no longer richest blue but stained by smog—filth from the North, from swarming people everywhere, from the goddamn tourists.

Valley Forge was a failure, and I was a failure too. Or so I regarded myself.

The story—the product of extensive research, enormous effort, and great pain—was drowned in words. Rejected by the original publisher, the book was issued by another, and it sank. Dad felt that he was sinking too. He couldn't accept the thought that his prose had curdled, victim of his ancient addiction to rhetoric, and blamed lack of success in this current world to fashion. He believed that, since he had had no major commercial success since *Andersonville*, editors and reviewers might be prejudiced by the sight of his name, those two words which had long ago seemed, and to him still seemed, so glorious. MacKinlay Kantor. In a sad, elaborate scheme, which he revealed to none of us, he submitted—over and over again—the manuscript of what he thought to be a "contemporary" novel to various publishers. Under a pseudonym. The novel was short and bad, and it was rejected again and again. He went on humming and smiling, and walking Maury. Working endlessly, and staving off creditors.

He still insisted on going out to dinner almost every night, and eating only vichyssoise or oyster stew, but mostly he fed upon dreams. He had, *goddamn it*, written *Long Remember*; he had, *goddamn it*, written *Andersonville*; he had, *goddamn it*, written *Spirit Lake*; he had, *goddamn it*... A couple visiting from Sweden had told him that he was still being mentioned in Stockholm as a candidate for the Nobel prize.

And I—in all ways I had failed. Ruth and I had finally said good bye to our marriage in September of '74. (We were not formally divorced for over two more years, at my request, for I shrank from the lawyers' bills.) Foolishly, I had told myself that I could keep the marriage alive through sheer strength of will, but I had failed, and the effort had exhausted me. Exhausted us all. I was at work on a second novel, but I couldn't get an advance. I sold a few articles and a few pictures, and I kept on working as best I could. I still saw the kids on weekends, but I was in a state of savage, almost emasculating, depression. I drank too much and, when at last

I fell asleep, I was tortured by uncertainty and strange, impossible choices, all through the night.

I was frustrated in all respects. I went without making even verbal love for almost two years.

I noticed her ass before I noticed her mind, which was as Valorie had intended. It was late July of '76, and I was coming once again alive. I was working on the first of what I hoped would be a series of articles— interviews with people in all states and conditions of life—for the *St. Petersburg Times*. (Make, for God's sake and my own, a little money!) I thought that an interview with a divorcée might be of interest, might be compelling, and so I called a friend who was socially active, and had a large acquaintance.

"Know any divorcées?"

"My God," said she, but I explained, and she gave me the names of two. Valorie was the first one on the list, and she was a lousy interview. She'd only been divorced a few months, she'd suffered small trauma in the process, and she was happy with her state. She did not fit the conventional image of the divorcée, there were no children involved, and there was no chance at all for me to show compassion and understanding, no great agony to share with the reader. (The real agony would come later, and to me even more than to her.) But Val was looking for a casual someone, just as I now was. She had asked our mutual friend about me, had gone to the library to take out *Hamilton County*, and she was interested even before I walked in her door. She was petite, her hair was short and soft and dark, and she was very pretty, even beautiful. She wore a blue halter top over her small bosom. (Later I would discover that her breasts were tiny, but that did not bother me at all. All my life I have tended to be attracted to women with small breasts; perhaps that has something to do with the pain of nursing, long ago.) She also wore a pair of very brief white shorts; they were called "hot pants" then. After I'd taped our unsatisfactory interview, and we'd started to talk about other things, Valorie found occasion to hunt for a book in the shelves she'd assembled along the very bottom of one wall of her apartment. When she bent over, as Val was well aware, the cheeks of her ass peeked out of her hot pants and winked at me.

"Are you free for dinner?"

"I can't make it tonight." Very slowly she straightened, turned, and smiled. "But tomorrow night I'm free."

* * *

Soon we both were bound. Her love, in childhood, had been betrayed, and Val was chary of giving it free reign, but she was in lust, "in love," with me. My love was not so fettered and, for the first time in my life, I experienced the nature of real, of total love—emotional, intellectual, and physical—which a man can feel for a woman. Complete acceptance of the other. The package accepted, unblinking, in its entirety. Strength and wisdom, weakness and childish asininity, known and understood, with no thought or dream of alteration. She would run from me—ah, like a fish on a line—and there would be great blathering about fear of "involvement" and "commitment." I would spend a few sobs, a few tears, wait a week, and then I'd reel her back.

Because I loved the woman she was. I loved her virtues, which were many—her mind was as supple and as wiry as her dancer's body, of which Val took great care, and in which she took great pride. And, alternately amused and annoyed, I accepted her failings, for she lacked perfection, just as all humans do. A few months before I met her, as I was first beginning to come out of the pathetic, shameful doldrums in which I had allowed myself to wallow for so long, I had met another, younger woman and had promptly fallen—quite literally—madly in love. The woman was pretty, was bright, was inappropriate, but I felt myself coming alive and I stole time from prose to write love poems. And now that I had met this not impossible and quite magnificent she, I wrote more poems, and Valorie was pleased. But I stimulated a nerve I had not known was there, and Val started to reply in kind. She had the gift for concision, for tight language, which poetry demands and, after a few months of admiring the beauty of her words, I realized that I did not.

I said, "Honey, from now on I'll stick to prose. The poetry is your department." She was pleased and proud and, the next weekend, she wrote a poem which was even better than any that had come before.

It was an exciting time. Together, or even during her agonized, agonizing retreats, we were coming to know one another. The St. Pete *Times* accepted my proposal for a series of articles, and she and I held grand celebration. The editor had told me on the phone that they wanted one article a week for their Sunday *Magazine*, and that meant that I'd be making an adequate living. A few days later the editor wrote and told me she had misspoken.

She had meant one article every four weeks. I plummeted to earth like lead through clouds, Val's snarls of outrage echoed mine; her love restored me.

It was a sad time as well. Dad was obviously failing, to a point where friends, and even Mother, Layne, and I—who had so long believed in his invincibility—could see. (My camera had seen it two years before, when I shot his portrait for the back of the book jacket of *Valley Forge*—tired old soul, still defiant but, oh, so tired, glaring out from a crumbling face—but I had refused to accept the understanding which my lens offered me.) Yet still he insisted on taking Mother out to dinner at night—vichyssoise for him, or perhaps a bowl of ice cream—and sometimes Val and I went with them. And then he would want to go on to sing, on to reach an audience. Often he would sing some portions of the "Tourist Song," and I think that Valorie found them tasteless, even shocking—one shouldn't lump all tourists together, one shouldn't damn them all—which was foolish of her. I think she also thought Dad pathetic, which indeed he was. Weary old man; voice all gone.

Yet there was something gallant in the way he still strove for applause, and something remarkable, and comforting to him, in the fact that he still gained it.

Months later, and it was a Special Occasion. Dad was sitting—drifting, dozing—in his favorite chair in the living room, his nakedness wrapped in a white sheet. But Mother, Layne, and I were gathered out on the old side porch, with the breeze of early April gentle on our skin and in our hair. Layne and Mother were sitting on the rattan couch with its aqua cushions, and the doctor was sitting in a chair. I was also seated, facing him—and thus my face to his face, almost on a level—and we were having a Conversation.

"I'd give him ten days, two weeks at the outside," the doctor said. "He's got congestive heart failure, which is depriving his brain of the oxygen it needs, but also he's suffering from inanition." I had looked up that word six months before. "He's starving himself to death."

So much achieved through desperate struggle in his young manhood. *He had no satisfactory world, no satisfactory being, of his own. But perhaps he could shape them, out of words.* So much glory gained in his middle years, and so much failure since. And now he shrank, defeated. But thought of his voice, his eyes, the man himself—so vital once and so easy—enveloped me still, and warmed me with remembered fire.

*   *   *

Mack was sitting—drifting, dozing—in his favorite chair in the living room, his nakedness wrapped in a white sheet, and he became aware. He felt the fabric of the sheet, he opened bleary eyes to see the whiteness wrapped around him. A phrase came to his mind. "Winding sheet," he thought. "They have wrapped me in my winding sheet. Why don't they wind me now away?"

He had always loathed the thought of a lingering death, of a long time dying. "*I'd make a lousy old man.*" He had said that when he and Mother got too goddamned old, they would board an airplane in company with other "old farts," flown by a pilot with an incurable heart disease, and fly high, and laugh and drink (the flight attendants would also have terminal ailments) until they plowed into a mountain.

Mother hadn't liked that notion very much, but now he was beyond any plowing, and she didn't like this process much better. For his body persisted, even after his brain had gone wandering and his soul had surrendered. There would come "good days," when friends came to call, and his mind might clear for a moment. The friends would say, "Hi, Mack," and he'd moan in response. Sitting in that chair of his—it was lavender in color, a faded lavender—wrapped in his sheet, eyes closed, drifting. The visitors would sit and talk with Mother and, at some point, mention would be made of some happening in the long ago, and perhaps his eyes might open, and his frail voice—voice which used to thunder—offer, "That was in March of '28. I remember..." And he'd be right.

After a sentence or two his voice would trail away. People would say, "That's right, Mack! How wonderful that you remember." But he'd be asleep again. Adrift.

By then I thought it fortunate that I had only one interview to do each month, to tape, transcribe and edit, and only one portrait to shoot. The portrait had been the editor's idea, and raised the price that I was paid. The first published interview, with the other divorcée, had been excellent—full of color, full of sadness, even desperation. But the *Sunday Magazine* had wanted a portrait to go with it, and that interview had been granted on condition of anonymity, so Valorie had been my model. Head bent, hands pressed to her eyes to hide her face—it had been a hell of a picture, for she was a hell of an actress.

But now I had become, with Mother so wearied and torn, almost a full-time male nurse. They call it role reversal. "Hush, Dad. Here, let me help you. No, don't drink out of that glass. You just took a leak in it. I'll get you another."

Maury, old brindled hound with grizzled snout and noble soul, had been ailing for a long, long time. He had rheumatism, and had difficulty clambering into the chairs Dad had insisted be set aside for him in the bedroom and the living room, or the chair and sofa which were his in the workroom. He was also going blind, and would blunder into the doorjamb when he tried to go outside. No longer king of the beach, he was not a happy dog. In late May or early June, Mother, Layne, and I debated, briefly, and decided that he should be put to sleep. Leaving Dad dozing, inane, in his own chair in the living room, I led Maury out to the car and lifted his weary old body onto the back seat. When we got to the veterinarian's clinic I lifted him out and helped him inside. I talked to him, and stroked his ear (Maury always liked that), while the vet gave him a shot and killed him.

I wished I could be as kind to my father.

"This, this, is disgusting!" I was startled, for he had not spoken intelligible words in days. He had cried, "*Aaanh, aaanh!*", upon occasion (all of us cry when we come into this world, and many cry when they depart), but that was all. I had wiped him free of excrement, and had washed him, and had lifted his poor body—as emaciated as that of any prisoner at Buchenwald or Andersonville—and settled it upon the bedside potty. Now I was dealing with the dung-covered sheets.

I turned to face him. "What's disgusting, Dad?"

With his bony arm he gestured toward the bed. "This!"

Oh, ruined king of mine. Pathetic manikin. "Ah, it's not so bad, Dad. These things happen." I dealt with the ugliness and then I made the bed. When I was through, I turned to speak to him again. But he'd gone back to roaming in his mind, and so I settled him on the fresh linen.

"*Aaanh.*"

It had been four months since we'd been told "ten days," but still his stubborn body persisted. That afternoon I called a doctor I knew, who was familiar with Dad's condition. I named the three medications Dad was being given, and asked him if deprival of those pills and capsules would cause discomfort. There was a long pause, and then the doctor said no.

But despite lack of medicine and lack of food—he had long since stopped eating—the living death continued.

In September, while walking on the beach—she walked there daily, to give her own trim body exercise, and her mind relief—Mother tripped and fell. She broke her wrist, and it seemed that, outworn by grief, she broke her mind as well.

She went into the hospital, and Dad didn't even notice her absence. A few weeks later Layne-o and I agreed that I couldn't care for Dad properly, and he went into the hospital also, and then to a nursing home. On the eleventh of October 1977, he died, and Layne and I sighed and hugged and almost smiled, and used the telephone.

That night I took my father's bed, and my mother's, for my own. I did so without any conscious Oedipal desire, for the room was much larger than the guest bedroom, and cooler, and three walls were lined with mirrors. The mirrors were on closet doors and so arranged that, if the doors were opened at certain angles, when one sat or knelt or half lay on the love seat in the center of the room, one could see one's image reflected back from all directions. Years later I asked Mother if she had had those mirrors placed there for the reason I suspected. She was a little embarrassed—nice girls hadn't done such things, designed such rooms, when she was young. She said, "Well, of course they did make the room look larger." But then she paused, and smiled a tiny, wistful smile, and nodded her head.

Valorie had been on vacation when Dad died (though she had supported me loyally, bravely, through almost all of his long death), but she came back to town a few days later and, night after night for two glorious weeks, we made use of those mirrors. Posing, admiring our myriad carnal images in a world of glass, we rid that room of death. With my father looking on, youthful, and smiling, and applauding every move. Almost I could truly see him, and almost I could truly hear him laughing, and saying, "That's right, kids. That's the antidote; that's the answer to death. Go to it."

And we did.

17

Echoes

Mother came back from the hospital within a month, but she was in dreadful shape. She seemed to have lost all zest, and all intellect. She railed at "Mack's desertion," she moaned in self-pity, her gait was reduced to a tiny, uncertain shuffle, and constantly she forgot that she had taken her medicine, and so she took it again. I had to hide it away.

It was my belated questioning of the pills, which had been destroying her, which saved her in the end. There had been a confusion of doctors, because of a confusion of vacations, when she first broke her wrist and her will. Eventually I called the psychiatrist who, acting for a colleague gone to attend a seminar, had first seen her after her accident. I named the three drugs she was taking, on prescription and by direction, and he was appalled. "I tested her with those, and she had reactions to each. And I relayed that information. She shouldn't be taking any of them!" I robbed her of her pills, with better hope than when I had robbed my father, but nothing seemed to happen. After two weeks my sister and I agreed that she was beyond our help, and should go to a nursing home. We selected the finest in the area, I signed the papers, and I took her there. She shuffled into the place in her halting step, holding on to my arm, took one look at the lingerers gathered there, and shuffled out.

The administrators were shocked, even outraged, seeing a potential paying customer depart. "Mrs. Kantor, you can't leave. The papers are all signed!"

I shrugged my shoulders, and I laughed. I said, "It seems she doesn't want to stay."

The next morning she made breakfast for herself, for the first time since

September, and three weeks later—because she disapproved of the stuffing I had planned to make—she prepared and cooked the Christmas turkey.

I have not painted her well; not as well as she painted portraits with the oils she used. I have made her subsidiary to my father in this tale, as indeed she was in life, and perhaps the slight distance which I maintained, the result of early rivalry and earlier pain, affected the telling also. Yet the word *distance* makes me pause, and smile, and shake my head. If I maintained any distance at all, it was slight indeed, and I made up for it otherwise. About a year after Valorie had run off, flown off, to New York, I got to thinking about her—hardly a half day passed when I did not do so—and a thought occurred to me which never had before.

"You know," I said to my sister, proud of my new understanding, "she was a little bit like Mother. I don't mean just physically, always so dainty and trim, but in other ways too."

Layne and Val had been fond friends, and now Layne looked at me, unbelieving, and burst into laughter. "You mean you never realized that before?"

Mother was a charming, valiant, gifted lady, and the many friends who survived her still honor her memory with admiring words and fond smiles. And, my God, she was patient—she had to be, to live with Dad. But also, he had spoiled her rotten. As he had spoiled himself and me, by living, and giving, to the very limit of his income. By, in bad times, always convincing himself that next year would be better. And so many "next years" had been. (Toward the end, when he was failing badly, Layne-o was talking with him as he sat at his big desk. Desk covered with bills. She said, "Honestly, Daddy! I think you believe in miracles." He thought of riding a day coach across Iowa, with an envelope clutched in his hand; of another coach, sitting in Pennsylvania Station, and a young man coming toward him down the aisle; of fouled-up orders, and watching a '17 burn at Chelveston; of happy news he and Reno had first heard while sitting in the bar of the Prince de Galle. He smiled, and nodded his head. "Oh, yes," he said.) But he had been depression-burned, and cautioned, frightened, by the manipulations of his father. He had not believed in investment, he would *always* make money, and the only estate he left to Mother were royalties from his stories and books—and only a few of the stories, and *Andersonville*, continued to sell—and their house and three hundred feet of beachfront property on Siesta Key. When the property and house were sold they provided her, along with Social Security, with a comfortable income, but she was used to more than comfort and she was furious.

"How your father could have done this to me!"

And yet, despite all loss and petty anger, she came to thrive. She had never learned to balance a checkbook—Dad had always done that for her—but, with chiding, instruction, and encouragement from Layne-o, she learned. That gave her reason to be proud of herself, in ways she had not been before. The house she had lived in for so many years, and which she had redesigned, had been "our house," and she bitterly rued its loss. The house she rented next was "this house." But when Bill Shroder—who was divorced from Layne once their kids were grown, but remained as fond and caring as any son-in-law could be—built her a house, with no fee for himself, and on land of her own choosing, that was "my house."

She traveled a little. She had lunch or dinner with old friends. She worked constantly at her painting, and studied to learn more. She cherished, she delighted in, her grandchildren; the very thought of them made her glad. And always in her mind was remembrance of the miracle which she thought that she had lived—the hurts and blessings of the love which she had known. *"I love you, Irene!"*

After the house—their house, our house, all those dreams—was sold, I moved into an inexpensive, falling-down, old-Florida-style apartment house. It had once been very impressive indeed, the first fancy apartment house in town, and I live there still and am very fond of the place. It, along with books on the shelves and artifacts on the mantel, connects me to the past. But it was the present I needed to be connected to in 1978—the present, and an income. After over a year my series of articles for the *St. Petersburg Times* Sunday *Magazine* was canceled—and not too long after, the magazine itself was, quite deservedly, canceled also. I wrote articles and made photographs for some regional magazines, and even a few small national ones. I couldn't support my kids properly, I borrowed from my mother, and I was quite ashamed.

Years before, friends had said, because of my voice and my gift for blather and for blarney, "You ought to be on radio. You ought to be on television." It had been a common cocktail party remark, which I had totally dismissed. I was a photographer. But now I didn't regard myself as a photographer any more, I was having trouble making a living as a writer, and Valorie made the same suggestion.

I said, "Television? Who'd want to look at my homely face?"

"Darling, you may not be handsome, but your face is *most* expressive. It's one of the reasons I love you."

By happenstance I became host of a call-in talk show on local radio for a few months and, for an amateur, I was pretty good. By luck and determination I then got a daily interview show on local cable TV, and slowly I learned to be better. Few people watched such local shows but, after a time, many watched mine. I fed off the community, of course: the lawyer with a cause, the doctor with a passion, even a very articulate man who killed cockroaches for a living. Sarasota also has a number of writers, painters, and cartoonists of not only local but national reputation. And it has an extraordinary number of institutions and resorts which draw celebrities in every field. Many of them appeared on my show. I had the typical good journalist's ragbag of information tucked inside my head, so I was able to conduct sensible interviews, not foolish ones. But while Sarasota has a sophisticated citizenry, its business community has—with certain noble exceptions—a largely redneck mentality, and it wasn't until after almost three years that, through a grant from a corporation hungry for local gratitude, I gained full sponsorship.

Within six months (as soon as I could afford it) an audience survey showed that, in prime time, I was affecting the networks' share of the local ratings. It was wearying, but it was fun in a way. Once I had thought that I might "own" New York, and now I almost "owned" Sarasota. I thought the trade unequal.

Sometimes, when I was doing commercials or public-service announcements—looking and talking earnestly, or smiling disingenuously, into the camera—a ghost from the past came nudging from the bottom of my mind. While I talked and smiled, or looked especially sincere, I would think, "Now I'll *sell* them. Now I'll con them. For just this minute, I'll be like Grandpa!"

In the summer of '78 their mother had taken our girls up north. (Jeffrey was already on his own.) Mother was devastated, and so was I—never see my kids no more. But late the next summer, not long before her thirteenth birthday, the elder, Lydia, decided that she missed her friends, her school, too much, and insisted upon coming back to Sarasota. She was, and is, a willful person, and she had her way. And so, for three years, I had the dubious, delightful pleasure of being a single Daddy. I kicked her behind around the block a few times, and she kicked mine. I hugged her on occasion, and she hugged me. We got to know one another, and she decided that I was not quite the monster she had thought I might be.

Jeffrey, on his own, and Melissa—in part because of our summer meetings, in part because of Lydia's reports—came to feel the same.

*   *   *

On April 30, 1980, Valorie went away. I would say, "Ran away," except that I drove her to the airport in Tampa. We embraced, and made vows for the present and the future. I watched her plane take off. On the way back to Sarasota I turned on the radio, and they were playing John Denver's "Leaving on a Jet Plane." I didn't know when Val would be back again, either.

She told me that she cried all the way back to New York. Two months later she called it off.

Eventually I met another lady, and I went on with my show, went on with my life.

And Mother went busily on with her life, until June 16, 1982. That afternoon I got a call from a fine painter, Jack Bailey, who had taken her as a student. "I went out of the room for a minute and came back, and found Irene sitting on the floor. She still has a paintbrush in her hand, but she can't get up." I got over to the studio as soon as possible. We carried her to my car, and I drove her to the hospital. While they were treating her in the emergency room I called my sister (she had become an attorney after her divorce—a public defender, and a fine one). When Layne got to the room where Mother had been installed, the doctor told us, "Irene has had a stroke. Her speech is slurred, she's paralyzed on one side, and she's blind. Do you want us to take extraordinary measures?"

I thought of Maury, and we both thought of Dad. We knew too much about extended death. Our voices chimed together as we said, "No!"

Mother was still half lucid. She had been planning to fly to New York in two days' time, and visit an old friend. The last words I heard her say were, "This is a hell of a time for something like this!"

Within nine hours she was dead.

Mother had been in the habit of writing notes to herself, during the long, lonely hours of the night. In the drawer of her bedside table we found a few lines she had scribbled not long before. The handwriting was not as firm as when she had written, so many years ago, "You are part of me—the sweetest and most thoughtful lover and husband a girl could ever have." But the sentiment was just as touching, just as sure.

> *Vivid dream*
> *Mack had been up*

doing something—
he jumped back into
bed.—his top bare—
young solid chest as
when young
against me
a happy dream

Starting at least as early as Thorne Smith, back in the twenties, Sarasota has always attracted writers. It's a nice and private place to work. In December of 1952, three "local" writers—Richard Glendinning, John D. MacDonald, and Mack Kantor—met for lunch on a Friday and, all unwitting, started an institution which is no institution, a club which is no club and has no rules, which has lasted ever since. It is variously called "the writers' group," "the Friday lunch," or "the Liars' club," though never the last by Dick Glendinning. He says there are probably Liars' Clubs in Peoria, and there should be none in Sarasota. But Dad liked the thought of going to the Liars' club, or lunch, and he went whenever he was in town.

The only rules for nonmembership are that the individual make, or have made, his living through the use of words; exceptions are sometimes made for those who currently only struggle and aspire to do so. Writers of all sorts, and all degrees of fame and success, have sat at that table through the years, and cartoonists, editors, and agents as well. The individual must also be first invited by a nonmember in good nonstanding, and be reasonably intelligent, reasonably amiable, and, if the danger is seen in time, not a boor. And he can never be a she, for the group is blatantly sexist. Lillian Hellman was visiting town once, and wished to come, but she was not invited. And my sister is still furious because, after the publication of her novel, Dad never took her as a guest, though he took me a few times even though I was only a photographer. (In later years I tried to stage a palace revolution and change that all-male notion, but I lost.)

There is considerable wit at the table, considerable kindness, and nastiness is frowned on. There is a little shop talk—"Hurray, I finished the book!" or "What my goddamn publisher did to me!"—but mostly the talk touches on the world at large, and gossip, and politics and other forms of obscenity. And liars' poker is played with the serial numbers of paper currency to determine who pays for the drinks. It is played with ill will, cunning, and glee.

After Dad died, a silly little person, who was on the fringes of the group, bustled up to me and said, "Now that Mack is dead, you must come to lunch in his place. You belong. You're his son." I quite properly ignored that foolish invitation but, a few years later, I was invited for myself, for words I spun on television and words I wrote, and I've been going ever since. The weekly ritual interchange with intelligent men of uncommon common interests has helped to sustain me during difficult times. It has helped to keep me sane.

The group was very important to Dad also. From the beginning, he played the role of grand man of the table. He was then the best known of them all and, after a few years, he had the Pulitzer Prize to mention with a not-so-casual shrug. But, usually, he played his role with grace, and almost always with fierce charm. Through the years since I've been there, his name has been mentioned frequently. All of the veterans have a "Mack story" to tell, and all of them also have another story to top the last one. The telling frequently brings laughter, but it is laughter tinged with fondness and respect, and that gives me pleasure, adds to my pride.

One November, while I was working on this book, and suffering agonizing financial strain, I was invited to share Thanksgiving dinner with a couple I am very fond of. I was also to spend the night in their guest bedroom. I accepted eagerly, and looked forward to relaxing. I hoped for nothing but amusing talk, and distracting laughter. My friend Jim is a very gentle man, but at that time, because of certain factors in his life, he had little snakes of anger coiled within. After the other guests had gone we sat below, next to the room where I would sleep, while his wife cleaned up in the kitchen, which was on the main floor of the house, one flight above.

We sat and talked and drank. I noticed that the jug of vodka we were pouring from was closer to empty than it ought to be, but I thought little of it. At last my friend went up the stairs to bed, while I nursed a final drink and played with ideas for my next chapter.

"Put it down, Jim!" The voice of his wife came down the stairs. "Jim, put down that gun!" I went up those stairs, fast, to find Jim, wearing only shorts or pajama bottoms, standing in the bedroom door and holding a gun. His eyes were dull and out of focus, but the hand that held the revolver was steady, and the gun was pointed at his wife.

I said, "Give me the gun, Jim," and he turned his face and the gun toward me. Slow and easy, with my feet and with my voice, I approached him, saying, "Jim, give me the gun." By the time I said that phrase again, the gun barrel was jammed into my belly, but I was able to twist it aside and high and out of his hand.

Jim went back to bed and passed out. After a few words with his wife, I went down to my borrowed bed and sat there, thinking of nothing. After about half an hour I examined the gun. It was a Colt .38 Airweight. When I broke it open and ejected the bullets, I started shaking. They were hollow-nosed Police Specials—the kind that leave a hole as big as a hand when they exit the body. I shook for half the rest of the night, and then I went out and stowed revolver and bullets in the trunk of my car. I went back in and slept for three hours.

That morning, in dramatic tones, I told Jim that I was confiscating his gun. He only shrugged. "That's all right," he said. "I've got a .357 Magnum in my glove compartment."

At writers', Friday, Liars' lunch that day, I told the others of my adventure. They were properly sympathetic, and they praised my nonexistent courage. I said, "What was I going to do? Run back downstairs, and wait for the sound of shots?" (Or—as my sister cheerfully suggested when I reported the incident to her—wait, as I ran, for a bullet in the back?) They agreed that I'd only done what was necessary, and they laughed at and with me at the anticlimactic story of the Magnum.

"You know," one of the old regulars said, "that reminds me of the time Mack had to take a gun away from Borden Deal."

That I had not known about. It had happened when I was still in New York. Borden had been a well-known novelist, and a regular at the Friday lunch for years. He and Dad had been friends, and one night his wife had called Dad and said, "Mack, please come over right away! Borden's drunk, and he has a gun, and he's threatening us and waving it around." Dad, I was told, had gone over and taken the gun away.

I thought, "My God, I'm caught in an echo chamber. For all my life! I not only hear echoes of my father but, even without knowing, I act them out."

Echoes. I have lived on them, shaped my life around them. Echoes of the past, and of each day's, each hour's, dreams of—payment toward—the future.

I think our lives are made of echoes—bright and golden, grim and gray.

Some time ago, *Tropic*, the Sunday magazine of *The Miami Herald*, ran an article I had written about the making of this book. I had never known that

John Kantor had another grandson, from a later marriage, but he had. And another granddaughter also. They apparently had a happier experience with John Kantor than those in my family had, and they had been upset by some of the things I said in the article, have said in this book, about him. My cousin, or half-cousin, wrote the *Herald,* and asked that I get in touch with him. He gave his phone number in his letter, and I called him. He was a most engaging man and, though our experience and memories were different, we had a pleasant conversation for half an hour.

About ten minutes into our talk he said to me, "You know, you sound almost exactly like Grandpa."

Like John Kantor.

And perhaps my father sounded more like John than he cared to own. We are, all of us, entrapped by the past—chained, warped, made true or false, by our early shaping and our genes. And sometimes genes can assert themselves by more than echoes in the voice. I, out of obsession, have written this book. My sister, when young, wrote a novel. Her younger son, Tom Shroder, is a fine writer and a very successful journalist. And my own daughters are dangerously infected with the virus also. They write well.

We are all prisoners in the cage of time.

I have a novel to do, and I hope other books after that. I wish to see my children thrive. And somewhere there is a lady to love. I am eager for the future.

But I know that there is a part of me that still yearns to be awakened by the boom of a rough and vibrant voice. *"Goddamn it, you kids, wake up!...It's six o'clock and the morning's bright and there are things to do. We're going on a picnic!"*

Briggs' Woods would be a wonderland.

We'd have a fine time that day.

July 13, 1987

Sources of
Quotations

pp. 1–2: *But Look, the Morn*, by MacKinlay Kantor (Coward-McCann, 1947)

p. 15: *Valedictory*, by MacKinlay Kantor (Coward-McCann, 1939)

p. 16: *Rolf in the Woods*, by Ernest Thompson Seton

p. 16: *Under the Lilacs*, by Louisa May Alcott

p. 20: *Gentle Annie*, by MacKinlay Kantor (Coward-McCann, 1942)

p. 34: "Daniel Boone," © 1933 by Rosemary and Stephen Vincent Benét

pp. 35–36, 51, 59, 63: *But Look, the Morn*, by MacKinlay Kantor (Coward-McCann, 1947)

pp. 68–69, 72–74, 75, 78–79, 81: *The Maples Were My Gods*, by MacKinlay Kantor (unpublished ms)

p. 91: quoted by MacKinlay Kantor in *I Love You, Irene* (Doubleday, 1972)

pp. 96–97: *The Maples Were My Gods*, by MacKinlay Kantor (unpublished ms)

p. 97: *"Purple,"* by MacKinlay Kantor

p. 101: "For a Fifteen-Year-Old," by MacKinlay Kantor, republished in *Turkey in the Straw* (Coward-McCann, 1935)

p. 102: "Floyd Collins's Cave," by MacKinlay Kantor, republished in *Turkey in the Straw* (Coward-McCann, 1935)

p. 107: letter written by Irene Layne Kantor, in family keeping

pp. 112–113, 121, 123–125: letters from MacKinlay Kantor collection in the Library of Congress

pp. 126–127: *Long Remember*, by MacKinlay Kantor (Coward-McCann, 1934)

p. 133: "Notes to Be Left in a Cornerstone," ©1936 by Stephen Vincent Benét pp. 144, 145, 145–146, 147–148: correspondence by Margaret (Peggy) Leech Pulitzer, in family keeping. By Permission of the Estate

p. 157: letter from MacKinlay Kantor collection in the Library of Congress

pp. 170, 172–173, 177, 179: "Bailey, Who Burned?" by MacKinlay Kantor (Curtis Publishing Company, 1943), republished in *Glory for Me* (Coward-McCann, 1945)

p. 174: cablegram from MacKinlay Kantor collection in the Library of Congress

pp. 188, 189–190, 198–199: *Glory for Me*, by MacKinlay Kantor (Coward-McCann, 1945)

pp. 194–195: letter from MacKinlay Kantor collection in the Library of Congress

pp. 208–209: *But Look, the Morn*, by MacKinlay Kantor (Coward-McCann, 1947)

pp. 211–212: *Sarasota Herald-Tribune*, September 26, 1956

p. 213: letter from MacKinlay Kantor collection in the Library of Congress

pp. 234–235: The story about the bowl of milk and the girl is an excerpt, slightly revised, from an unpublished novel by Tim Kantor, and it initially appeared in print in *U.S. Camera Annual*, 1977.

p. 235: *In Russet Mantle Clad*, by MacKinlay Kantor (unpublished ms)

pp. 242–243, 244–245: letters from MacKinlay Kantor collection in the Library of Congress

pp. 275–276: note written by Irene Layne Kantor, in family keeping

INDEX